HISTORICISM ONCE MORE

Whatsoever oracles the human heart, in all emergen-
cies, in all solemn hours, has uttered as its commen-
tary on the world of actions,—these he shall receive
and impart. And whatsoever new verdict Reason
from her inviolable seat pronounces on
passing men and events of to-day,
—this he shall hear and
promulgate.

RALPH WALDO EMERSON, "The American Scholar"

We sympathize
in the great moments of
history, in the great discoveries,
the great resistances, the great prosper-
ities of men; because there law was enacted, the
sea was searched, the land was found, or the
blow was struck, for us, as we ourselves in that
place would have done or applauded.

RALPH WALDO EMERSON, "History"

ROY HARVEY
PEARCE

Historicism
Once More

PROBLEMS

& OCCASIONS FOR

THE AMERICAN SCHOLAR

PRINCETON UNIVERSITY PRESS

PRINCETON, NEW JERSEY

1969

FOR

*"Chemistry! the elevating, beautiful
study! which only the vulgar think technical, because they have not delved into
its capacious recesses. Chemistry—that
involves the essences of creation, and
the changes, and the growth and forma-
tions and decays, of so large a constituent part of the earth, and the things
thereof. We can well imagine how a
man, whose judgment leaps over the
mere artificial, can be an enthusiastic,
life-devoted, student of this noble science."*

FOREWORD

THE ESSAYS reprinted here are informed by a conviction that works of literature, precisely as they are events occasioned at a particular time and in a particular place, have the power to carry with them, beyond their time and place into ours, a continuing sense of the occasion. So considered, they are not perfected but are instead perfecting and may continue to manifest to the properly instructed reader a lively sense of the possibilities for belief and commitment which they express. The conviction is, I think, nowadays a common one, deriving in good part from our attempt to move beyond both the reductionism of positivistically inclined historiography and the formalism of *explication de texte*, each pursued as an end in itself. Historiography and *explication de texte* in their various modes are absolutely necessary conditions of literary understanding. But they are nonetheless only exegetical—our means of preparing ourselves to engage the texts we would understand, and understanding, would interpret. The critical essays here reprinted, then, are attempts to manage such occasions as will hopefully enable a reader to meet the texts dealt with on their own terms—interpretive occasions which will be for him consonant with the literary occasions which have called them forth. The verdicts they strive to pass are set by the critic's obligatory question—not right or wrong, but *how* right; and further, what were the conditions of rightness? What do those conditions have to do with ours? The utopian end of such an enterprise, for those who would share in and contribute to it, is as full and complicated a sense of the past and present as we can contain in our critical imaginations. Accordingly, in the four essays which come first in this volume—all by-products of the work which went into the essays of Part II and into other critical work of mine—I have tried to deal with some of the problems of method and procedure which are entailed by my sense of that utopian end and by the conviction which I have said informs the separate critical essays.

I have done my best to avoid second-guessing myself. For the most part I have left the essays as originally published, although here and there I have made such changes as will render them truer to their original intentions. I have indicated such changes in two ways: by giving at the end, in addition to the original date of the essay, the date of the changes; and by adding bracketed footnotes when it seemed necessary to take into account studies written after the publication of the essays in question.

The one essay which is in effect new is "The Metaphysics of Indian-Hating: Leatherstocking Unmasked." In it I have brought together portions of and added substantively to "The Leatherstocking Tales Reexamined" (1947), "Melville's Indian-Hater: A Note on a Meaning of *The Confidence-Man*" (1952), and "The Metaphysics of Indian-Hating" (1957). The second named has already been reprinted in somewhat different form in the revised edition of my *Savages of America: A Study of the Indian and the American Mind* (1965). I borrow from it again to put its substance into a larger context.

In "Hawthorne and the Sense of the Past" (1954), I have incorporated a section from "Romance and the Study of History" (1964). And I have made no attempt to update the references to popular culture in "Mass Culture / Popular Culture"—on the grounds, the phenomenon being what it is, that the updated references would be out of date by the time they got into print.

The essays were originally printed and copyrighted as follows:

"The Leatherstocking Tales Reexamined," *South Atlantic Quarterly*, XLVI (1947), 524-536.

"Melville's Indian Hater: A Note on a Meaning of *The Confidence-Man*." Reprinted by permission of the Modern Language Association from *PMLA*, LXVII (1952), 942-948.

"The Metaphysics of Indian-Hating," *Ethnohistory*, IV (1947), 27-40.

"Historicism Once More." Originally published in the Autumn 1958 *Kenyon Review* (pp. 554-591). Copyright © 1958 by Kenyon College; reprinted by permission of the publisher.

"Literature, History, and Humanism: An Americanist's Dilemma," *College English*, XXIV (1963), 364-372; reprinted by permission of the National Council of Teachers of English.

"Mass Culture / Popular Culture: Notes for a Humanist's Primer," *College English*, XXIII (1962), 417-432; reprinted by permission of the National Council of Teachers of English.

"Robin Molineux on the Analyst's Couch: A Note on the Limits of Psychoanalytic Criticism," reprinted from *Criticism*, I (1959), 83-90, by permission of the Wayne State University Press.

"Hawthorne and the Sense of the Past; or, The Immortality of Major Molineux," *ELH* (The Johns Hopkins Press), XXI (1954), 327-349.

"Romance and the Study of History," *Hawthorne Centenary Essays*, ed. Roy Harvey Pearce (Columbus: Ohio State University Press, 1964), pp. 221-244.

"Hawthorne and the Twilight of Romance," *Yale Review*, XXXVII (1948), 487-506; copyright Yale University Press.

"Whitman: The Poet in 1860," published as the Introduction to Walt Whitman, *Leaves of Grass*, Facsimile Edition of the 1860 Text (Ithaca: Cornell University Press, 1961), pp. vii-li.

"Henry James and His *American*," published as the Introduction to *The American*, Riverside Editions (Boston: Houghton Mifflin Co., 1962), pp. v-xxi.

"Wallace Stevens: The Last Lesson of the Master," *ELH* (The Johns Hopkins Press), XXXI (1964), 64-85.

"Theodore Roethke: The Power of Sympathy," *Theodore Roethke: Essays on the Poetry*, ed. A. Stein (Seattle: University of Washington Press, 1965), pp. 167-199.

"Whitman and Our Hope for Poetry," *The Poetic Tradition*, ed. D. C. Allen and H. T. Rowell (Baltimore: The Johns Hopkins Press, 1968), pp. 123-140.

I am grateful to the editors and publishers concerned for permission to reprint. Copyrighted material in the essays is quoted with permission as follows:

ROBERT DUNCAN:

"The Opening of the Field," by Robert Duncan, copyright © 1960 by Robert Duncan, published by Grove Press, Inc.

THEODORE ROETHKE:

"The Cycle," copyright 1941 by *The Virginia Quarterly Review*, The University of Virginia; "The Return," copyright 1946 by Modern Poetry Association, Inc.; and "Wish for a Young Wife," copyright © 1963 by Beatrice Roethke as Administratrix of the Estate of Theodore Roethke; and lines from the following poems: "Feud," copyright 1935 by Theodore Roethke;

"Night Journey," copyright 1940 by Theodore Roethke; "Open House," copyright 1941 by Theodore Roethke; "Weed Puller" and "Moss-Gathering," copyright 1946 by Editorial Publications, Inc.; "The Lost Son," copyright 1947 by Theodore Roethke; "Cuttings" and "Cuttings (later)," copyright 1948 by Theodore Roethke; "Praise to the End" and "Where Knock is Open Wide," copyright 1950 by Theodore Roethke; "Bring the Day" and "Oh Lull Me, Lull Me," copyright 1951 by Theodore Roethke; "The Waking" and "The Vigil," copyright 1953 by Theodore Roethke; "I Know a Woman," copyright 1954 by Theodore Roethke; "His Words" and "The Exulting," copyright © 1956 by The Atlantic Monthly Company; "They Sing, They Sing," copyright © 1956 by Theodore Roethke; "In a Dark Time," copyright © 1960 by Beatrice Roethke as Administratrix of the Estate of Theodore Roethke; "The Pure Fury," copyright © 1958 by Theodore Roethke; "The Young Girl," copyright © 1961 by The Curtis Publishing Company; "The Far Field," "The Marrow," and "Once More, the Round," copyright © 1962 by Beatrice Roethke as Administratrix of the Estate of Theodore Roethke; and "The Chums," "The Abyss," "Her Longing," and "The Rose," copyright © 1963 by Beatrice Roethke as Administratrix of the Estate of Theodore Roethke; all from *The Collected Poems of Theodore Roethke*. Reprinted by permission of Doubleday & Company, Inc. and by Faber and Faber Limited.

WALLACE STEVENS:

Quotations from *The Collected Poems of Wallace Stevens* and *Opus Posthumous*, by Wallace Stevens, are protected by copyright and have been reprinted by permission of Alfred A. Knopf, Inc. Copyright 1954 by Wallace Stevens. © Copyright 1957 by Elsie Stevens and Holly Stevens. Reprinted by permission of Faber and Faber Limited.

Robert Penn Warren:

Many friends have over the years read versions of these essays, and I thank them once more. I am most indebted to my constant readers, Robert Elliott and Stephen Gilman, who have always done their best to help me write better than I know. I am, as ever, grateful to R. Miriam Brokaw who suggested that some of my essays be reprinted and helped me design the selection and to Eve Hanle who graciously took it from there; an American scholar could ask for no better editors. My dedication (the words of course are Walt Whitman's) is intended to thank a number of my La Jolla colleagues, past and present, who have proved to me that if we do not in fact have one culture, we have none.

CONTENTS

xiii

I

Problems

"ONCE YOU LEAVE YOU'RE OUT IN
THE OPEN; IT RAINS AND IT SNOWS.
IT SNOWS HISTORY. . . ."

Bernard Malamud,
The Fixer

1

HISTORICISM ONCE MORE

"Por el examen de su conciencia histórica penetran
[los hombres] en su intra-historia y se hallan de
veras. . . ." Miguel de Unamuno, *En torno
al casticismo*

"If one can really penetrate the life of another age,
one is penetrating the life of one's own. . . ." T. S.
Eliot, Introduction to Ezra Pound's *Selected Poems*

Early in Georg Simmel's great *Sociology*, there is an
excursus into a question fundamental to the general
inquiry which that book undertakes. The excursus is
called "How Is Society Possible?" And it might well
furnish us a paradigm for initiating still another inquiry into the theory of literature and criticism. How,
indeed, is literature possible? Such a question is entailed by another, one which it has been our particular
compulsion to ask in this Critical Age: what is literature? But, like Simmel, we may find that it is one
which we can ask properly only if we at the same time
ask one which it entails. Thus: how is it possible that
literature should be what it is?

Consider how, asking only what literature is, we find
ourselves regularly confronted by answers set in terms
of a series of either/or propositions—critical purism *v.*
critical pragmatism, the autonomous *v.* the instru-
mental, the individual *v.* the societal, the poet *v.* the
period, foregrounding *v.* automatization, texture *v.*
structure . . . and finally, art *v.* life. Those who confront us with such propositions, of course, most often
strive to show how one element of a given proposition

3

is resolved into the other, so to achieve that "higher" synthesis which is marked by tension, ambiguity, irony, and the like. But, asking how it is possible that literature should be what it is, I wonder if such a synthesis is achievable, or even desirable. Might it not be that the function of the literary work is to show us that such a synthesis is, in fact, impossible of achievement; that there is a constant and necessary dialectical opposition between the very categories we would synthesize; that in a realization of this opposition lies our fullest and richest sense of the quality of high art and, beyond that, of our sense of the highest possibilities of ourselves as critical readers?

Here I think of another of our either/or propositions: literature *v.* history. And I wonder if it is not the case that literature is possible precisely as it is because it is in its very nature a way, perhaps the most profound, of comprehending that dialectical opposition which characterizes our knowledge of ourselves in our history; and that that opposition is one which subsumes all those I have noted above. Thus, the proposition should read: history (*our* history) via literature. If this is so, then we shall have again to develop a kind of criticism which is, by definition, a form of historical understanding.

In point of fact, we are doing so. We move toward a kind of criticism which is historical in not the usual sense of the term. For we have regularly used it to refer to the historical placement and elucidation of the literary work. This "new" historical criticism would go somewhat further and establish between ourselves and the literary work a direct, existential relationship. This is, I take it, essentially a form of what is usually called historicism.[1] Hence my title. This historicism assumes

---

[1] There is an annoying semantic problem here, of course: What, actually, does "historicism" mean? What kind of critical philosophy of history does it entail? The question centers on the kind of rela-

4

that the past, by virtue of its very pastness, becomes an aspect of the present. In effect, a literary work carries the past into the present—and not just as a monument endowed with the sort of factuality from which we may infer its previous mode of existence, but rather as a somehow "living" thing from whose particularity of form we may apprehend that existence and to a significant degree share in it.

I grant at the outset that the historicist critic as I have envisaged him would not have been able or in-

___

tivism which the historicist assumes. It is my own sense that positivistically minded historians have adopted the term as a means of supporting an illimitable relativism, although they would surely be uncomfortable to discover that this can easily lead them to the kind of idealistic view of history expounded by, say, a Croce. On the other hand, it would seem that "historicism" can be expounded as having always settled itself upon the bedrock of a "universal" theory of human nature. If the latter is the case, then there is no necessity for qualifying "historicism" with "existentialist," as, following the example of some recent Hispanists in particular, I am tempted to do. The best brief account that I know of the problems here involved is Friedrich Meinecke's "Values and Causalities in History," as translated in Fritz Stern's *The Varieties of History* (New York, 1956), pp. 268-288. See also Rudolf Bultmann's 1957 Gifford Lectures *History and Eschatology* (Edinburgh, 1957), especially pp. 140-142. [My understanding of "historicism," I would add in 1969, is confirmed by the following account of the thought of Leopold Ranke, from whom all modern historicism is said to flow, in Gerhard Ritter's "Scientific History, Contemporary History, and Political Science," *History and Theory*, I (1961), 264-265:

Ranke's objectivity, which became the model of all scientific history, has been all too often misinterpreted as mere neutrality. Granted, he declined to act as judge of the past but declared that he only wanted to report it "as it really happened." In contemplation of the grand drama of world history he wanted most to "blot out his self"— not, however, to stand by as the disinterested observer but rather to be able to dissolve completely in the reliving of the awesome events. Not neutral indifference but the opposite—the most intimate, enthusiastic participation, the strongest involvement in the course of events and in the inexhaustible complexity of their manifestations —is the spiritual posture in which he confronts world history. In the last analysis his objectivity stems thus from the universality of his conception of history. He keeps himself free (at least in principle, that is, insofar as is at all possible for a human being) from all commitment to any particular interests, to any particular intellec-

clined to compile an *NED*, do a critical text of *Beowulf*, initiate a *Variorum Shakespeare*, travel the *Road to Xanadu*, or, for that matter, fully determine the fateful tensions and paradoxes of "The Rape of the Lock" or calculate precisely the component of the personal and impersonal in "Lycidas." Moreover, I freely admit that such jobs still need doing and are being done, though, I suspect, more and more rarely and with increasingly diminishing returns, I assume, in short, that our relation to our literature has changed as we have changed, that the needs accruing from that relation have changed too, and that the changes point us toward what can most accurately be called historicism. In turn, as they come up, the relevant questions are: how has this taken place? what does it mean that it should take place? what does it mean to be, shall we say, a "critical historicist" instead of an "historical critic"?

Now, this historicist tendency in our criticism is by

---

tual currents, to any historical epochs—even from commitment to his own fatherland, to his own religion, to his own times. Not only are all epochs for him equally "immediate to God" (in his famous phrase), but likewise all nations and ultimately also all great movements and trends of the human spirit which have become historically significant. Scientific history, so understood, is fundamentally unlimited in its quest for knowledge. It by no means restricts its choice of material in the manner which is often set as an ideal today: to choose out of the past only that which has continued up to the present, that which is important for our immediate self-understanding. Its fundamental aim is rather to illuminate the entire cosmos of human cultural strivings and thereby to enlarge our little selves into the unmeasured, thus meeting a deep and genuine need of the human spirit. Ranke once formulated its highest aim thus in a letter: "To understand and capture all the deeds and sorrows of this wild, passionate, violent, good, noble, peaceful, of this sullied and pure creature that we are ourselves, in their genesis and in their configuration." It must be understood that this is not a question of a kind of historical anthropology, of exhibiting what has always been the same in human nature, but rather of the opposite: to bring to light the inexhaustible variety of the potentialities that man possesses in the struggle with his fate to create his civilization.]

no means a unique or isolated phenomenon, not just another specialized product of the scholar-critic's specialism. Quite the contrary. It can best be understood as one of the most complex and sophisticated aspects of a problem that now generally tries our soul—that of the nature and the import of our sense of the past. We recognize that at the most the past has done much to make us what we are and has given us much of what we have—our modes of hope, aspiration, and responsibility. And at the very least, we recognize that the past is the one thing we cannot change, that it is *just there*, absolutely given. Our problem is to understand it, which should mean to accept it—which is *not* to say approve of it. Whether with a Frank Yerby we play with libidinal fantasies about the past; or, with a Bruce Catton we lose ourselves in its sheer factuality; or with a Robert Penn Warren we conceive of its chief protagonists as a series of Adams, in whose fall/ we have sinnéd all—however we look toward the past, we cannot free ourselves from the fact that it is somehow here, now, built into our sense of our time. Our sense of our time seems these days inevitably, with ever-increasing intensity, to involve a sense of the past. And literary criticism is answering to that sense too.

Our criticism and the scholarship that buttresses it are certainly now mature enough to assume the burden that our culture has forced upon it: not only to see literature in history, but to see history in literature; to understand that the art of reading a poem is an act of at once appropriating and being appropriated by its history; to declare that a poem is an expression of the highest humanistic import, as it is an expression of a man whose very humanity is defined both by the fact that he is a man and that he is a man in a particular place and at a particular time. When will our criticism fully assume this burden? When it understands that it has already begun to do so, or at least recognized

7

that it needs must do so. The immediate task is to describe the conditions of doing so. How is historicism possible? How is criticism possible?

2.

The problem of history, to be sure, has been central to the formalist criticism which gives our age one of its names. But it has been a problem stated in such a way as to obscure the terms and conditions of its solution. There is, for instance, the great example of "Tradition and the Individual Talent," with its insistence that the poet is he for whom history, or at least the history of literature, is totally and immediately available. If the tendency of that notable essay was to imply somehow that the poet was a prophet through whom history spoke, Eliot corrected it in his many brilliant essays of formal explicatory analysis, essays in which his interest was the way a poet "uses" the history which he is given to know better than the ordinary run of men. Yet the problem of history *qua* history, of what part history itself has in the meaning of poems, has always been present in Eliot's thinking about literature. It is there particularly when he speaks, as he so often does, of the poet's concern for "language."

"We may say," he writes in "The Social Function of Poetry," "that the duty of the poet, as poet, is only indirectly to his people; his direct duty is to his *language*, first to preserve, and second to extend and improve. . . ." This is, as I shall maintain, an auspicious beginning, since it is on the consideration of the poet's relation to his language that there must be centered any examination of his relation to history; for language must be for the poet the principal vehicle for history; through language history gets into literature. But here, as elsewhere, Eliot goes not much beyond this sentence. And of course, when, as poet, he most starkly

8

confronts the problem of language, he does so as a Christian for whom the problem of history, and thus the problem of language, is resolved in the dogma of the Word. The dogma may or may not be correct; as far as Eliot's religious commitments are concerned, one must grant that it is so. But there remains the problem of how a reader who is not of Eliot's persuasion can be brought to grant that it is so. There remains the problem of how Eliot's dogmatic view of language (and history) can be made convincing to a reader who is concerned not so much to agree or disagree with him but to understand him. There remains, in short, the problem of understanding in what sense Eliot's views, as his poems project them, are themselves segments of history—not only his history, but also ours as his poems may make it ours.

I instance the views of Eliot here as being seminal for that formalist criticism which has helped many of us to learn how to read. Language is a primary concern of all that criticism; but almost always it is a curiously non-historical language, overripe with its accumulated load of meanings, which it is the poet's obligation to preserve, extend, and improve and the critic's to explicate and perhaps to generalize. In their formalist *vade mecum, Theory of Literature*, Mr. Wellek and Mr. Warren distribute most forms of historical study among the various levels of that Hell they call "The Extrinsic Approach." They do, however, detach from historical scholarship the study of the language of poetry and admit it to that Better World they call "The Intrinsic Approach"—yet only under the name "Style and Stylistics." And even here they take a dim view of stylistic study when it goes beyond the descriptively formalist. Such work, they write, "often assumes that true, or great, art must be based on experience, *Erlebnis*. . . ." (Is this to say: poetry is an experience but is not based on one?) And, of course, since history

9

is merely a record of human experience, for Mr. Wellek and Mr. Warren it would seem to follow that if we attempt to know literature as a phenomenon in history and ourselves as readers thereby also bound up in that history, we must necessarily founder on historical reductionism.

The prime assumption is that the historical study of literature is necessarily reductionist. Going on this assumption, the formalist critic can do no more than make obeisance to the power of the language with which the poet must work and then hasten on to see how the work has been carried out. Thus it is significant, I think, that in his recent statesmanlike summation of the doctrines of those whom he calls the *New Apologists for Poetry*, Mr. Murray Krieger repeatedly is obliged to point out that, although the New Critics have given us a quite powerful and fairly consistent theory of the author's role in the creative process, they have never been able to deal adequately with the role of language in that process. He writes, for example: "Clearly, then, . . . language must be considered as a formative factor in the complex process of creation. I must say that the poet's original idea for his work, no matter how clearly thought out and complete he thinks it is, undergoes such radical transformations as language goes creatively to work upon it that the finished poem, in its full internal relations, is far removed from what the author thought he had when he began. . . ."[2]

[2] *The New Apologists for Poetry* (Minneapolis, 1956), p. 23; and cf. pp. 73-74, 97-98. It should be noted also that Mr. Krieger, in "A Note on the Objectivity of Value," pp. 158-163, defends the possibility of "objectivism" in value-theory as against extreme "historical relativism." He fully acknowledges the fact that literary conventions and the like are "historically relative" and indicates that his Apologists, or some of them, do also. But he does not go on to discuss the possible implications for the nature of the literary work and the realization of its intrinsic values which derive from such "objectivism." Once more, he limits himself to elucidating the poetics of

10

Now, Mr. Krieger nowhere specifies exactly what he means by "language." At the most he seems to mean, as so often with the New Critics on whom his study centers, "medium." And therein lies, for both the New Critics and him who is their apologist, the large difficulty. For "medium" carries with it in much New Critical (and other) aesthetic thinking a kind of mystique: something (its power as "symbol"?) in the medium, in language, works in such a way as to make for that sort of creative resistance to the artist's initial intuition which *must* contribute much to the production of the achieved literary work. Surely, the logic is essentially analogical: language (for all its power as "symbol") is like the stone, or clay, or paint with which the artist works. But, and herein lies the difficulty, the analogy holds only minimally. For language is obviously freighted with values to a degree and in a way which plastic substances are not.[3] This is, indeed, of

---

his Apologists. And this is only proper. I think, therefore, that had he pursued the subject further, he might well have reached conclusions of the sort I come to in this paper. Which is another way of claiming that the sort of historicism (which I take to be akin to his "objectivism") expounded here develops necessarily out of formalist New Critical poetics when it is considered in relation to the historicist theory of culture assumed in this essay. [Mr. Krieger's "objectivism" has entailed for him a conception of the use of language in poetry whereby it is dissociated from its historical matrix yet continues to refer to it. He would, as he says, explicitly affirm the "miraculous power of poetry" and insists that I and others are wrong in accepting the common-sense view, developed in much modern linguistic theory, that the language of poetry remains the language of ordinary discourse, but with an intensification of those aspects of usage (metaphor, meter, etc.) which make for fictionality. See his *A Window to Criticism* (Princeton, 1964), pp. 1-70.]

[3] Plastic substances as media (and also musical tones?) indeed could, at least theoretically, be held to be analogous to language as medium. For surely the historically definable conventions as to "suitable" uses of those media in the fine arts must have some significance for artist and beholder, critical and uncritical. But here again the analogy is minimal and of not much use to the theorist or critic. Mr. Krieger, however (footnote, p. 68), believes differently.

11

the essence of its power to symbolize. Language above all communicates values; and by "values" I mean both feelings of desirability and obligation and their negatives, and the very modes and forms by which those feelings and their negatives are expressed. (Perhaps it would be better to say values and valuations.) To reach this belief, one need not go so far as to accept as linguistic orthodoxy the theses of Benjamin Lee Whorf. Still, reading someone like Whorf might at least have a heuristic value, if only because it would serve to remind us that literature can never be as "pure" (i.e. freed of mundanely determined value-forces) as we, well instructed by Mr. Krieger's Apologists, might like it to be.

Mr. Krieger, then, can find among the New Critics, whom of course he studies in their own terms, no adequate account for this ("the linguistic") side of the creative process; he must make do with what he and his Critics have. But if he wished to move beyond his Critics' terms and categories (as he does not), he could well talk about language in its historical-cultural aspect. For it is in relation to its culture that language has its initial and minimal symbolizing power. Language is, as we regularly say, a system of symbols whereby, in great part, culture is historically transmitted. The values projected by a language (whether in a poem or any other form of expression) are not just initially and minimally, but also residually, the values of the culture whose language it is. Indeed, it is the force of this residual power which, in the making of a poem, gives to language a creative power analogous to the poet's. The power is ultimately that of the poet's culture as, through its historical development, it has made the world in, about, and for which he writes. The study of language, thus, is a form of the historical study of culture. So that in the end, Mr. Krieger's remark about the New Critics' concern with

12

"language" is one about their concern with history. But
it remains a concern limited by their strangely unsophisticated conception of language—unsophisticated
because it is a conception set by an assurance that the
historical dimension of language is not finally relevant
to the meaning and import of the literary work. We
come, then, to a version of the complaint regularly
set forth by antagonists of Mr. Krieger's Apologists:
that they are inadequate as historians and therefore,
in all their brilliance, incomplete as critics.

Still, I should say that in general the antagonists
have not argued their case well enough. True, they
have caught the Apologists in a number of factual
errors. But for the most part they themselves have
either conceived of history as being merely a "setting"
for literary works and then have tacitly admitted that
it is much more interesting to study the setting than
the works; or they have so confused works with setting
that the works have become for them just dim spots
on the historical horizon—so dim that it doesn't seem
to be worthwhile to distinguish one from another; so
dim that critical explication is at best an adventure in
uncontrolled impressionism. From such (at their extremes) antiquarianism and reductionism the New
Apologists set out to rescue us, and in great part did,
but only at the expense of tearing the literary work out
of its historical-cultural context and putting it entirely
in ours. Although this was a desperate measure taken
to save the literary work from the disappearance into
context which seemed to threaten, it was nontheless
one that now appears a little prideful and comports
strangely with the Apologists' vaunted sense of order,
continuity, and tradition. The Apologists respected language, yet do not seem to have wanted really to understand just what it was that they respected. Perhaps, in
order to do what they did, they could not afford to want
to do so. Perhaps their great success could be achieved

13

only at the expense of this, their great failure. Precisely because they succeeded, it seems to me, we can see wherein they failed; we may even avoid such failure ourselves. This is *our* chance—or one of our chances—for success. I daresay that this is a task set for us by our situation at our moment in history.

Studying language, we study history. We study history, so that we can study language. (There are other ways to do so, of course, as there are other institutions which make for the historical continuity of culture; but this one is our major concern, because it is our artists'.) Studying history, we study culture. Studying a culture, we study its poetry. Studying its poetry, we study its language. The system is one and whole. If it is closed, that is because it encloses us. And even though we may prefer to work within any one of its segments, we must not confuse the segment with the whole. Nor must we forget how and to what purpose the other segments exist.[4]

It is not enough to protest, as have many of the New Apologists, that they regularly go to the *NED* or that they can read *The Great Chain of Being* too. This is to yield to the conception of history as "setting." For the questions immediately arise: to what critical use are the *NED* and *The Great Chain of Being* to be put?

[4] Cf. Allen Tate's remarks, at the end of his "The Man of Letters In the Modern World" (1952): "It is the duty of the man of letters to supervise the culture of language, to which the rest of culture is subordinate, and to warn us when our language is ceasing to forward the ends proper to man. The end of social man is communion in time through love, which is beyond time." Mr. Tate's man of letters, like Mr. Eliot's, seems not to be subject to the claims and demands of history as it is conceived in this essay. But this is so only because he has committed himself to a religion which subsumes the historical under the ahistorical. Thus a difficulty arises in some of Mr. Tate's criticism when, for example, viewing Poe and Emily Dickinson, *sub specie aeternitatis*, he cannot grant them any life except that which is of transcendentally immediate significance to him. The net result is to fail to see such poets whole and to be a victim of what the historicist might call the eschatological fallacy.

What happens to the historical-cultural ambiance of a word when it gets into a poem? Is the ambiance somehow left behind? Does it survive, but as entirely transformed? This last would seem to be the New Critic's answer. But it is an unsatisfactory answer; for it would do away with history as by a transformative fiat. Hence the historicist critic, meditating Mr. Krieger's argument, would take the matter one step further and ask: to what degree is language, or culture, or history, qualitatively *in*, existentially *in*, a literary work? By virtue of being there, what does it do? Then: in what sense do we, as we read critically, actually engage ourselves to the language, the culture, the history, which is there? If language, as we must say, has an active, creative role in the making of the literary work, then the effect of that work on us must be in some part the effect of language—of the specific values with which it is charged and of the form which values took, and so of the period in which those values had their existence. Somehow, it would seem to follow, we are made to be vitally committed to those aspects of the period out of which the literary work has come. Somehow, we have come to be relativists of a sort—historicists, that is to say—which above all the New Criticism would seem to want us not to be.[5]

[5] The New Critical treatment of the implications for literary criticism of Professor Lovejoy's work is a useful, because extreme, instance of its anti-historicism. More than once (most influentially by René Wellek and Austin Warren, *Theory of Literature* [New York, 1949], p. 109) there have been quoted, out of context, the following words from the introductory chapter of *The Great Chain of Being*: ". . . the ideas in serious reflective literature are, of course, in great part philosophical ideas in dilution. . . ." The rest of the sentence is significantly left unquoted; indeed, there is usually no indication that the sentence does not end here. The rest of it reads: "—to change the figure, growths from seed scattered by great philosophic systems which themselves, perhaps, have ceased to be." Thus Professor Lovejoy would appear to be saying that although he, as an "analytic" historian of ideas, is interested in his work only in the ideas themselves, they nonetheless, when present in literary struc-

15

We may not go all the way with historicism as it has usually been defined; but our way of thinking has been fatefully conditioned by a kind of thinking so close to historicism that we must use it as a means of defining our own position. For classically historicism holds (and I quote here a "neutral" definition, that of Maurice Mandelbaum in his *Problem of Historical Knowledge*) "that . . . every set of cultural values [is] relative to the age in which it is dominant."[6] (The question here, of course, is the meaning of "relative." If it means "relative to nothing but," we would balk and say "relative to, among other things. . . ." But it is not entirely clear that the classical historicist would push us into balking thus.) Insofar as language creates, the fact of creation is inextricable from the point in time of creation; and insofar as we know a literary work, we know, among other things, its time. Not—and this is the main point—as exotic information, as something totally apart from our time, but as something

---

tures, are involved in "growths" which are quite obviously, as the language indicates, somehow different from and not reducible to the "seed" in which they originated. That Professor Lovejoy means such an interpretation to be put on his words is clearly indicated in a couple of sentences he quotes approvingly from Whitehead toward the end of the paragraph in which the supposedly heretical initial statement about "dilution" occurs: ". . . it is in literature that the concrete outlook of humanity receives its expression. Accordingly, it is to literature that we must look, particularly in its more concrete forms, if we hope to discover the inward thoughts of a generation." My point is that, misinterpreting Professor Lovejoy's assertion as they have characteristically done, the New Critics have cut themselves off from a possible way of developing a sense of the past, a way which in itself would let them more fully evoke that concreteness and particularity which they insist is primary in the quality of a literary work.

6 *The Problem of Historical Knowledge* (New York, 1938), p. 89. This is meant to categorize statements like the following from Karl Mannheim ("Historicism" [1924], *Essays on the Sociology of Knowledge*, trans. P. Kecskemeti [New York, 1952], p. 86): "The first approach to a historic mode of thought and living lies . . . in the ability to experience every segment of the spiritual-intellectual world as in a state of flux and growth."

which, as we know it, is at once of its time and ours. Pastness in a literary work is an aspect—a vital, authentic aspect, a *sine qua non*—of presentness. The work of art may well live forever as the creation of a man like other men before and after him. But an integral part of its life, of its formal quality, will derive from the fact that it was created at a time, and for and of a time. Thus, and only thus, is literature possible. Thus, and only thus, does it become what it is.

3.

We must, therefore, consider the literary work as it is a kind of statement which can never be dissociated from either the time in which it was made or the time in which it is known: i.e. when the work was written or when it was (or is) read. Let us say of a literary work that it is a form of a conditional contrary-to-fact statement of the order: "If there had been such a person as X, living in a specified situation, etc., he would have acted in this way." The literary work is thus, as we say, not "true"; it consists of a series of hypothetical situations, imagined and motivated in such a way that, within their confines, we can accept as necessary the actions and responses into which the situations— and the imagined human beings in them—are made to issue. What primarily interests us in "created" situations of this sort is, of course, not their inevitable relevance to factuality, but their possibility: their resonance with our deepest sense of ourselves. And it is this interest in possibility which lets us willingly suspend our ordinary disbelief in such imagined situations and accordingly assent to them as fully as an artist can compel us to. In effect, we compact with him to go as far as he can take us into the realm of human possibility. Indeed, we say that what differentiates him from most of us is his possession of a superior degree both of awareness of such possibility and of ability to ex-

17

press that possibility in language and all the formal, constructivist means which language bears within itself. This is what we mean when we speak of a writer's sensibility.

I am aware that to put such a complex and parlous matter so briefly is to run the risk of oversimplification. Nonetheless, I think that what I have said is, so far as the task I have set myself is concerned, not only correct but adequate. For it takes us into the heart of our matter: if the literary statement is contrary-to-fact and if, further, it defines the conditions under which the facts might have been otherwise, i.e. "true to life," then its attraction and power for us must lie in the fulness of the definition. For a literary work does, indeed, define the conditions of our existence as it *might* have been: which is to say—if we will look as profoundly into our situation as the literary work would have us— as it is. So far as our lives have meaning, we are what we aspire to be—what the literary work tells us we might have been, under the conditions which would have made such an existence possible. In literature, then, we believe in our own historical, existential possibility as the writer's use of language defines it.

Such belief is what I have previously called, borrowing a phrase from Américo Castro, a "commitment to a vital possibility." And at this point *a fortiori*, we must take into account the specific moment in history at which the work was made. For the language of the work is bound to that moment, as are all the substantial compositional elements which the language is made to render. In assenting to the actions and responses developed in the literary work—and, moreover, in being satisfied, by virtue of the hold the formal structure of the work may have on us, to look at it in and of itself—we likewise assent to the beliefs and the values which those actions and responses manifest. That the assent is an as-if assent (to a conditional

18

contrary-to-fact statement) makes all the difference. The difference is that, moving toward such an assent, we are fully prepared to take into our purview, as a vital human possibility, all the historically definable forms of life in which that possibility is made operative. Such an assent entails no "practical" decision and consequent action on our part. For it is grounded on the crucial fact that the past world realized for us is a possible world, not a real one, however much it may seem like that real past world of which we can learn in historical works. Knowing this, now thereby freed to conceive of the past world not as one which did happen but as one which could have happened, we do indeed commit ourselves to its vital possibility. In this way literature "teaches" us.

It is, I should say, this as-if commitment which obliges us to conceive of the literary work as necessarily at once of its time and ours. For although the form of the commitment is defined by the modes of possibility manifested in the work, still the object of the commitment—that toward which our awareness of possibility draws us—is that portion of the past which constitutes the concrete and infinitely particularized substance of the work. *Hamlet* is not true, we declare, but it is true to life. Reading the play, we assent to the possibility that a man could have been like this one, at this time, in this place. That to which it is true is the sense of possibility which is at once ours and a Shakespeare's (or ours as a Shakespeare, in all his creative genius, can evoke it in us), but which we can realize only as a Shakespeare can make it charge a particular Elizabethan situation with the life of art. What is true of *Hamlet* is true of a poem written an instant ago. Criticism is thus a form of historical study—perhaps the purest of historicisms.

This point or a point quite close to it has been made before, of course—most handsomely, so far as my read-

19

ing goes, by Lionel Trilling in his essay, "The Sense of the Past." But the tendency has been to think of Mr. Trilling's essay and the criticism which it has generated as being, somehow, apart from that of the proper New Critics. My point is that it is not apart from their work, but that it grows out of their work, and necessarily. But then, if we can deduce an editorial principle from the kind of criticism filling our quarterlies and journals, we can find evidence of a need to go beyond anti-historicist formalist criticism into something more truly responsive to our need for a criticism which will take into account what Mr. Krieger calls the creative role of language—and what I have ventured to define further as the creative role of historically determinate culture.

I mean here the criticism of those whom I shall call the New Mythographers, I cannot, of course, go into the perilous ramifications of mythographic criticism. What I wish to point out is something quite simple: that our New Mythographers have been concerned to go beyond textual explication and to locate in literary works some substantial center whereby such works may be realized as specifically cultural products. It is as though they had sensed the need to demonstrate how the literary work, by virtue of its activity as literary work, has historical import. They would account for its informing and assent-commanding power by pointing to something beyond (or antecedent to) the creative act of the author. And they point not to language, or culture, or history (for these entities are for them too large, inchoate, and amorphous) but to myth. As to the source of that mythic power: well, therein lies the tremendous range of their interests and commitments—from, say, the frankly theistic, proto-religious criticism of Philip Wheelwright to, say, the frankly naturalistic, proto-anthropological criticism of Stanley Hyman, and beyond. And further, the senior

New Critics themselves—Mr. Ransom, Mr. Tate, and Mr. Brooks, for example—have as often as not had recourse to the concept of myth when they have come up against the necessity of accounting somehow for such informing power in literary works as they could not trace in the exquisitely creative manipulations of the author. In fact where the Old Critic has had recourse to history—to sources, background, and biography—the New Critic has had recourse to myth.[7] He

[7] Thus the attraction—or should one say the felt authenticity—for the New Critic of Christian myth, which is *par excellence* that myth which would completely absorb history into itself and has thereby been taken to transcend it. Objecting to Douglas Bush's kind of historical criticism and Leslie Fielder's extreme mythographic criticism—both of which yield, in his view, to the temptation "to find in literature a support for religion or perhaps a surrogate for religion"—Cleanth Brooks points out that "it is no accident that so many of the formalist critics either hold, or are sympathetic to, an orthodox Christian faith" ("A Note on the Limits of 'History' and the Limits of 'Criticism,'" *Sewanee Review*, LXI [1953], 129-135). Mr. Brooks, in the historicist view, is perfectly right in his desire to avoid both "ersatz religion" and "ersatz poetry." But he offers, so far as my reading of his work goes, no adequate account of the quite obvious historical otherness of poetry, because, one supposes, being a good Christian, he cannot conceive of a component of otherness as radical as that which the historicist would discover in the literary work. Saying this, however, the historicist must add that Mr. Brooks's way with history and its existential actualities is not the only way for the Christian. Another way is that of William F. Lynch, S. J., in his "Theology and Imagination," *Thought*, XXIX (1955), 529-554. Father Lynch writes, for example: ". . . the order of belief called Christology is a belief in the capacity of the human, and the actual, if we imagine and live through it, to lead somewhere. The essential meaning of Christ is that He rejected the way of tricks and magic and power and quick infinities as redeeming ways and chose instead to walk through the mysteries of man (thus I refer to the actualities of man and all the stages of human life) as a way into God. Thus all Christians talk about the 'mysteries of Christ' but they do not talk enough about the mysteries, I mean the realities, of man—through which He, Christ, walked and imagined as a path to freedom and the infinite. It is easy enough to believe in the virtue of infinities, but it is hard to trust in the finite and the actual as a way to them. A properly understood Christology should provide the theological energy required for that penetration for which we no longer seem to have the heart or the energy. I do not say that Christology must get into the poem or the symbol, but

21

has seen clearly that insofar as language (to use Mr. Krieger's term again) is creative, its power cannot be located in the manifold of the sort of social and intellectual history which has been the standard fare of so much Old Criticism. Nonetheless, he has been unable on the one hand to define clearly his sense of myth in its relationship to the hard details of historical evolution; or on the other hand, to generalize his sense of myth into a theory which would account for the sheer plenitude of that evolution—its quality of constant change, activity, and transformation, of vertiginously comprehensive fulness. He has failed, I would say, to take into account the very historicity of history. Mythographic criticism, then, on this analysis, is a proto-historicism generated by the New Critic's deep need not to be frozen into methodological orthodoxy. But, as so often happens, the means to avoid orthodoxy have themselves become orthodox. And the life of literature, which as teachers and critics we would evoke, is said to be compressed into so many archetypes and rituals whose secrets we must unlock if we are to show how they touch with their charismatic power the author in the act of making his work. *Where* those archetypes and rituals are, and *how* they are—this question thus far has not been amenable to historical study, as it should be, but only to psychoanalytic and theological exegesis. Looking to see whither it has gone, we see

---

what we may call the Christic act, the act of athletic and confident penetration of limit, of the actual, and the human, can again become the model and energizer for the poetic imagination and for the total act and attitude of any human culture. What other firmer *quid credas* could there be for the poet or for popular culture?" A little later Father Lynch says, "And we may briefly define the men of belief as those who, with every concomitant obligation, believe in and possess *historical* symbols." In short, Father Lynch's Christology holds inseparably in view history and man, and his eschatology is such that, so far as literature and the arts are concerned, it teaches man to trust in the finite and the actual.

only the withering away of the New Criticism into the New Mythography.

The Elder Statesmen of our New Criticism were so concerned to save literature from historical study—and one of the lessons of *my* life, in any case, is that it had to be done and they have done it—that they tended to hold suspect anything that smacked of relativistic historicism. Yet, if we are only willing to look into our situation deeply enough, we can see that this has been their share of one of the ills of our culture, the fear of history itself. And we can see that the New Mythography has been an attempt to cure that ill by fiat. Moreover, so intent have we been on doing our job as we have been taught to do it, we are hardly aware of other relevant approaches to our problem: for example, the iconological studies (however different one from the other) of Panofsky and of Gombrich and others of their groups, or closer to home, to the criticism, primarily in Romance Literature, of that part of the so-called New Stylistics which we in this country know mainly in Erich Auerbach's *Mimesis* and a cornucopia of essays by Leo Spitzer. Here we see a tendency to take language, culture, and history with a degree and kind of seriousness that we have got used to thinking is impossible. Thus, in *Mimesis*, Mr. Auerbach would show us precisely how the life of language—all that makes for Style—in a given series of works is a manifestation of the very reality principle of the culture in which they had their origin. In effect, the author is not so much agent as carrier; his genius inheres in the fact that he is sensitive to the creative possibilities latent in his culture, to be realized only in his art. Now, we might object that criticism of the sort which *Mimesis* typifies does not do enough to comprehend the creative genius of the author in his art. But at the same time we might well admit that our criticism correspondingly has not done enough to comprehend the creative genius of language in *its* art. I instance the work of Spitzer and Auerbach here, of course, not to expound it, but because it exemplifies a significant sort of critical study which moves in a direction other than the one in which we now tend generally to be moving—or better, which moves in a direction in which we seem to want to move. Indeed, I think that in some notable cases we *are* moving in that direction.[8] We are doing so when, as historical critics, we write of Shakespeare (as has J. V. Cunningham), or Donne (as has Rosemond Tuve), or Wordsworth (as has Josephine Miles), or Keats (as has Earl Wasserman), or Defoe (as has Ian Watt), or Cooper (as has Henry

[8] Réné Wellek has most notably set himself against our moving in that direction. See, for example, his *History of Modern Criticism* (New Haven, 1955), I, 183ff.; his discussion of Auerbach's *Mimesis, Kenyon Review*, XVI (1954), 299-307; and his memorial note on Auerbach, *Comparative Literature*, x (1958), 93-94. In his and Mr. Warren's *Theory of Literature* (New York, 1949), p. 157, Mr. Wellek dismisses cultural relativism of the sort I am expounding by quoting Troeltsch: "All relativism is ultimately defeated by the recognition [in Troeltsch's words] that 'the Absolute is in the relative, though not finally and fully in it.'" But it is my understanding that these words of Troeltsch's are consonant with his doctrine of "value-relativity," a mode of what Mr. Wellek elsewhere calls "perspectivism." Meinecke quotes Troeltsch as saying "Value-relativity is not relativism, anarchy, accident, arbitrariness. It signifies rather a fusion of the factual and normative, which is ever moving and newly created and cannot, therefore, be determined universally and timelessly." On this Meinecke comments: "Value-relativity, in other words, is nothing other than individuality in the historical sense. It is the unique and intrinsically valuable imprint of an unknown absolute—for this kind of absolute will be acknowledged by faith as the creative ground of all values—upon that which is relative and bound to time and nature" ("Values and Causalities in History," p. 283). The task of the critic, it would follow, is to expound literature as something "ever moving and newly created" even as it is "bound to time and nature." His faith will be in man's ability to sense in himself (however ultimately derived) "the creative ground of all values." [As of 1968, Mr. Wellek's views were best summed up in his Olympian refutation of Auerbach's—to me irrefutable—arguments for the historicist position. See his 1960 essay, "Literary Theory, Criticism, and History," in his *Concepts of Criticism* (New Haven, 1963), pp. 1-20.]

24

Nash Smith), or seventeenth-century prose style (as have George Williamson and Jackson Cope), or the nineteenth-century American compulsion toward the symbolic mode (as has Charles Feidelson), in such a way as to evoke our subjects "as they actually happened"—to use the much maligned (and much misinterpreted) historicist battle cry. Doing so, we strive to see how the very wholeness of a work of art is a product not only of an author's own creative activity but of the creative potential of his culture. Mr. Cunningham is spokesman for them all when he writes in his *Woe or Wonder: The Emotional Effect of Shakespearean Tragedy*: ". . . our purpose in the study of literature, and particularly in the historical interpretation of texts, is not in the ordinary sense to further the understanding of ourselves. It is rather to enable us to see how we could think and feel otherwise than we do. It is to erect a larger context of experience within which we may define and understand our own by attending to the disparity between it and the experience of others."[9]

4.

What we ask of the work of art is that it be, in its own terms, carrying its own values, *whole*. "Wholeness" is, of course, a tricky term; but it need not be so if we will be proper (i.e. properly qualified) historicists. This would entail a radical relativism, usually associated with historicism, as regards specific forms of value and valuation in the cultures out of which our literature has come. But it would entail one absolute, a mode of certitude not usually associated with historicism but nonetheless not necessarily excluded from it. (Indeed, as I point out elsewhere, such an absolute has been

[9] [*Woe or Wonder* (1951) is reprinted in Mr. Cunningham's *Tradition and Poetic Structure* (Denver, 1960). The quotation is from p. 141.]

25

for some historicists essential to their understanding of history and the historical process.) This absolute is that quite obviously set by the writer's primal intuition —a common sense so penetrating as to be beyond common sense—that man, the self, is at the center of all literature and that literary works are necessarily created in terms of a fixed, unchanging and unchangeable sense of what it is to be aware of oneself as a man, whatever one's situation in historical time. The writer's primal intuition becomes, as it gives pattern to his vision of his historical situation, that of the reader and critic. But he has a kind of access to it—what is called in recent psychoanalytic theory "controlled regression" —that they do not. What it is *to be aware of oneself as a man*, I have said, not what it is worth or what it may signify when measured in other than humanistic terms; for this latter is an affair, as we know, all too subject to historical change. A literary work is thus *sui generis* a densely particularized expression of what I can only call *humanitas*.

Here I do no more than remind my reader of a commonplace, so that, when he considers its bearing on his conception of the relation of history to literature, he will be in a position to face fully the obligation entailed in interpreting that conception. Thus when, as we have traditionally done, we require of a literary work that it be "whole" in order to be adequate to our (ideal) conception of it, we are requiring nothing less than that it be informed by its author's—and our—sense of what it is, in the circumstances with which the work puts us in touch, to be aware of oneself as a (potentially) whole man.

I am, as I have said, once more raising an old problem—one, in fact, whose resolution we seem to have decided is so easy that it no longer needs study. Yet only in relation to our resolution of this problem will we be able to put literature where it belongs, central among the panoply of our modes of knowing ourselves in history. Thus as critics and readers, we still must work with a traditional criterion: the ideal possibility that a work of art may or may not, or indeed may only partly, achieve wholeness. (To say this is, of course, to subscribe to a version of the "organismic" theory of literary form.) But I have hoped to re-define the criterion somewhat: first, by noting that historically contingent cultural data, through language, have a crucially significant role in the "meaning" of the literary work, in all its wholeness; and second, by noting that the literary work has as its end the objectification of such historical data as they may be formed into ideally possible wholes. The wholeness, as I have said, ultimately derives from the writer's (and reader's) sense of *humanitas*. As the literary work approaches the ideal of wholeness, so each of its component elements—controlled and made integral by the writer's development of his primal intuition—partakes of the effect of the others and thus makes for an object increasingly available to total aesthetic realization. Its component of *humanitas* ultimately furnishes the modes, devices, and techniques—the specifically *formal* elements—for holding the work together; its component of historical data furnishes the terms under which the holding-together can obtain. (The two components, however, are never so neatly separable as they are here, theoretically —for example, in the matter of conventions and literary "rules.") My account of the radical relativism which must hold as regards historical data, I take to be necessarily derived from our knowledge of cultures moving in history; my account of the ideal possibility which must hold as regards literary structures, from our knowledge of ourselves as men.

What must above all be remarked is that the ideal possibility of wholeness must always, by our definition of the function of literature, be historically conditioned in any of its particular expressions. And since in artistic wholes it is expressive forms—their "aesthetic" qualities —in which we are especially interested (or should I say which especially attract us?), we must always attend to that conditioning element which is a means, a means *sine qua non*, of creating our sense of those wholes and their import for us. Surely, to say this is to do no more than to try to sharpen our sense of the literary work as a "concrete universal"—universal as regards its tendency, derived from its vital center of *humanitas*, toward the ideally possible whole; concrete as regards its necessarily historically conditioned expressive form.

At this point, inevitably we must again turn inward, away from history and ask: what is this absolute *humanitas* which sets the creative writer's intention to create an ideally possible whole out of historically conditioned cultural data? (We do so, however, only so that we may turn outward again, toward history and its rich abundance of achieved literary works.)

I use the term *humanitas* not to beg questions but to indicate a way in which we might ask them—questions which rise inevitably when we assess ourselves in terms of those paradoxical qualities which mark us as men: reasoning, but not necessarily reasonable; irrational, but not necessarily victimized by our irrationality; aspiring, but nonetheless quite likely to fail; failing, but nonetheless quite capable of aspiring; knowing, understanding, expounding what we are even as we fail to achieve it. The qualities are as numerous as are the facets of our self-realization; and each carries its contrary imminently within itself. But they all have one thing in common: As we know them, as we assess ourselves in terms of them, they are integral with our capacity for inwardness. And holding them in perilous balance, we find them hard to bear. From this fact derives our ever-increasing difficulty in confronting them as such. We are somewhat comforted, for example, when we discover that those who some time ago called themselves New Humanists concluded by putting these qualities at the services of an inner (which was to say, in the long run, an outer) check. The New Humanists may or may not have been right, in the long run. But the authentic humanist, as I dare call him, must stay within the limits of the short run; for, as humanist, whatever his private long-run commitments, this is all he is given. And this is all he can be sure that he has in common with other humanists, who may well have their own long-run commitments. If this conception of *humanitas* is narrow, so are our lives as humanists; but as this conception is deep, so are our lives. And it has served us well. For centuries we have been able to realize the total humanistic power and relevance of literary works whose authors' long-run commitments are often utterly alien (sometimes even offensive) to our own. Herein we know that this conception of *humanitas* has served us well—in spite of all our efforts, deriving from our inevitable concern for our private long-run commitments, to prove that it will not. The inevitability of both our effort and its failure—so that we are capable of taking the highest pleasure in works whose values we know are alien to us: such a paradox it is which, as it makes for the existence of such contrarieties, uniformly characterizes *humanitas* as we know it.

Of this *humanitas*, then, we can say at the very least (and I think here that the least will suffice) that it derives from our awareness of our private and often burdensome existence as men: our sense of our opposing selves, as Lionel Trilling has called it. He has put the matter quite bluntly: "The function of literature, through all its mutations, has been to make us aware of the particularity of selves, and the high authority of the self in its quarrel with its society and its culture." This statement, from Mr. Trilling's *Freud and the Crisis of Our Culture*, may well serve as a focal point for the wide-ranging literature on the subject, moving from psychoanalytic theory at one extreme to existentialist theology on the other. Further, it will help us see why so many recent behavioral scientists have found in literature extraordinary resources in documenting their researches in self-systems, personality structures, political commitments, and the like.[10] For them literature, because it is literature, can take us directly into the forms of selfhood which have emerged out of those cultures whose behavior in history they would understand.

In a recent book, *The Tower and the Abyss*, Erich Kahler has even more precisely defined our sense of the self and its ineradicable *humanitas*:

> When I try to delve into my innermost feeling, my initial feeling of self, I find at bottom there is not just a feeling of sheer existence, or of sheer thinking, the Cartesian *cogito*. There is immediately and simultaneously, something more. There is implicit in my feeling of existence a feeling of *organic* existence, or organicity, of *wholeness*. Distorted, stunted as it may be by the wear and tear of modern life, the original form is still traceable as it was present in the bud of youth; a ball radiating strength and capacity; all-sidedness, all-potentiality; coherence, correspondence. . . .[11]

[10] I think of such recent examples of studies of this kind as Nathan Leites and Elsa Barnaut, *Ritual of Liquidation* (Glencoe, Ill., 1954); Henry Murray, "Poetry of Creative Dissolution," *Wake* II (1950), 95-106; Leo Lowenthal, *Literature and the Image of Man* (Boston, 1957); and Harry Jaffa, "The Limits of Politics: An Interpretation of *King Lear*, Act. I, Scene I," *American Political Science Review*, LI (1957), 405-427.

[11] (London, 1958), p. 250. In n. 13 of Leo Spitzer's review-article on Stephen Gilman's *The Art of La Celestina*, *Hispanic Review*, XXV (1957), 19, there is a valuable list of major thinkers whose work must be consulted if one is to understand the movement in intellectual history of which Mr. Kahler's statement, as he tells us, is but a culminating expression.

We are, then, inescapably aware of ourselves and of those qualities of selfhood which I have called our *humanitas*. At the center of that awareness, we know ourselves to be, momentarily at least, neither conditioned nor contingent. But at the perimeter of that awareness, we know ourselves as in all things conditioned and contingent. On the one hand we are vital existences who may well be perverted or glorified, but nonetheless never deprived of our individual vitality, so long as we have at least the awareness that we exist. On the other hand, we are acculturated creatures whose least gesture can always be accounted for in someone's encyclopedic register of the life-style which obtains at our particular moment in history. We are both of these at once; so it has always been, so it must always be.

Our humanistic disciplines may be specifically arranged and tabulated as they focus on the kinds of relationships which hold between these two aspects of ourselves. The relationship on which literature focuses is that in which our *humanitas*, in all its historical conditioning, is shown as it might realize itself, were it powerfully operative in a way in which in common-sense reality it never is. This strange as-if power is a direct product of the nature of the literary statement as I have already translated it analytically: "If there had been such a person as X, living in a specified situation, etc., he would have acted in this way." Making a statement of this type, the artist is as free as he can be to do as he likes with the data of his culture (and I mean here literally the worldly riches which his sensibility is *given*). He can do as he likes, however, only so long as he does it in accordance with a a sense of possibility consonant with the *humanitas* which it is his gift to know better than other men of his age. In literature, we could say, *humanitas* triumphs over history, even as it triumphs by means of history. His-

31

tory, in a grandly fictive act, is made to be at its service. But history, to be sure, claims its due. Which is this: that the triumph of *humanitas* can never be acknowledged except in such terms as history has given it. The triumph of *humanitas* in literature, then, is a triumph of self-limitation and self-definition. The limits are those of history, as are the terms of definition. And he who, as casual reader or earnest critic, would know the triumph can, by virtue of a dialectical *force majeure*, know it only as it is limited and defined.

Humanitas, that is to say, insofar as it can be operative, is the agent of human freedom. But when any man would even tell another man what it means to be free, he must meet that other man on the common ground of what, coming after the fact of the meeting, we call history. We call it history; if he is a poet, he most often (at least recently) calls it language. And the fact of history, because it is a fact, is limiting and defining of freedom. (Indeed, could we not say that the masterplot of masterplots is that of the artist declaring our freedom in the very terms that limit it?) History limits a poet's freedom too, of course. (Let "poet" be our word for literary artist.) Only, he pretends that it does not. Or rather: the kind of statement he would make gives him the license, the poetic license, to pretend that it does not. This is one of the characteristic contrarieties of *humanitas* which he pushes to an extreme. He makes history, he says. We may well say that he is wise to believe that he does make history; for this is how he best manages to be true to his sense of his self and his vocation. But we can afford, as he cannot, to know better. (This is surely one of the chief rewards accruing from the critical reader's subordination to the artist.) We know that as the poet has used history, so he has had to let history use him; and that what the poet has created is not a pure, ahistorical, timeless expression of *humanitas*, but rather a confrontation of history on behalf of *humanitas*. *Humanitas* itself—or that one of its contrarieties which stands over against man's drive to be absolutely creative—sets such a limitation. And we, if we read wisely and well, if we can perceive whatever degree of wholeness there is in the poet's creation, we will rejoice to note that here at least the result has been a stand-off. And we will know that there are, of course, other means of confronting history, but none which does so specifically on history's own terms, as those terms are carried in that language concerning which the poet is professionally so solicitous. The other means—philosophy, direct historical study, theology, critical theory of the sort which this essay aspires to be, etc.—confront history by translating it into their own special terms: which, for all their import for us, accounts for their "insubstantiality" as compared with poetry. Poems, thus, are not a means of transcending history (as has recently been maintained) or of submitting to it (as used to be maintained), but rather of meeting it. At least, this is how it must be for poets when they are looked at by readers.

For readers, poems are, whatever else, a means of knowing history well enough to bear its burden. "I wish to see how much I can endure," Max Weber is declared to have said in the course of justifying his way with history. So it must be with us, justifying our way with the riches of literature which have come to be our heritage and our responsibility. For us, the vital center will be *humanitas*. And literature will be nothing more, and nothing less, than a prime mode of evoking the possibilities of that *humanitas* as it has moved through the terrible complexities, often the *inhumanitas*, of the historical structures, literary and otherwise, which it has created for itself.

To say this is, I think, simply to generalize upon the poetics developed in the work of many recent critics and theorists of criticism. One could fill a common-place book with statements like these:

> *Works of genuine poetry* . . . lay open to [the] sympathetic understanding *human being in its possibilities as the possibilities that belong specifically to the one who understands it.* [The italics are the author's.]
>
> Rudolph Bultmann, "The Problem of Hermeneutics," *Essays, Philosophical and Theological* (London, 1955), p. 246.

These deeds and events [among which are works of literature] trace out the peculiar physiognomy of a people and make evident the "inwardness" of their life, never identical with that of any other human community.

> Américo Castro, *The Structure of Spanish History* (Princeton, 1954), pp. 32-33.

For surely, the most highly alembicated and sophisticated work of art, arising in complex civilization, could be considered as designed to organize and command the army of one's thoughts and images, and to so organize them that one "imposes upon the enemy the time and place and conditions for fighting preferred by oneself." One seeks to "direct the larger movements and operations in one's campaign of living." One "maneuvers," and maneuvering is an "art."

> Kenneth Burke, "Literature as Equipment for Living," in *The Philosophy of Literary Form* (New York, 1957), p. 257.

"Poetic truth," which seems so difficult to bring to earth, to isolate, to state clearly, and which is also so strangely intimate, has its roots in a sense of communion with other persons, persons perceived through masks, yet somehow decidedly there, who have believed in us enough to invite us to this uncommonly intimate response, and in whom we, in turn, are called on to believe.

34

Walter J. Ong, "Voice as Summons for Belief:
Literature, Faith, and the Divided Self,"
Thought, xxxiii (1958), 60-61.

Such statements are of interest to us not only because of their tendency toward some form of *Lebens-
philosophie*, but because the eschatological commitments of their authors have not much necessary relationship. Such commitments are, as it were, so many
a priori ontological foundations of a common view of
human nature, existentially defined. And, as we must
constantly remind ourselves, literature is, in this sense
at least, nothing if not existential. Its essence is not
to be of the essence.

The value of a literary work, we can conclude, may
be measured precisely as it is a whole structure whose
very ordering into wholeness is set by its realization of
its potential of *humanitas*. Literature is not an expression of (or above) history, but rather an expression *in*
history. The greatness of a literary work is an index
and an assessment of the possibilities for greatness of
the culture out of which it has come. Literature is for
both writer and reader—although in different measure
and to differing immediate ends—an act of commitment to, and a full and humble acknowledgment of,
that possibility. Artistic greatness, then, is the ideal
result, characterizing the degree of realization of an
ideal possibility, of the aesthetic "It ought to be" which
is consequent upon the writer's initial and initiating
humanistic "I am." All cultures, thus, through their
great writers, manifest the *possibility* of greatness.
What art teaches us is the degree to which that possibility has been realized.

Thinking about literature in this way, we would
perhaps cease to look primarily for specifically cate-
gorizable effects (tension, paradox, ambiguity, generi-
cally determinate unity, etc.), and give our attention

to literary structures as they achieve relative degrees of wholeness and correspondingly relative degrees of the autonomy that certainly is a signal criterion for artistic achievement. We would take tension, paradox, etc. as so many *means* to this end; and we might well expect to discover many other such means. For they are, from the point of view of this essay, means whereby there may be achieved the formal resolution or the containment, or both, of those existential contrarieties which, as it is endowed with *humanitas*, the literary work manifests. Thus we would take literary work as, in the largest sense, ways of coming to know the world fully enough to celebrate our own existence in it. We would take it that one of the glories of our critical endeavors, like that of an artist's creative endeavors, is that they are never-ending, never completed, never completely fulfilled, never perfected. Acknowledging this fact, we would—as readers and critics, as historians, as men living in the present—commit ourselves (however temporarily) to the living possibility, to the living uniqueness, of such literary works as we should study, or teach, or write about. We would, in the process, attend to the component of creativity, of the full-flowering of *humanitas*, which derives from the culture in which the work has its initial being. We would, in a sense, be in and of that culture as we read the work. In and of that culture, to be sure, in a way that none of its members could have been in and of it; for we would be in and of it aesthetically, able to attend to just those of its values on which the author's creative sensibility was selectively and triumphantly operative. We would be achieving, let me say it again, *historical* knowledge. We might, for good cause, have reason to hate the specific values of the culture; still, unless those values immediately threatened ones we hold dear, we could yet experience their attraction, power, and compelling force—their charge of sheer human possibility.

In criticism, of course, we always return to the eternal verities—*plus ça change* . . . —as in anthropology, sociology, and psychology we always return to the psychic uniformity of mankind and to cultural universals. That is to say, at the center of the artist's vision as the critic knows and elucidates it is *humanitas*, even though the center as he knows it exists only as it is defined by and gives wholeness to the perimeter of historically contingent data which surround it. The special emphasis in historicist criticism—that which gives it its excuse for being—is on that sense of our involvement in historical-cultural otherness which we gain by virtue of the literary work's rediscovery of those eternal verities. Hence, the literary work, properly read, would be our means again to affirm that rule which our own culture, in its fear of difference, variation, and the like, trembles to affirm: value-charged then; *therefore* value-charged now. This is not other-direction, but rather an inner-direction of such a degree of certitude that it can, without fear for its own well-being, willingly confront an authentic existence of the other and willingly assess the import of the latter existence for its own.

5.

Let me venture an example of the sort of problem which proper historicist criticism would turn up and the sort of solution it might propose. Among critics of *The Scarlet Letter* there is a notorious tendency to refuse to fit the novel into its own integral, historically definable (and therefore limited) system of values. On the one hand, there are critics who claim that the novel exhibits a kind of libidinal timorousness on Hawthorne's part; he was fascinated, so they claim, by dark ladies and all the sexuality and power that they embodied. Yet he feared them, and so had to destroy them, thereby distorting his sense of self and making

37

impotent a portion of his creative imagination. On the other hand, there are those critics who would somehow bring Hawthorne into the fold of one of the Christian orthodoxies, especially that one which in our time would graft the thought of a Niebuhr on to that of an Eliot. For them *The Scarlet Letter* must be made to point to some kind of redemptive *dénouement*; they would interpret this *dénouement* as altogether a *felix culpa*. Now, these approaches to *The Scarlet Letter*, in their very extremism, have yielded up valuable insights for us. But essentially they have not dealt with *The Scarlet Letter* so much as with its import and significance for the culture of its critics. They are deliberately ahistorical and must be accepted as such. I do not wish to dismiss such views but rather to suggest the possibility of another, superior to them at least in its attempt to make its center of interest the novel in relation at once to its historical situation and to ours, not just to ours. I should think that such an alternate view of *The Scarlet Letter* would fully grant that Hawthorne's culture had its constraining libidinal timorousness and its recusant Calvinism, but only to ask: what meanings could he create by evoking the possibilities for authentic human existence which that timorousness and that recusancy shaped and directed? What does it mean (not "how was it actually"—for these are different questions) to have existed in that Boston which Hawthorne's New England gave him the materials to create? How was it possible to *live* then? How was it possible to live in and through the forms (repressive and expressive) peculiar to *that* civilization? What sort of vital structure does Hawthorne create and how does its vitality partake of the vitality of his own culture and that earlier one which his own gave him to envisage? A larger question would follow automatically—a question to which one could propose a private answer precisely because a novel, a work of art, had let him conceive of asking it: how is it possible to live authentically in and through the forms peculiar to *our* civilization? The historicist might or might not venture to answer such a question. His primary task, however, would have been, through his criticism, setting the occasion for our asking it, and asking it in such terms. Studying the Then, making us know it as literature gives it to us, he would help us free ourselves to study and know the Now.

Nachbilden ist eben ein Nacherleben, said Dilthey: to reconstruct is to re-live. Collingwood's variation on this statement is: "The value of history . . . is that it teaches us what man has done and thus what man is." This is, I take it, a proposition whose truistic nature, as Collingwood's and Dilthey's own work shows, literary art most fully demonstrates. ("Art," so Collingwood's famous words go, "is the community's medicine for the worst disease of mind, the corruption of consciousness.") We all know that one of the central problems of our time is to relearn this proposition in such a way that we may live by it. It seems to me that our criticism is now trying, however hesitantly, to help us learn this proposition anew. I only suggest here that we make quite sure of what is involved in the learning and face up to its implications and difficulties as best we can—which is to say, with our clearest insight and intelligence. An adequate critical historicism would be governed by the certitude that formalist criteria for truth, in poetry as in other institutions, are the necessary, but not the sufficient, condition for literary understanding. Such criteria, being formalist, enable us to note only where the literary work ends. Only a deeply matured sense of history, and of men moving in history, will enable us to note where it begins.

Formalist criticism, as it has been refined in our time, can with masterful delicacy describe and elucidate what it calls the texture and structure of a liter-

39

ary work. But trying to account for the life-principle of the work, it must always evoke terms like organicism, symbolism, etc.: all, strictly speaking, terms of analogy, and, like their archetypal paradigm, the "I am" (an "I am" curiously drained of its existential quality) of Coleridge's secondary imagination, deriving their power from that to which they are analogous, not from anything intrinsic to them. Poems (again, our shorthand term for literary works) begin with persons in history. And however those persons, and their history along with them, are transmuted when they appear in poems, an inseparable portion of the form and energy whereby the transmutation is brought about derives from what they were in the beginning. It is much too easy, much too inviting, to say "In my end is my beginning" and leave it at that. Whatever relevance this has to our eschatological understanding of ourselves, it has at best a secondary relevance to our aesthetic-humanistic understanding of ourselves. Yet it too might well furnish an a priori ontological foundation on which still another theory of the person in history, the person *making* the poem in history, could be constructed. And, of course, the Coleridgean doctrine of the secondary imagination itself could furnish another such foundation; but we would require of it a shift in emphasis from ontology to existence. As a result, our interest in that a priori would have shifted from its eschatological import to an existential view of the poet as person in history: from theology and metaphysics to critical historicism. What such a view gives us to see is not where the person began or where he will end, but rather how it is to be between the beginning and the end. If this is a least common denominator, let us make the most of it.

In a poem there is outline, texture, form; and there is something happening. The important point is that there is something *still* happening, and the organicity and wholeness which formalist criteria will help us remark are such because, as the poem first happened, it still happens. As it still happens, it brings, inseparably, the life of its culture with it. If we accept the form, we accept the life. If we accept the life, we accept the culture. This is historical understanding and historical knowledge.

As a result of the encounter between the creative potential of language as it is given to the poet and the creative potential of his sensibility, there emerges the poem, doing its work as poem. As its maker's fine understanding of *humanitas* urges him to compose in such a way as to make his culture's language consonant with that understanding—as this, the writer's creative act, takes place, so will the reader's complementary creative act take place, but after-the-fact and from a perspective in which he can comprehend the consonance of language (i.e. history) and *humanitas*. We shall see, as so much recent criticism has taught us to see, that the poem is out there, an object existing solely for us to realize and to elucidate. But we must acknowledge that, in the very nature of the poem, "out there" means "out there in a historically definable time and place." As we realize and elucidate the poem, so will we realize and elucidate ourselves, or that aspect of ourselves which, being our *humanitas*, lets us know the infinitude of shapes and meanings *humanitas* can assume. That infinitude is nothing more or less than the infinitude of history: which is, so far as it is the locus of our poetry, an infinite series of exemplars of what we would possibly have been, were we not what we are.

6.

We have come, therefore, to the deep end of critical historicism. And it should be abundantly clear that I have done no more than suggest the range of theoretical and practical considerations which may well encourage him who would be a critical historicist to go to this point. In critical theory it is not possible to do much more than suggest the obligations entailed by asking and answering the question: how is it possible that literature should be what it is? Hence, at this stage of the argument we touch upon the kind of commitment which, even as he tries to justify it, the critical historicist can only refer to, describe, and perhaps illuminate. Following out that commitment—this is surely a matter of the deepest and most private personal concern and can be understood and tested adequately only in the actual doing. Still, by going to literature for a parable—this by way of a brief exercise in the sort of hermeneutics which, because he would be a critic, the historicist also feels is at the heart of all criticism—he just may communicate a sense of what it might well mean to be what he would be.

In the second poem in the title series of Robert Penn Warren's *Promises*, the poet recalls that as a boy he would listen to one of his Confederate elders rambling on in great and particular detail about the War Between the States. And he recalls that:

> In the dust by his chair
> I undertook to repair
> The mistakes of his old war.
> Hunched on that toy terrain,
> Campaign by campaign,
> I sought, somehow, to untie
> The knot of History,
> For in our shade I knew
> That only the Truth is true,
> That life is only the act
> To transfigure all fact,
> And life is only a story
> And death is only the glory

42

Of telling the story,
And the *done* and the *to-be-done*
In that timelessness were one,
Beyond the poor *being done.*

This is the mind of the proto-mythographer (is it significant that the poem makes it out to be an adolescent mind?) going to work on the discrete facts of history.[12] But then, there is a moment of revelation. The old man has had to explain guerrilla warfare and how he and his soldiers had been obliged to ambush guerrillas and to dispose of them:

"By the road, find some shade, a nice patch.
Even hackberry does, at a scratch.
Find a spring with some cress fresh beside it,
Growing rank enough to nigh hide it.
Lord, a man can sure thirst when you ride.
Yes, find you a nice spot to bide.
Bide sweet when you can when you ride.
Order halt, let heat-daze subside.
Put your pickets, vedettes out, dismount.
Water horses, grease gall, take count,
And while the men rest and jaw,
You and two lieutenants talk law.
Brevitatem justitia amat.
Time is short—hell, a rope is—that's that."

This is the end of the old man's account; but, for the poet recalling his boyhood, somehow this episode would

[12] The exegetical historicist might well recall at this point how another Southerner, Thomas Wolfe, in *The Web and the Rock*, under the *persona* of Monk Webber, listens to his teacher, Edwin Greenlaw, under the *persona* of Randolph Ware: "Get the Facts, Brother Webber! Get the Facts . . . I am a Research Man! . . . I get the Facts!" "What do you do with them after you get them?" asks Webber. "I put salt on their tails and get some more." Of this man, Wolfe-Webber in his concern to project even this Grandgrindian *done* and *to-be-done* into mythic timelessness can say only, "He was gigantically American."

43

not end. He recalls that the old man had finished by
saying to him:

> "By God, they deserved it. . . .
> Don't look at me that way. . . ."

And now somehow the facts of this War, or any War,
come alive for the boy. He recalls how at that moment,
"The world's silence made me afraid." He has a nightmare vision of the old man as a young officer riding
on, the air about him filled with the "outraged" faces
of hanged men:

> The horseman does not look back.
> Blank-eyed, he continues his track,
> Riding toward me there,
> Through the darkening air.

The past, as the tenses and the action indicate, is now
present. The horseman, in his world of hanged guerrillas, in his world of quick justice, in his world of
"queasy" stomachs and consciences, must ever ride
toward and into the lives of those Southerners, those
Americans, those men, who come after him and live
as they do because of what he has done, because of all
he has done. There is a final concluding line—a verse-
paragraph in itself—stark in the sense of ultimate true-
ness it would precipitate:

> The world is real. It is there.

The problem, as so much of Mr. Warren's poetry and
fiction demonstrates, is that of historicism. One suspects that, were he to write his essay "Pure and Impure
Poetry" now, Mr. Warren would account for the nexus
between purity and impurity by the fact that man can
discover his purity only in meditating the impurity
which is his burden in history and transforming it into
poems. Is not something like this the meaning of the
prefatory lines with which Mr. Warren puts us on our

44

way toward understanding his *Brother to Dragons?* "Historical sense and poetic sense should not, in the end, be contradictory, for if poetry is the little myth we make, history is the big myth we live, and in our living, constantly remake." This is but a variation on "The world is real. It is there"—a sentiment which, tied to that sense of the *"being-done"* which gives rise to it, might well be a working motto for a critical historicist. For the critical historicist is convinced, simply enough, that we must know that it is there before we can know that it is real.

1958

2

LITERATURE, HISTORY, AND HUMANISM:
An Americanist's Dilemma

> "An artist's use of language is the most sensitive
> index to cultural history, since a man can articulate
> only who he is, and what he has been made by the
> society of which he is a willing or unwilling part."
> F. O. MATTHIESSEN, *American Renaissance*

As MY TITLE indicates, I write as an Americanist. So
my focus will be somewhat narrow—but not too narrow, I think. For I am convinced that the Americanist's
burden as teacher is to that of his non-Americanist colleagues as American literature is to British literature—
indeed, as it is to Western European literature generally. As Americans we are surely but Western Europeans *in extremis*. I want then, from an Americanist's
point-of-view, to consider our situation as teachers of
literature, consider it as an aspect of the condition of
our culture in the 1960's. Indeed, I am sure that the
shifts of emphases in our teaching during the 40's and
50's most clearly manifest the way that our tasks have
come now to be defined for us. Or rather, our tasks
have come now to be *set* for us. It has been up to us
to define them; for in defining them we in fact perform
them. My words then are to be taken as an exercise
toward definition.

I begin by recalling the fact that one of the concerns
which gave impulse to the New Criticism—I should
prefer to call it the New Formalism—was its ambiguous
feeling about the relation of the study of history to the
study of literature. On the one hand there was the New

Critics' belief that the Old Critics were increasingly tending to lose sight of the unique and intrinsic quality of the literary works which they so carefully put into proper texts and for which they so fully recreated the socio-cultural milieux. On the other hand, there was the New Critical belief that literary works themselves constituted history: that, by virtue of the creative acts of their makers, they somehow appropriated and totally transformed the past, or that portion of it which was worth saving, and made it totally available as something existing in the present—its mode of being set by whatever formal quality (irony, ambiguity, generic consistency, etc., etc.) might distinguish it as art. That the first of these beliefs was substantially correct is demonstrated, I think, by the revolution in the teaching of literature which has been brought about in our own time. Hardly anyone I know even admits (or, perhaps, can remember) that he once taught literature in anything but fundamentally explicatory and formalist critical terms. But the second of these beliefs—involving at its most extreme the major theses of say, "Tradition and the Individual Talent," "The Intentional Fallacy," and "An Outline of Poetic Theory"—continues to raise problems which are as yet unresolved. We have as yet had no satisfactory account of what is called the New Criticism's "Contextualism." In short, the New Criticism—or, the New Formalism—has taught a lot of us that we must read literary texts intrinsically; we decline to make them out to be mere vehicles for the cultural and intellectual history in which they had their initial life. And yet, we would grant that history is as much *in* our literary texts as our texts are in our history. A full "contextualism" would have to take this fact into account. And it is at this point, with this proposition, that this essay properly begins.

For I take it that the criticism which now attracts

many of us is a product of the compulsion (the disciplined compulsion, I hope) to say what I shall say. Think of the work of Lionel Trilling, Erich Auerbach, R.W.B. Lewis, Leslie Fiedler, Father Walter Ong (the names I cite are at random) . . . think of this work and you will note that it assumes, with formalist criticism, that poems do not mean, but are; and then goes on to ask what poems do. Asking what poems do, those I cite are in effect asking how poems teach, and how such teaching is related to other kinds of teaching: in all, how poems enable us to know something of that dilemma entailed by the fact that man lives always in a culture alive with its past, present, and future; that dilemma, in short, which has urged us to claim that literature (literary study) is central in the humanistic studies.

What does it mean for us, coming at our time in history, at once possessing and possessed by our sense of past and present, to say that literary works have as a necessary condition of their own intrinsic value the fact that they both implicate and are implicated in the conditions of the time and place in which they were created—in their history, that is to say? We grant that literature, as we can know it now, in the continuing present, nourishes our sense of the past. How is this possible?

Let me put this question in operational terms, terms which reflect the sort of teaching and writing which many of us would do. (I should admit that I think of my own teaching and writing, not to say my speechifying, as being recto-verso aspects of the same operation.) How are we going to write criticism and to teach in such a way so as to use properly the sort of historical evidence available to us? Alternatively: what sort of historical evidence does literature constitute? What kind of history does literature make, and how are we to understand it? How may we proceed so that literary history and historical criticism become one?

Yet there is a prior question, or series of questions, I think; and they must be answered before we can even try to answer such questions as I have posed. Are we clear as to what asking such questions entails? Why, indeed, should such questions as I have posed be so central for us, living as and where we live? Who are we that we ask such questions? And what do we want to achieve by asking them? What does it mean for *us* to ask them?

First, then: *Some notes on the theory of literature (and I would add, the theory of criticism) in the United States.*

From the beginning, recall, we have not had a body of writing which we could classify once and for all as "literature": something which, however produced and by whomever, would be set down on the assumption that it must and will have a leisured and intelligent readership committed to the intrinsic value of *prodesse* and *delectare*. I need not go through the evidence from our colonial and provincial history. I need only recall that later, as our literature had its national origins in writers who wanted to be literary men in the traditional sense of the phrase, it reflects in its substantial and formal qualities the fact that such men had to write in a language fatefully conditioned by the assumptions of a culture even whose elite members on the whole expressed no deep or abiding concern for the integrity of the literary man's vocation and the meaning of that vocation for their lives. Literature, in point of fact, has never been for our society the kind of institution that it has been for others—older, traditionally allowing for, expecting, and demanding the existence of an intellectual elite (or opinion leaders, as they are now called).

(Let me pause parenthetically to define "institution,"

49

since, as with other such terms which we have begun to find so useful, we must constantly remind ourselves precisely to what we are committing ourselves when we use it. I remind you of Harry Levin's justly celebrated essay, "Literature as an Institution"; and then, to get that essay's substance into my remarks here, I quote from an essay by Talcott Parsons: An institution is a "system of patterned expectations defining the proper behavior of persons playing certain roles, enforced by the incumbents' own positive motives for conformity, and by the sanctions of others." Thus to say of literature that it is an institution is to say that it is the product of men who, in the society in and for which they write, are expected to achieve certain clearly definable ends which may be clearly related to the ends achieved by men playing analogous roles in the same society.)

Hence, I repeat: literature has never, for good and for bad, been in our society the kind of institution that it has been for others—not even as an institution for an "elite." It has been all too characteristic of Americans either to be disinterested in a literature with "clearly definable ends" or to be suspicious of and uncomfortable with such ends precisely because they are claimed to be clearly definable.

Yet literature has had its own kind of institutional status in the United States; and I think that it is a full and frank recognition of that status which is the necessary condition of the proper historical critic's proper interpretation of American literature—and beyond that, for our understanding of the nature of our criticism and the kind of teaching it points us toward. Failing of adequate general acceptance and sanction (even among the intellectual elite), our literature has tended to be that parodoxical thing, a "private" as opposed to a "social" institution. At its best, it has sought its sanction (as Tocqueville long ago observed) in the nature and aspiration of the individual man, not of the community. And as in modern times the forces of American—as of world—history have further and further separated the individual's idea of the good life from that of his community, as societies have tended increasingly to become mere collectivities and not true communities, literature has perforce been biased toward the "private" as opposed to the "social." In the United States literature has never really "belonged," as fully articulated institutions—mediating more or less justly between man's need at once to be "private" and to be "social"—seem usually to "belong." The paradox of its status in the United States lies in the fact that its not "belonging" has come gradually to characterize it as an institution: made for its institutionalized non-institutionality, so to speak. Thus we say of its authors—caught up in this paradox—that as authors (not always as private individuals) they are alienated.

Here, of course, I am thinking particularly of the achievement and fate of writers of the first rank like Poe, Emerson, Hawthorne, and Melville. As for writers of the second rank—for example, Bryant and Cooper—their interests in the political and moral problems entailed by the development of their own (and our) culture took the place, I think, of an interest in being primarily literary men, and caused them to produce poems and fictions whose power—which is there, assuredly—derives from their direct and pragmatic involvement with such explicitly political and moral problems as were set by the nature of their culture, not by their sense of the radically humanistic requirements of art. If any of them had that sense in abundance, it was surely not available to him; of the reasons why this was so perhaps we may never be altogether certain, but surely a closer study of the workings of nineteenth-century culture will let us approximate such reasons. As for writers of the third rank—Longfellow and Lowell, for example—their noble hope to produce an adequate popular culture for a democratic society, which meant, we can see now, to mediate btween high culture and low (or no) culture, this noble hope was productive of poems and fictions whose least-common-denominator effect excluded a vital sense of the depths and complexities of "private" human action. Maybe I put the matter too strongly here. But one thing, I think, is certain: Longfellow and Lowell, and others like them, of course, did nothing in the long run to establish the positive and assured role of the serious imaginative writer in American culture. With the noblest of intentions, they tried to compromise that role. And compromise in these matters would seem always to mean if not destruction or dissolution, at least transformation. Come to think of it, we do not yet know much about this transformation of the writers' role in American culture. We do not yet know much about literature as an American institution—through its makers, living out its life, sometimes half-life, in a society in which it has no properly secure station.

I forbear further examples. If what I say has any novelty at all, such novelty derives not from my pointing to facts of which we are not all aware, but rather from my interpretation of their significance for the modes of literary history and criticism intended properly to deal with them. The history of these modes from the beginning almost up to our own time is dealt with at large in Howard Mumford Jones's *Theory of American Literature.* I have been encouraged to say what I have to say by Professor Jones's fine study; yet, of course, I want to go a little further than he does. I want to go into the consequences for our criticism, especially the recent consequences, of the fact that literature has never had a clearly institutionalized status in our culture.

Let me begin, where most of my teachers seem to

have begun, with Parrington and his dismissal, not at all casual, of what he called the belle-lettristic. Parrington, in brief, decided that literature was actually but a branch of politics. The necessary condition of that decision, I suggest, was his total, uncritical, perhaps unconscious, acceptance of the apparently non-institutionalized status of literature in American culture. He looked for a traditional social institution and could not find it. Temperamentally he was disinclined to take seriously "private" institutions—if, indeed, he could even see them. Or perhaps it was his Jeffersonian-Populist faith which assured him that there need be no conflict between public and "private" institutions. So he decided that American literature *did* have a social role, but rather as politics than *belles lettres*. In effect, it was for him a new kind of public institution— as I have said, specifically a political institution. Thus he was able to disregard that amalgam of public and private values and criteria which had served traditionally to define the function of literary institutions, and to search for other, more "pragmatic" values and criteria.

It was at this juncture that the New Criticism began its tremendous work—to save literature from politics, as from all extra-literary, history-centered considerations: not only in fact from Parrington but from the genteel tradition-oriented literary historians and positivistic reductionists whom he too had found unsatisfactory. In effect, the New Critical effort was to restore literature to its status as an institution whose nature was unique and irreducible to anything but itself. New Critical criteria and standards were self-consciously "traditional" ones and tended always to be rigidly unequivocating, inadequately taking into account the "Americanization" of literature as an institution. The New Critics worked toward a critical mode which would in effect take American (and, of course, other) literature out of history; would make history "extrinsic" to literature and make the most of it as an institution—a traditional institution—which, if touched by politics, moral philosophy, and the like, was nonetheless able to absorb and transform all that touched it, so that the end-product was an object above and beyond the pressures of history and historical issues. The effect of such pressures, if yielded to, was in fact taken to be deleterious. (Read, for example Blackmur on Melville or Tate on Emily Dickinson, or Winters on almost anybody to see what I mean.) If for Parrington, literature simply didn't exist as a separate and unique institution, for the New Critics it existed as an institution which in all times and all places had and would have a separate and unique function. Parringtonian and New Critical zealousness made for an apparently irresolvable dilemma.

Yet it *was* resolved, at least in part. I think that it was the greatest achievement of F. O. Matthiessen to work (or work toward) the resolution. Matthiessen, as he said, was concerned to establish a more independently positive role for literature as literature than Parrington (and the Parringtonians, I should add) would allow. And against the New Critics, he was concerned to show how literature, as literature, *is* a special sort of political instrument and thus is, in a special way, integrally tied to the historical situation in which it exists. It was, surely, Matthiessen's clear understanding of the poetics of organicism (itself a New Critical preoccupation) which allowed him to do what he did. In Matthiessen's great work the methods of the New Criticism were used to modify and enlarge the methods of the political and social historian, and vice versa. The hopes of the earlier Van Wyck Brooks and his peers were finally realized. Orthodox literary history was, in effect, rejected, as was orthodox literary criticism. It no longer really mattered whether or not Whitman wrote any particular form of verse or if Hawthorne and Melville were really novelists or if Emerson was a philosopher or a *littérateur*. In effect what Matthiessen showed was that literature in the United States had an institutional status, but one which was somehow different from that it had in other older, more tradition-oriented cultures; that part of the formal meaning and import of American literature derived from the fact that its major producers were forced into the status of "marginal" men; that as such they could not rely on the traditional power of traditional forms; that they saw that the individual accommodated himself to the collective only at his great peril, that art was a means of expressing a sense of that peril and surviving it; that the creation of continually new and renewed forms was demanded of them, as custodians of the individualism of the literary-esthetic in a mass society—or at least in a society which was moving rapidly toward massiveness.

And the recent major advances in our understanding of our literature and its role in our culture have come from scholar-critics whose work can be at best fairly called post-Matthiessenian. (I say this, fully acknowledging that I have rigged my scheme here and made it overly dialectical. But I would claim that, within its limits, it is valid.) I think of studies of our fiction in relation to the tension between the novel and the romance; of the import of the symbolic mode for our writers; of interest in the relation between "mythic" commitments, literary expression, and social belief and action; of the conception of the writer as "sage"; of the notion of the American writer's ambiguous relation to the ideology of the culture of which, although it more or less sustains him, he must be suspicious. What such studies indicate is this, I think: that we have accepted the fact that our literature, never having had the clearly articulated social-institutional role of the literatures of older western European societies, cannot be properly studied primarily in terms appropriate to the study of such older literatures—that such terms, when and if used, will have to be vastly modified, adapted "organically," so to speak. Moreover, we have accepted the fact that the means to studying our literature in its historical development must be integrally related to the more general study of our history; that we must develop techniques, strategies, and categories which will let us discover and evaluate those qualities of our literature which, in their distinctiveness, give it its unique power and import. Further, we have realized that we must learn to be better comparatists—to proceed from a sense of American distinctiveness to a sense of French or English or German distinctiveness, and then—and only then—to relate them. We have realized that we must learn to see how the relative lack of traditional, overtly institutionalized literary sanctions in the United States is coming to be one of the recent harder facts of life in older societies, although it is a fact which nonetheless makes headway but slowly against the fact of their age and the traditional sanctions for literature which that age carries. In all, I should say, we have realized that we must learn to be proper historical critics.

Thus I come to the second topic to which I must address myself. *What is the nature of this integrally compounded literary history and historical criticism which we so badly need? What sort of teaching and study would it produce?*

I suggest that it is a history and criticism whose method must be such as to keep in view the fact (for I take it as a fact) that literature—any literature—is at once in history and above it; that it is generally a means of getting perspective on man in history and also of assessing the cost of being a man in history; that it is particularly an expression of the unique perspectives which come in given cultures to be available to the men of high imagination who would adopt them, and is also, for such men, constituent of the very terms given them to assess that cost. The impulse to literature must surely be universal; as the expression of a universal impulse, literature is always *immanently* an institution; but the form that impulse takes, the degree to which it may achieve institutionalized realization—these are matters to be understood only by a study of literature as the concrete and particular element of a concrete and particular culture. And as a crucial dimension of culture is history, so it is of literature. For us it must follow that, however sure we are that our literature is expressive of a universal, substantially fixed impulse to deal imaginatively with man and his world, nonetheless we accept as a fact of our life that the forms in which our literature have been expressed are of a kind limited and shaped by the nature of the culture whose individuals' impulse to literature it expresses. This indeed is a fact in the nature of man in this world—a condition of that humanity the understanding of which gives literary study its central position in the curriculum.

A brief example. *The Adventures of Augie March*, let us say, is as a work of art presumably of universal significance. But its achievement is not the product of its being at one extreme a recent variation on, say, the picaresque nor at the other of some absolute intuition of its author into the human situation. Rather, such novelistic form as it has is a product of its author's striving to express the universal, man's truth, in terms constrained by the culture in which that truth is, as it were, revealed. (As *humanists* we may call the truth about ourselves "revealed" whenever it is possible for us to see all of it—to know it as an aspect of what Melville called our "apprehension of absolute condition of present things.") The fact of the constraint, then, comes to be integrally and necessarily part of the meaning of the book—the difference it makes to and in us. And we find that the direction of Augie's adventures, his point of view, the sensibility with which he is endowed, the purview which his author gives him—that these are products of an imagination (Bellow's, not Augie March's) striving to realize itself in the context of a society for which neither the symbolism of the romance, nor the rigidly controlled perspectivism of the Jamesian novel, nor the common sense of "realistic" fiction, nor the seemingly uninterrupted and unarticulated flow of "naturalistic" fiction will suffice. Nor will the Kafkaesque manner of Bellow's earlier work suffice. There must be evolved a literary form which will allow the protagonist to endow the world as he discovers it with a curiously irresponsible charisma—Augie March's, not Bellow's. For it is this charisma—Augie's abundant awareness of his superb authority as a person—which, so Bellow's art would direct us to discover, characterizes those individuals in our world who have learned that life, if it is to be lived at its fullest, must be lived on the margin. Thus the compulsive, lyrical, obsessively autobiographical form of Bellow's novel—deriving from his sense of how a marginal man, if he were sure enough of his overplus of humanity, might plunge into the world and yet not lose his marginality; the lack of sharp points of transition, clearly articulated notions of status and social style, progress; what might be called Bellow's charismatic naturalism, whereby Augie's world, not Augie's self, is revealed to us as, under his aegis, it changes its shape. Thus finally, a certain weakness—perhaps Augie's, perhaps the novel's, perhaps Bellow's. For Augie March must, in the nature of his adventures, compromise himself, by surrendering his critical faculties, even when his creator (to whose sense of life here high irony is irrelevant) would appear to want him to seem to be holding on to his integrity for dear, very dear, life. The sentimentalism of the novel, along with its heroism, holds only when seen as a formal quality of a fiction created in Bellow's (and our) world and at Bellow's (and our) moment in history. The sense, for well or for ill, is that of the creative imagination as it takes its substance from the time-bound world in which it has its being. In this novel—as in this our world—Don Quixote proves to be a pseudonym, or an alias, for Sancho Panza.

Indeed, writing out someone's search for a genuine identity pushes Bellow to even further extravagances in *Henderson the Rain King*. Here the format and gimmicks of a Tarzan story—written, as it were, by Henry James Senior—become appropriate vehicles for the adventures of a Christopher Newman who fears all along that his real name might turn out to be Tom Sawyer.

But I do not mean to make my slight example into a critical essay. What I have tried to sketch here is a portion of the sort of notes a teacher writes to himself when he is trying to decide on the direction in which he wants to point his class and some of the things, not to say landmarks, he'd like them to see on the way. Once he and the class are on the road, who knows?

From the point of view of literary criticism as, put into action, it becomes the discipline we would inculcate—from this point of view, what I have said amounts to this: that when we come to try to understand our literature in our history and our history in our literature, even when—I daresay *especially* when—we are dealing with products of our own time, we have to be ready to see new forms, new modes, new styles emerging and to realize how all that is new results from from a particular confrontation of his culture made by a particular man at a particular time. We must be ready to see that, whatever else it is, criticism is ineluctably a mode of historical understanding—and

59

thus a mode of history itself. It might well be that in implicating criticism in history and history in criticism, we wish to transcend both, to achieve a *tertium quid*: an act of critical confrontation of man in his history which literary texts exist to make possible. Thus, guided by such an integrally compounded historical criticism, we would confront ourselves as Americans, only to discover that we are men of the world: at long last, humanists all.

On an occasion like this one, I can risk a formula: we would seek to combine a Parringtonian sense of the informing power of the historical-cultural situation with a New Critical sense of the informing power of the creative imagination. To say this, I trust, is not simply to utter another NCTE- (or MLA-) type piety. Nor is it to be provincial. For even as I refer and have referred to such men and movements as we know best, I would suggest that we need to learn about other men and movements which also would teach us to restore literature to history and history to literature. Who among us reads, or reads those who read, Curtius or Lukacs or Ingarden or Alonso or Castro or Bachelard—to drop just a few names? We must, in any case, cease considering the two powers alternatively, so as to make for that layer-cake arrangement of history and criticism whereby we manage to assign literary works two lives: one in history and one out of it. History must be for us not milieu but ambiance—not setting but the very atmosphere which the man of high imagination breathes so that he can live and do what he must do.

Let me put the matter down in a series of theses:

1. In its perdurable humanism, literature at once expresses and measures the capacity of the culture out of which it comes to sustain the specifically human. Our joy in art, then, comes from our being involved in its measured expressiveness.

60

2. In literature the specifically human is identified as a self whose power for selfhood, centering on the fact of consciousness, enables men to wrest meaning from the flux of existence. It is a power whose literary-artistic manifestation we can assent to because, guided by the very "formalism" of the manifestation, the work of art, we can be brought to imagine it as possibly ours. The self is the author's, as a man speaking to men. The selves which make up his speakers and casts of characters are functions of his self and, through his art, can become functions of ours. He discovers them, as though for the first time—and so do we, so can we. We can discover them only in their world and in their history. As we are moved to assent to their very existence (an actual existence in art, a possible existence in life), somehow we come to incorporate their world and their history into ours. Reading a work of literature is a transaction with persons in history, a continuing dialogue. Mastery of the theory of this dialogue—which would be a plenary theory of historical criticism—is a problem to be solved by a psycholinguistics and a poetics as yet beyond our ken.

3. In literature this self, the created and creating self of the author, is made to live out its adventures, which become *our* adventures, in and through *language*. For the writer, culture is, in the largest sense, language, the sum-total of modes of communication. A writer thus always begins, wherever he may end, with the historically bounded facts of language. And readers must begin with him there, wherever they may end. It might well be that in Utopia our central discipline is a true, all inclusive general linguistics, one which would encompass that future psycholinguistics and poetics which I have mentioned.

4. We ask of a literary work that it be at once perfected and perfecting in its own terms—that it realize

what we can know at the outset (on second reading at least) is its own capacity, in means given it by its medium, to realize the specifically human.

5. By understanding and interpreting such perfection in literature, knowing the work formally, we can know further how the culture which has set those terms at the outset has at the end at once allowed and constrained the realization of the specifically human. The literary work, as a product of man's capacity to make fictions, mediates between outset and end, its culture and ours. It thus *makes* history and is central to our grasp of tradition and continuity—thereby of the oneness of the world. Here I can best quote once more some words of Robert Penn Warren: "Historical sense and poetic sense should not, in the end, be contradictory, for if poetry is the little myth we make, history is the big myth we live, and in our living, constantly remake."

We must, that is to say, all be philosophical anthropologists first and critics second—as we would ask of, say, historians or sociologists or whatever that they likewise be philosophical anthropologists first and historians or sociologists or whatever second. For we, like the others, have above all to deal with the simple, separate person—who is yet, as the poet insisted, democratic and en masse. In short, we must develop that flexibility and adaptiveness—that sense of the life of literature, not just its form—toward which *American Renaissance* so notably pointed us. Hence at this point I can do no better than recall a couple of crucial sentences from the chapter on "Method and Scope" in that book. "An artist's use of language," Matthiessen wrote in the words I have used as epigraph for these meditations, "is the most sensitive index to cultural history, since a man can articulate only who he is, and what he has been made by the society of which he is a willing or an unwilling part." And to read cultural history thus, he said, a few words later, is to "feel the challenge of our still undiminished resources." I comment. Do we yet know how to define the terms "artist," "use of language," "sensitive index," "articulation," "being a willing or unwilling part"? Do we yet understand what it is to be "challenged" thus? Have we understood what it means to have "undiminishable resources"? I am not at all sure that we do, although the record of criticism lately shows that we are beginning to try. In any case, Matthiessen's work has itself come to express that challenge too. I have meant here to account for and make explicit some of the problems it raises, in the hope that we will learn better how to meet it—and meeting it, to meet our students.

1963

3

MASS CULTURE/POPULAR CULTURE:
Notes for a Humanist's Primer

". . . limits
are what any of us
are inside of."
CHARLES OLSON, *The Maximus Poems*, 5

THINKING about mass culture these days, we seem increasingly to want to take a second or third or fourth step before we have taken the first. Or so I think a careful study of our essays and studies shows. Perhaps we fear that that first step is a step backward. And so it is—into ourselves. For once we admit something so overwhelmingly simple as the fact that we must live together in our community, we shall be obliged to inquire into what Edward Sapir long ago taught us to call the genuineness or spuriousness of our culture: that which gives our community such wholeness as it has. We say that our culture, any culture, is genuine to the degree that it allows full play to our sense of the dignity of man, spurious to the degree that it narrows or distorts or inhibits that sense. Hence we can do no less than begin at the beginning, within ourselves in our community, however narrow, distorted, or inhibited we may be. But it has been ever thus in the humanistic studies.

I mean to suggest in these notes that in the beginning and at the end the study of mass culture is the business—in our time a necessary condition—of the humanistic studies. So far we have not been able to envisage the end clearly because we have not sufficiently considered the beginning. I do not mean to exclude the middle—the myriad essays, books, meditations, editorials on mass culture. I mean only to get them into focus, to set them over against the image of man in which they must be conceived if they are to have any validity whatsoever. I am sure that most of those who have given us the essays, books, etc. have proceeded out of their faith in man. But on most humanists the net effect of their work, since it is so often programmatic and artificially particularized, has been to confuse the issue by simplifying it. To be sure, the simplification is often merely strategic, or "heuristic." Yet as often the stratagem has involved losing sight, if only temporarily, of him on whose behalf the issue has been raised, in whose image the issue must be conceived.

For the humanist the overwhelming consideration here derives from his vocation as teacher. In our world, humanists, whatever their special fields, are almost invariably teachers. The humanist's subject-matter indeed is his students; in the field of his special expertise, he is concerned with object-matter. In his meetings with his students, the humanist must inevitably put to the test the image of man as his special knowledge of his special field empowers him to. I mean by humanist, then, the worker in the humanistic studies, who, whatever else he is, is a teacher and must accordingly face the fact day-to-day that his students, his audiences in general, have had their lives and sensibilities markedly formed by mass culture. This is an aspect—unhappily, a necessary condition—of their life-styles. I suspect that it usually turns out that the humanist soon enough discovers that his life and sensibility have been so shaped too. He need not have any particular "professional" interest in mass culture, but he needs to learn how to think about it, how to interpret the burgeoning "profes-

65

sional" interest in it, as it bears on his role in the teacher-student relationship.

1.

The central fact is quite simple: We do *not* live, alas, in a world we never made. Maybe we did not *really* make it; but it is ours, and it is pointless to conceive of ourselves in another world. As this world is ours, we are this world's. As we have taken the good things it has given us, as we have perforce had to take the bad things which have inevitably come with the good things, so we must pay for them. Drive as hard a bargain as we can, we must, nonetheless, pay for them: pay by knowing them and living with the knowledge. Let us freely admit that on the whole mass culture is one of the "bad" things. But let us drive ourselves to go all the way in knowing it—to ask what it is, how it has developed, what it can do *to* us, what it can do *for* us.

By now these questions have all been pretty satisfactorily answered. And I shall give the answers in summary fashion, and then consider a question which the received answers make inevitable: what we are to do with what we know—then to act? I shall not be able to answer this last question satisfactorily, of course; I know of no one who has. But I am impressed by the fact that he who asks that question inevitably is asking a question about himself *in* his culture. Indeed, it is the implications of that word "in" which give rise to these notes.

WHAT IS MASS CULTURE? The products of the imagination and intellect—at some stage mass-produced, of course—which are intended to image life's possibilities for men whose lives are for the most part dominated by such rationalized and technified modes of behavior and governance as have increasingly ensured (and also endangered) the continuity of society since

66

the Renaissance. The song suits the singer; and its creation and production are set by the same pattern which sets his character. Neither song nor singer is marked by much of that *human* impulse, as we like to think of it, to rise above one's cultural matrix, comprehend it, and so become a better, fuller, more comprehensive person. The song, confirming the singer in what he is, seems then inevitably to exploit his anxieties, disable him, and make it all the more difficult for him to conceive of any way of life but his own. So that his life style, insofar as the songs he sings are involved, will become all the more rigid, all the less flexible, and he the less able to conceive of the genuinely new in life's possibilities.

How has mass culture developed? The answer, of course, is implicit in my brief definition. The necessary condition of mass culture is technology, as this is the necessary condition of mass man. The outcome of the technification of society is what Marx called "alienation," meaning thereby to indicate the fact that, as mass production techniques take over, the worker loses a sense of genuine participation in the product of his work. At its worst, mass culture is thus "alienated" culture: a contradiction in terms, really. Our songs are not made for us as persons, but as members of a group, *consumers* all, our functions dominated by whatever the group must get done in order to keep up with the demands for production which we let our technology set for us. According to this way of thinking, he who makes our songs (or writes our stories, or produces our TV programs, or whatever) can do so only if he lets himself be alienated from that which he produces. The apparatus whereby the songs get from writers to audience is such as to demand of the writer that he produce not for persons, but for groups, masses, crowds. The faceless middlemen who form the intervening invariables between writer and audience know what the audience wants, and therefore what the writer must produce. But they know in reality only what the audience has previously consumed (which they have previously supplied), and so the point of the least common denominator is soon reached. It is incorrect, then, because irrelevant, to say that today's mass culture is simply analogous to yesterday's—this century's to the eighteenth century's, or the nineteenth century's. For, so far, the level of mass culture has descended, precisely as the role of technology in making it available has ascended.

WHAT CAN IT DO TO US? WHAT COULD IT DO FOR US? To ask this question in such an alternative fashion is to catch a glimpse of a ray of hope which comes from the candle which the lords of the media have not yet been able to extinguish. What mass culture can do *to* us is sufficiently evident in what I have said already— and in the nature of the things which bombard us day by day. To reinforce what I have said, let me quote the words of one of the writers of the most successful rock-and-roll songs of our day: "Basically, these songs are a means of escape from reality. We write lyrics deliberately vague. The songs are egocentric and dreamy. Lots of basic blues ideas wouldn't work as rock-and-roll ideas because the blues are too real, too earthy. You have to make them dreamlike and very moral. That's why you're rarely going to hear even a plain, *happy* rock-and-roll song, because happiness is a real emotion."[1]

The cold, calculating calmness of these words induce in me, at least, much more anxiety than do the icy hallucinations of *The Thief's Journal* or *Naked Lunch*. They call for a straightforward indictment. Let me quote one such, which is intended to be a general indictment of the media of mass culture, from Father William Lynch's noble *Image Industries*:

[1] *Esquire* (March 1961), p. 71.

1. The failure, on a large scale, of these media to differentiate between fantasy and reality; the result is a weakening, throughout the nation's audiences, of the power to differentiate between these two things.

2. The weakening and flattening out of the area of feeling and sensibility in the public consciousness.

3. The extent to which freedom of imagination is being restricted, not by the morality of the censor, but by the purveyors of all the techniques for the fixation of the imagination.

4. The "magnificent imagination": the spectacular projection of the dream on the screens of the movies and TV, in which all the true lines of our human reality are lost.[2]

In short, the world of this song-writer is the one of official Hollywood, whose productions—according to the language of a 1960 release of the Motion Picture Producers Association—are based on the notion that "drama . . . almost always deals with the unusual, the unique and the departure from normal human experience." The "normal" is not to be enhanced, our sense of it deepened; it is uninteresting. The consonance of normality and individuality (i.e. uniqueness) presumably has been proven (by market analysis?) to be the stuff that humanistic-type daydreams are made on. The screen-writer, like the song-writer, is supposed to live in a world in which alienation from reality is the rule—in which through some anti-miraculous genetic transformation, men are born lobotomized. Or should be.

But of course they are not. And the nature of mass society induces in them—which is to say in us—a whole complex of anxieties (beyond tranquilizing) over the establishment and preservation of their (which is to say our) identities as what Whitman called in more

[2] (New York, 1959), p. 20.

hopeful days "simple, separate persons." The anxieties seem to be the necessary product of our lives in a mass society, the psychological form of that alienation which technology is a prime agent in bringing about. And here, I should say, mass culture can do something *for* us—and does, if not often enough. Its products can be composed so as to take into account our anxieties, our concern to establish and confirm our positive identities, even as we enjoy (as we should) all the material goods that technology gives us—and have the increased leisure to enjoy them. It can engage us in our spare time in such a way as to let us enjoy the realities, even the trivial realities, of our lives—not necessarily going deep, or seeking to enhance or enrich or transform our sense of reality; just letting us coast along, storing up energy for those moments when we can look deeply into reality and allow ourselves to be guided by poets, storytellers, philosophers, intellectuals, what Melville called "thought-divers." Mass culture can be *fun*—easy play, as against the harder ritualized play of higher forms of culture, with our sensibilities loosened and relaxed, our reality-principles neither exploited nor fully and drivingly engaged. And it can be *serious*, as we contemplate in general terms matters of import to the lives of our spirits. In either case, it can be charged with "real emotions." It could be, and it must be. (When it is, as I shall suggest later, it perhaps had better be called "popular" culture.)

2.

As educators, we know well the bitter truth—that for good and for bad, mass culture is a corollary of mass education. Here are some wise words, spoken by the Dean of Columbia Teachers College in June 1960:

> Much of our civilization rests on mass production of identical units and merchandising them through mass-produced reactions in people.

70

The implications for schools are broad and deep, confronting us immediately with paradoxes. For one of the principal aims of education is to make people alike. . . . The object is to help the child by increasing his power to communicate, to understand, and to live efficiently with his fellows, to stress what is possessed in common and makes a community possible.

But the coin has another side. For while the common characteristics of people make a community possible, it is their uncommon qualities that make it better. Variety, innovation, leadership and progress come only from individuality. The danger is that we may become so fond of and so dependent upon the mass production of both commodities and consent that we shall forget where to stop. What makes it all so difficult to control is our feeling that there is nothing so bad about being alike. And there isn't, of course. The trouble is that it keeps us from being different—and when we lose our differences, we lose our individuality.[3]

The humanist, of course, grounds his vocation in a commitment to the idea that men are alike above all in their capacity to be different, "en masse" (to use Whitman's words again) to the degree that they can realize that they are "simple and separate," "normal" to the degree that they can be "unique." (He knows too that in our culture he most likely would be unable to be indignant about mass culture if he were not the recipient of a mass education.) That is to say, simply enough, he would understand mass culture, so to transcend it. But he would, or should, admit that even he cannot transcend it all the time—perhaps even most of the time. What he wants is to insure that there always will be the possibility for the transcending; in short, that mass culture has a viable relationship with *elite* culture.

[3] I quote from a mimeographed copy of Dean John Fischer's remarks.

71

I emphasize: *elite* culture. Let us not be irresponsible, or cowardly, and call it *high* culture. Let us not conceal from ourselves the fact that, like mass culture, it must always involve the problem of social status, measured some way or another. For "elitism" carries responsibilities which mere "height" does not. In cultivating his responsibilities—a measure of *his* dignity—the humanist will perforce cultivate his elitism, and so do what he can to work toward the production of not mass but *popular* culture.

I suggest that when mass culture is healthy, when a good part of its health derives from the fact that it has a viable relation with elite culture, it is, or could be, *popular* culture; and that it might well counter, or at least slow down, the forces of depersonalization and alienation which threaten us. I shall suggest that one of the necessary conditions of an authentic community is a *popular* culture—an authentic people's culture.

In the nature of modern life such a culture—popular or elite—must be accessible to all; and although it is likely that the great number of men will for the most part be capable of only popular culture and that there will be the usual minority whose capabilities direct them for the most part to elite culture, nonetheless the general rule will be that even that minority will (simply because men are not highpowered enough to live with elite culture alone) find itself increasingly involved with popular culture. As humanists, we work in the hope that most men will be of that minority. And one of our tasks, whether professionally or as an aspect of our day-to-day lives, is to see to it that there is kept going that viable relationship whereby we are assured of a popular, not a mass, culture. The possibility of the withering away of popular culture seems to me to be so distant right now—granting the fix we are in—as not to be worth speculating about. I am a short-range utopian, I suppose: characteristically a mere humanist.

3.

I defined *mass culture* toward the beginning of these notes. Let me venture some related definitions. I mean to give some criteria for the various modes, or levels, of culture and to suggest their socio-cultural origins and implications:

A FOLK CULTURE is one whose homogeneity is inclusive, and is such that close, almost anonymous identifications are possible by the terms set by the quality of its homogeneity. It is non-urban, usually village, preliterate, minimally technological. Its artistic products, whatever their range of complexity in technique, tend to be thematically simple (i.e. non-complex—reflecting the assurance in person-to-person relations of both artist and him toward whom the artist directs his work). In fact, the artist is only minimally, if at all, differentiated as artist. His work, thus, is directed at a whole community, to the vitality of whose being all of its members are felt genuinely to contribute. The artist is *merely* one of those members.

AN ELITE CULTURE is one whose homogeneity is exclusive, and is such that identifications within the terms set by that homogeneity must perforce be particular and individualistic—some of its well-endowed members being set apart from the ordinary run of their fellows. The artist is thus one specialist among many, even though the intended import of his art is nothing if not general. For the elite exists because, in the mass of society above or beyond which its members must place themselves in order to be themselves, identifications are not, as it were, automatically guaranteed; identifications are not an assured aspect of intra-group understanding. Rationalization, bureaucratization, and the like preclude this, and the artist must adapt to the fact. An elite culture's artistic products are contrived so that, through their technique—indeed, *only* through

73

their technique—their necessarily difficult and complex themes may be perceived. The themes are necessarily difficult and complex because they derive from the artist's elite understanding of complexities of socio-cultural and "spiritual" behavior which the very nature of mass society (without which there would be no occasion for an elite) somehow conceals from the vast majority of its members. Even literacy and all that it promises is under the aegis of rationalization and bureaucratization. Technical (in the sense of "technique") expertise, self-consciously cultivated, becomes a necessary means of assuring that the artist's special insights cannot be in any way reduced to those of the mass of the members of his society. Any member of the society who wants to gain those insights must himself somehow join the elite—or, rather, that segment of the elite whose insights (and roles) he aspires to. Technical expertise, thus, becomes a means whereby the artist (and likewise those to whom he would speak) can differentiate his special product from that of all others, even from that of other artists. It is his lead which humanists follow when they ask what is entailed by their commitment to the idea that men are most valuable when they would realize their likeness in terms of their differences. I should guess that these observations apply, with some shifting of terms, to all members of the "intelligentsia."

POPULAR CULTURE represents the attempt, under the increasingly stratified, non-homogeneous (but increasingly homogenized) conditions of modern society, to achieve something like a folk culture to parallel and perhaps interact with the elite culture to which such conditions, in their very nature, give rise. It is increasingly produced for a mass, not a public. (A "public" has a character; a mass is denied one.) The producers of such culture (who may well nominally be members of the elite) assume and accept (what else can they

74

do?) the social and technological arrangements which an elite culture, particularly in modern times, must surmount; moreover, they *may* assume that those arrangements are such (or can be made such) as to create a satisfactory substitute for the totally permeating, conventionally stylized person-to-person communication which makes for a folk culture and for the marginal, unconventionally stylized communication which makes for an elite culture. Thus the problem for him who would participate in the creation of a popular culture is to make the technology of mass production (of books or whatever) subsidiary to the techniques of individual composition and production: to compose and produce in such a way as to reach the reader whom mass production makes possible, meantime not diluting or weakening the product while it moves between writer and reader. The problem is to design a work of "popular" art which has built into it safeguards against that further dilution-on-the-way; or which, as is more likely, somehow anticipates those dilutions and the nature and qualifications of the reader for whom they are to be made—anticipates them in such a way as to guarantee the preservation of such integrity as the artist, accepting fully the conditions under which he writes, has put into his work in the first place. Such dilutions—which above all characterize popular culture —must be made on behalf of the popular reader, with his nature and his needs in mind, not on behalf of the technological apparatus whereby the work will reach him. It may still be possible to distinguish between "public" and "mass." It is one of the ironies of modern life that only an "elite" is in a position to do so—to stem the drift of the "public" toward the "mass."

4.

We must remember that in times long past when our society was dominated by a political elite, the members of such an elite not only conceived of themselves as but actually were members of a cultural elite—not only patrons of art and artists but genuine "consumers" of their work. Domination passed in turn to an economic and then—in relatively recent times—to a power elite. For members of the economic and power elites, to rule society came less and less to entail seriously encouraging and cultivating its arts. For a member of the economic elite—say, a nineteenth-century entrepreneur—the arts were to be cultivated by sheer accumulation of art objects; the artist was supported, but out of a sense of a dimly remembered obligation, inherited from the era of political elitism. The outcome of this situation, ironically enough, was the development of the fellowship and foundation system in our society. More recently, members of the power elite have had even less to do with the arts. The role of the cultural elite has become free-floating, assumed in turn by, say, an academic intelligentsia and a non-academic (or anti-academic) avant-garde, who between themselves have divided the role of a member of the cultural elite into that of the critic and artist. They quarrel constantly—not seeing clearly that neither is in a position to do his job successfully without the other; that they can be effective only if they are allied. Thus in our own time, when we do have such an alliance, it is under the constant tension of a pull from the one side by the sort of artist who boasts that the only thing he has to defend is his ignorance and on the other by the sort of critic who doesn't dare admit that he is ignorant of anything. But the alliance can be strong, especially when it occurs in the academy—the one thing artists and critics being able to agree upon being the fact that members of a cultural elite are nothing if not teachers, humanists all. Now, I am suggesting by this little disquisition on elitism that it is a primary task of those who live in this alliance to dedicate themselves to the cause of a genuinely popular culture. Indeed, anyone who is dedicated to the cause of a genuinely elite culture shirks his duty if he does not also dedicate himself to the cause of a genuinely popular culture. Disengagement is possible only in theory; and we have had a good deal of that—essays, for all the sharpness and acuity of their particular critiques, wherein, between generous mouthfuls, the writer disclaims a taste for the cultural fruits of our mass society. Indeed, it would be interesting to study the by now wearisome, because irrelevant, argument typical of such essays: in which, out of an unhappiness we can only share, the writer is driven to claim that modern life is a game of Russian roulette which he will not play. (We might call this his conspicuous assumption.) Meanwhile, back at his ranch, he shoots sitting ducks, mass produced. He has succumbed to the greatest temptation for the humanist in times of crisis: marginality. For the humanist, if he be true to his vocation, must will himself to be at the center of his world, in the heart of the man in whose image it must be shaped. The American humanist, in point of fact, can best understand the problem of mass culture and so participate in its solution, because his is the society in which mass culture has taken deepest root. He is at once its most characteristic beneficiary and its inevitable victim. Its history is his, writ large—as is its life.

5.

Although the rise of mass culture is surely a worldwide phenomenon, Europeans are fond of equating it with "Americanization," a nasty term. In reality, it is a corollary of technology, as I have remarked; and it just happens that our culture was more amenable to rapid technification, and all it implies for social, economic, and artistic matters, than were other so-called tradition-rooted cultures. So we get blamed a little un-

77

fairly. Yet we must admit that ours is the place and the occasion where the problem of mass culture can be re-marked most clearly—as in this passage by an English architectural historian, meditating on our landscape:

> I am inclined to think that the diseases of the American environment are a disaster of the same magnitude as an H-bomb explosion—but, alas, far more subtle. All we shall see, and we are seeing it already, is a smoothing down into sameness and monotony and unrelatedness of every type of human activity, and hence slowly, gently, insidiously, of people themselves. Ten percent will always rise above the common standard as they would anywhere; the great human problem is whether the ninety percent become beasts of burden or achieve their own self-realization to the limits of their abilities. And the sense of place, of identity, of belonging, is essential to the ninety percent.[4]

As Gertrude Stein once said, the United States is the oldest country in the world, because it was in the twen-tieth century when other countries were in the nine-teenth. And so we have in the passage I have quoted a European trying to kill, or exorcize, a son grown too soon into a father-figure. Moreover, the son is not old enough to know how to be a father; and he is surely not ready to die. He is the victim of his own drive to pioneer, having begun to lose sight of the cause, taught him by *his* father, for which he pioneered. The cause, curiously enough, involved what I have called a *popular*, not a *mass*, culture. And the humanist should know more of the original conception of the cause than he seems now to.

6.

One of the great hopes in post-Revolutionary Ameri-

---

[4] Ian Nairn, "The Master Builders," *Punch*, June 1, 1960, p. 750.

can culture was for an authentic people's poetry. This is an aspect of the quest for a national literature which has been the object of much recent literary-historical study. Everything seemed to favor the rise of such a poetry; a new land, a new government, freed from its ties with Europe; a new social system, as it was felt; enough land to guarantee good fortune to all; an intention to educate all. The Jeffersonian hope for a natural aristocracy soon came to be a hope for a universal, leveling aristocracy. There were conservative doubts, to be sure. But they were at most cautionary. By the 1840's this could be said—and it is only one such statement among many:

> . . . the national literature could only be enriched if American "scholars" would abandon their "lone reveries" and "scholastic asceticism" and rather seek their inspiration in the "thronged mart" and "peopled city," in the "really living, moving, toiling and sweating, joying and sorrowing people around them." . . . "To obtain an elevated national literature, it is not necessary then to look to great men, or to call for distinguished scholars; but to appeal to the mass. . . ." When genuinely "*American* authors appear . . . They will form a most numerous class, or rather be *so numerous as not to form a class*"; . . . they will utter "the best thoughts of us *all.*"[5]

It all looked so easy; and it is precisely because it looked so easy that the history of popular culture in the United States is the great paradigm case for the history of popular culture in Western European civilization. The statement I have quoted is a reconstruction from a group of essays by Orestes Brownson, who was

[5] Benjamin T. Spencer, *The Quest for Nationality* (Syracuse, 1957), p. 113. In what follows, I summarize the argument of my *Continuity of American Poetry* (Princeton, 1961, rev. ed., 1965), pp. 192-252.

then in his radical, transcendental phase. It is matched, as I have said, by many others—usually by radicals and liberals in politics, the most famous exemplars being statements by Whitman, beginning with the preface to the 1855 *Leaves of Grass*. It is worth recalling these words from "Democratic Vistas":

> The word of the modern . . . is the word Culture.
>
> We find ourselves abruptly in close quarters with the enemy. This word culture, or what it has come to represent, involves, by contrast, our whole theme, and has been, indeed, the spur, urging us to engagement. Certain questions arise. As now taught, accepted and carried out, are not the processes of culture rapidly creating a class of supercilious infidels, who believe in nothing? Shall a man lose himself in countless masses of adjustments, and be so shaped with reference to this, that, and the other, that the simply good and healthy and brave parts of him are reduced and clipp'd away, like the bordering of a box in a garden?

Ironically enough, we might well apply Whitman's words to the danger of mass culture in our times, although he was attacking elite culture in his time. In any case, we must be still urged to engagement on both fronts.

For what actually happened? We have that curious phenomenon of a group of poets, almost all of them radical or liberal in their politics, discovering gradually that to make authentic poems they had somehow to disengage themselves from their politics, or transcend them; at best, they hoped through their poems to transform excessively political (and therefore partial) men into whole men. I think of Emerson and even Whitman himself. But note that Poe too felt himself to be a liberal, sometimes a radical. And, beyond poets, note that both Hawthorne and Melville were good lib-

80

erals, at the same time as they were writing the stories and novels which put them out of the reach of the very popular audience with whom they shared their liberalism. In all, they became to some extent "private" artists. As their correspondence and journals tell us, they had to, in order to survive as artists. The humanity which they wished to put into their poems and stories could not be trimmed to fit the political beliefs which, as men living and acting in society, they were quite willing to make the best of.

Yet during the period of Emerson and his peers—radicals and liberals whose art was not consonant with their politics—during this time, a people's poetry, an authentic popular poetry did rise, along with a vulgar imitation of it, in the scribblings of Mrs. Sigourney and her kind. The "authentic" popular poetry was Longfellow's, Lowell's, Holmes', and Whittier's. The first three were conservatives all the way. (Lowell wavered a good deal, however, but he was a notable trimmer.) And Whittier was in a way, after his earlier abolitionist phase, curiously a-political. The first three of these men were academics, Boston aristocrats; the fourth, Whittier, became their patriarch, the man whom they admired most. It was these men who constituted the Fireside Poets, the Schoolroom Poets. Their poetry assured their readers that life was not an empty dream, that all was real and earnest, that the natural world was as it was to give men lessons-by-analogy, that their Snow-Bound reveries were means of getting perspective on the actualities of their day-to-day life. They reminded their readers regularly that their origins were in virtual folk cultures—small communities in which inter-personal relations were stable and assured; they idealized such origins. And these poets were popular in an even more modern sense. They sold well; they were all deeply aware of the fiscal problems of the

81

market for popular books; they took their publishers' advice as to what would and would not sell; they let their publishers mediate between themselves and their readers. But note, withal: they meant to "minister" to their readers' needs. They brought elite culture (in their translations from European literature in particular) to their readers. And they struck out against those other popular writers who would exploit their readers' needs. Their record is one, whatever we can say against them, of patriarchal responsibility. They seem to have been born graybearded, hanging in portraits over the ordinary man's fireside: *lares* and *penates* for readers who would be frightened of sublimer gods.

But in their success and the way it was achieved lay the undoing of their kind of poetry after their own time. The rest of the story takes us into our time: with, above all, the publisher and his staff constantly searching for the least common denominator at which books can be sold, now not advising the writer but telling him what to do, what to write. The publisher is himself a victim of the technological demands (the get-out figure, it is called) of the market. Moreover, there are the magazines which exist primarily as advertising organs and which require, occasionally, poetic squibs to fill out their columns. In this case, publisher and editor are selling to advertising men, who gauge the market, then instruct editor and publisher on what is needed, and so on down the line to the writer—separated by an iron curtain of economic, technological, and even psychological factors from his reader. So that the Longfellows of our time have shifted from Evangelines to paperbacks, TV scripts, and magazine pieces. Or perhaps the Longfellows of our time have either taken shelter in the academy (where misery finds company) or have joined up with the publishing apparatus, having given up hope of licking it.

7.

My example out of the nineteenth century is perhaps too simple. But, as I have said, I think that it can be a paradigm case for our thinking about the problem of a popular as against a mass culture—the crucial concept in developing the one as against the other being that of "responsibility." We must not forget how difficult it was for the "serious" writer who, producing genuinely popular work, wanted to do more.

The American situation was characteristically more extreme than the British—where a Dickens, for example, could manage to use the vehicles of popular art to carry stories which, upon examination in depth, turn out often to have been elite art of the most demanding kind. Indeed, we must recall that the novel as a genre came into being as an essentially popular form; and that its greatest practitioners were often able to do what Dickens did. And to our own day the novel remains the only form in which literary art seems at once to be popular and elitist. Only *seems*. For in the later nineteenth century, it too was increasingly refined into the "difficult" form it is at its best today—such refinement being the writer's way of avoiding being homogenized by the demands of the mass market and its entrepreneurs. And the popular novelist, instead of transforming the popular into the elitist, now superimposes elitist conceptions of fiction onto an essentially popular form and makes for that special version of mass culture, the middlebrow. The most notorious example, of course, is Cozzen's *By Love Possessed*. There are others, Cheaper by the Dozen.

But now I begin to run into the problem of classification, gradation, and the like. And I shall not go on. I want to point out, indeed, that in matters of this kind, we are too prone to classify, pigeonhole, file away, and so say we have done our duty. This is, I think, one of

83

the easier ways of becoming morally indignant. And I am proposing a more difficult way—that of confrontation and evaluation, the humanist's first step.

Thus I think that a good deal of the contemporary debate about mass (or popular) culture is beside the point. Opponents in the debate have accepted—too soon I think—somewhat simplified versions of the historical situation which has made for mass culture and then gone on to show how the products of mass culture demonstrate the horror or the glory of the historical situation.

If history evidences progress, mass culture must somehow be a "good" thing: if it evidences regress, mass culture must somehow be a "bad" thing. To show that it is good, you point out how many good LPs, good paperbacks, good prints are selling and you bring up the fact of our museums-without-walls. To show that it is bad, you point out how much trash we are exposed to, how the purchase of good LPs and the like may be simply marks of longing for status; and you bring up the fact that in the museum-without-walls the great painting, cut down to its viewer's size, may function merely as a decorative plaque, part of the wallpaper. And of course, both sides of the debate are right insofar as their evidence is concerned. Strangely enough, they often interpret a given piece of evidence identically and then proceed to evaluate it in diametrically opposed fashions—according to their progressive or regressive theories of history. The debaters (they are lined up neatly in the Rosenberg-White 1957 *Mass Culture* volume and the Spring 1960 issue of *Daedalus*) are not really quarreling with each other; they are quarreling with history—with the fact that they, like the rest of us, have been born into this world. The net result is the fact that nearly everyone is now his own mass medium; that writing about mass culture has become a form of mass culture; and that whereas we may well be satisfied by a given writer's account of the intrinsic nature and quality of a given item of mass culture, we may well be dissatisfied with his account of the implication of that nature and quality for our quite concrete and specific existential problem: what is mass culture to us and what are we to mass culture? The problem, I suggest, is one of attaining a perspective that will not allow us to escape the fact that, like it or not, we have to *live* with mass culture. We must take our history straight. Which is to say, take ourselves in our history straight.

8.

How, in the midst of the mass of mass culture, bowed down by its weight, seeing the hopes for a popular culture increasingly frustrated, how are we to know, judge, and discriminate? How are we to establish the means whereby such knowledge, judgment, and discrimination might not only preserve and inculcate the idea of a popular culture, but advance it?

My suggestions are humanistic, therefore academic. They consist essentially in learning how to think of mass as against popular culture, then—and only then— to act as one can. Here I am concerned to set down some necessary conditions of the act.

HISTORICALLY. I have meant in my little tale of Fireside Poetry and in my comments on a too simple idea of progress (or regress) to indicate how such thinking might proceed. Such thinking, I am sure, will clarify our notion of the role of the maker of mass (and/or popular) culture and the special mode of responsibility he should assume. We will observe, I think, that even at its best popular culture is a peculiarly historistic thing —by which I mean to say that it is not intended to survive the lifetime of its immediate audience, or the phase-of-sensibility of its immediate audience. It gets used up, consumed, but it need not thereby be poison-

85

ous. Too, we will observe, of course, that in the nature of the increasing technification of the media, in the development of the mass media themselves, the possibility of such responsibility becomes increasingly difficult of realization. Careful, objective historical studies —sympathetic where sympathy is deserved—will at least sharpen and deepen our sense of the qualitative criteria of popular (as against mass) culture.[6]

SOCIOLOGICALLY. (I use the term in the sense of what Wright Mills calls "the sociological imagination" —which "enables its possessor to understand the larger historical scene in terms of its meaning for the inner life and the external career of a variety of individuals." For Mills "history" is essentially contemporary history— the way we categorize and comprehend our lives now, our experience, in our milieu as a somehow coherent complex of lived-through events.) The problem here is to isolate for study the relation of mass culture as produced and consumed (horrible words!) to the socio-political structure and function of our society. What is it, we ask, to be a mass-consumer? And inevitably our gaze is drawn hypnotically to the young, for whom the mass media have not only transformed a life style but have created one. Their character is one which is in great part fixed by the fact that everything—information, material goods, means of having fun, even the monuments of elite culture—seems to be available with

[6] A scholarly note. We have amazingly little knowledge of the history of mass/popular culture. And even at its best, it is, to my taste, too tendentious (I think of Queenie Leavis' *Fiction and the Reading Public* and the studies of Leo Lowenthal) or not quite tendentious enough (I think of Richard Altick's *English Common Reader*). These, and also a few scattered articles, are invaluable works—especially since so much historical study of the subject is merely pseudo-clever, sniggling antiquarianism: a particularly embarrassing form of *kitsch*. I suppose this is our abiding problem— about which we perhaps are necessarily under- or over-committed: how to be "objective" about something, our hopes for which have been so deeply disappointed.

the minimum effort on their part. They grow up very fast—having in high school worked through all the "activities" which used to be in the purview of college. They are trained to be consumers—their only consumer's guide the radio-TV segments which give the show a reason for going on. Their world view is fatefully conditioned by the idea of automation and of simultaneity of communication. Everything seems to happen, perhaps does happen, at once—yet the happenings are fragmented and the center will not hold. Perhaps there *is* no center, just a homogenized whole. Young people, as Paul Goodman says, grow up "absurd." Their need is to *fill* all the free time they have, not to *use* it; and their need is confirmed and deepened by the cultural fare they are offered. They become mistrustful of information as such, of words, of gestures, of ideas: all of which imply a central cultural style which they cannot sense. Unhappily, the more "insightful" among them are cynical, or at best disenchanted, about the possibility of a popular, as opposed to a mass, culture —about a popular, as opposed to a mass, education. They are so cynical that they don't bother to confront squarely the fact that their world has been transformed once and for all, irreversibly, into one in which the mass media, automation, and the like have freed them from some of the discontents of work. Surely their obligation is also to live in the world, even in that part of it we would teach them to earn the right to despise; they can't earn the right to despise it by disaffiliating from it. One way of living in the world, so even this sociological critique would seem to demonstrate, is to learn to think intelligently and critically about mass culture and to learn to differentiate it from popular culture.

FORMALLY. The problem here is one for the "critic," and involves his usual compulsion to see the relation of form to content. He studies an item of popular cul-

ture. Is this a day-dream, he asks, or a nightmare? Is
it held in proper check, psychically contained, by its
form? Is it related to reality? Or does the form serve
only to make it a substitute for reality? (Here, of
course, "reality" is the first term of Freud's "reality-
principle": what is, in the nature of man and his
world, humanly possible of achievement.) What portion of reality does it deal with and how? What are the
characteristics of its medium and what problems do
these characteristics pose for the popular artist who
would to his reality principle be true? What is the conception of human nature upon which the operation of
the medium is postulated? And then follows a question
as to the relation of particular forms as used in mass
(or popular) culture and their use in elite culture: the
question, of course, of what is called *kitsch*. Critics
have more and more observed how the objects of elite
art are imitated in mass culture, and in the imitating
drained of their integral value and import. Corollary
to this is the fact that objects of folk art too have been
imitated thus—from folklore to fakelore, as the saying
goes. Certainly, it is true that only the inauthentic—
mass culture at its most vicious—is produced when an
object of mass culture is offered as an easily earned
surrogate for an object of elite or of folk culture. But
I am not convinced entirely that the intelligent borrowing of forms and motifs from elite and folk art is necessarily vicious. After all, the wonderful popular songs
of the seventeenth century take much of their strength
from the folk songs which inspire them; and this is
true in our own time too. There is clearly a descending
line from the performance of a Mississippi chain gang,
to that of The Weavers, to that of The Kingston Trio.
Yet the performance of the latter still is not necessarily
offered as a substitute for the performance of the
former, but, as it were, only as an introduction to it.
And there might well be an *ascending* line. From rock-

and-roll to Washboard Sam and the country blues—who knows? The point is that the possibility of moving from a popular to a folk form is not foreclosed. In its not being foreclosed—this is perhaps the proper relation of popular art to folk art; and I should think something comparable holds for the relation of popular art to elite art: *My Fair Lady* to *Pygmalion*; advertising layout to Mondrian; Paddy Chayefsky to Chekov; Ted Williams to Nick Adams. When the possibility of moving from a popular to a folk or elite form is foreclosed, when there is no vital relation between the one and the other, then we have mass art for the mass consumer—not popular art for the popular auditor or reader or singer or whistler or whatever.

I think that just as the shift from a painting by Kandinsky, to a monumental building by Gropius, to a Tech-Built house is evidence of a vital relation between elite and popular art, so such a relation exists (and can exist) for our songs and stories. The relationship is possible, however, only if conditions are such as to let the maker's sense of responsibility to his audience predominate. Indeed, in the formal analysis of popular as well as of folk and elite art, what we mean when we speak of form or style, is the maker's means of being responsible in and for the portion of reality which his work comprehends. Some words of the great Finnish architect Alvar Aalto on the problem of mass housing today are relevant here: "Standardization . . . does not mean that all houses must be built alike. Standardization will be used mainly as a method of producing a flexible system by which the single house can be made adjustable for families of different sizes, various topographical locations, different exposures, views, etc."

Popular culture, considered formally, must be "standardized," so that through technology it can be made readily available to the popular audience. But, within the limits of its audience's sensibility, it can be made adjustable—so as to let members of the audience relax, refresh themselves, and simply enjoy the fact that what they have in common is the fact that they are different: their humanity half-engaged. And I should say that it is the corollary function of elite art to urge its audience to commitment, meditation in depth, so to contemplate the fact—so "real" as to be beyond enjoyment—that what makes its members different is what they have in common: their humanity *fully* engaged. Mass culture, of course, is humanity *disengaged*, atrophying—form exhausting content, content eating cancerously at form. It is predicted upon the existence of a world in which our central problem—holding together our images of the world we have and the one we ought to have—is as irrelevant as are those of us who would think about it. We intellectuals don't understand the mass audience, so proclaims Dr. Frank Stanton of CBS—and I am here paraphrasing some words of his published in the mass-culture issue of *Daedalus*. We are given part of CBS's time: so we should let the masses enjoy themselves. What Dr. Stanton doesn't understand is that willy-nilly we are part of the mass audience too. Only, being intellectuals, we know the difference between a mass and a public, a crowd and community, between aspirin and that stuff Dr. Stanton's clients would overcharge us for—the overcharge being our ticket of admission to Madison Avenue produced entertainments whose aim is to convince us that it is worthwhile being overcharged: proof positive of the value of the American way of life; brain-tinting out of the laboratories of Helena Rubinstein. Happily, there are a few (not many, but a few) self-parodists in the mass arts who know, or seem to know, the difference too—for example, he who creates Pogo; he who publishes *Mad*; and he who recorded a

90

couple of years ago chipmunk voices which are like Fabian's and Frankie Avalon's—only more so.

9.

Thus my three perspectives: *historical, sociological, formal.* It is obvious that each is a version of the other; and that the major student of mass and popular culture—he to whom we shall have to go to school—will work from all three perspectives at once and so discover the complexities of his humanism. The nearest things we have to inclusive studies of the sort I envisage are Raymond Williams' *Culture and Society* and his *Long Revolution*, Richard Hoggart's *Uses of Literacy*, Father William Lynch's *Image Industries*, Reuel Denney's *Astonished Muse*, and Gilbert Seldes' *The Popular Arts*; and all these are weakened, I think, by a curious foreshortening of their historical perspective. But they are powerful books; and I think that all humanists should come to know them. Their attitude toward the popular audience (with which their authors are quite willing to identify) is not that one of fearful contempt so popular among "critics" of radical and conservative persuasion, nor that one of unctuous submissiveness so popular among television and radio executive and advertising men. If they have an optimism, however muted, it is because they hold that every gain is not a loss; that if the losses outnumber the gains, nonetheless they do not obliterate them. And that is the best we can do—learn to tell the gains from the losses, so to hold on to them.

Third Programs (even on non-prime time!) are all very well. But the Home Service is for us too. I think that the mass-communications authorities among us make a slight error in emphasis when they concentrate almost exclusively on promoting the cause of "serious" TV. The Lively Arts—the popular arts at their possible

91

best—are increasingly neglected by such students, who are then forced into being too grateful for what the media men give us. The net effect is to indicate that they, therefore we, are "above" the popular (the mass) arts. It is the humanist's task to tell his mass-communications colleague that one can't get "above" his ambiance. But, of course, first the humanist must grant that the mass-communications man is not merely a lapsed humanist; and the mass-communications man must grant that the humanist is not just a frustrated elitist. I think that if they begin to talk with one another, they will learn that they both speak imperfect dialects of the same language.

Beyond this, there is social action—the general nature and direction of which I think is obvious enough from many of the second-, third-, and fourth-step studies I alluded to in the beginning. The danger is that we will try to take action without knowing why and on whose behalf. On *our* behalf—that's who; and that's why. We are all of us inevitably part-time members of the mass audience. We know enough to divide it, and ourselves as part of it, into the mass audience *per se* and the popular audience. And we know enough to promulgate the popular tastes to which we can allow ourselves to be committed.

So far we are losing the battle, because so far, we have in our panic not been quite able to conceive what it would be like to win it. Were we to be possessed of a truly popular culture as well as a truly elite culture, the condition of our lives would be such as to force us frankly to admit that popular culture played a significant part in our lives—as, in point of fact, it already does. In the unattainable utopia for which we must work (because if we are honest with ourselves, there is nothing else to do), the terms *popular* and *elite* would refer to books and music and pictures which differed in value not as regards the segment of the population which comprehended them but as regards the degree of comprehension which they demanded: *full* and *middle* culture we might call them; and have to add a third term, *minimal* culture. All segments of the population would have free access to all levels. In the nature of things, there would be more devotees to the last two than to the first; nonetheless it is most likely that a man devoted to full culture would give himself to middle and minimal culture too, and so strengthen them and the viable relationship, without foreclosure, which should exist among them. And it would happen, I suppose, that just because a man was capable of comprehending full culture, he would comprise part of an elite dedicated to serving his culture as a whole. From the *power* elite to the *cultural* elite; from *full power* as a mode of governance to *full culture*. For full culture would entail full responsibility, the fullest sense of humanity and community.

But, saying all this, the humanist is properly wary of his own speculations—lest they blind him to the facts of life. Yet he *must* speculate, in order that he may the more sharply look about him and see and assess and work to amend such facts. For he can't but know that the problem of popular as against mass culture is embedded in our task of salvaging our world. Which is to say, of salvaging ourselves. Mass culture most often is not only sub-culture but anti-culture. It destroys culture, our means of working out a relationship between what we are and what we ought to be, and so would destroy us, and deliver us packaged—to whom? That is the true horror. For the lords of the media and their minions are not satanic or dictatorial or consummately villainous. Indeed, they would destroy themselves along with us—and all without really knowing what they are doing. In our brave new world we have reached the stage where we can destroy and package ourselves to no purpose whatsoever. For there would be neither

sender nor receiver: just that glittering package. Mass
culture truly bores from within, bores us to death,
bores us in the name of entertaining us, bores us into
the state where we don't know that we are being bored,
where boredom becomes normalcy. Meanwhile, The
Package awaits.

10.

I conclude these notes with some words, published
in the mass-culture issue of *Daedalus*, which put well
the desperate hope (what else is open to us?) in which
we must speak about such matters. They are not mine,
but the novelist James Baldwin's:

> Perhaps life is not the black, unutterably beautiful,
> mysterious and lonely thing the creative artist tends
> to think of it as being; but it is certainly not the sun-
> lit playpen in which so many Americans lose first
> their identities and then their minds.
>
> I feel very strongly, though, that this amorphous
> people are in desperate search for something which
> will help them reestablish their connection with them-
> selves and with one another. This can only begin to
> happen as the truth begins to be told. We are in the
> middle of an immense metamorphosis here, a meta-
> morphosis which will, it is devoutly to be hoped, rob
> us of our myths and give us our history, which will
> destroy our attitudes and give us back our personali-
> ties. The mass culture, in the meantime, can only
> reflect our chaos: and perhaps we had better remem-
> ber that this chaos contains life—and a great trans-
> forming energy.

I can add to this only my conviction that the life and
the energy are such—as are we whose life and energy
they are—as still to make it possible for us to have a
popular, not a mass, culture: one which will let us live
our history and store up the energy for those high oc-

casions when we try to confront and understand it;
one which will give us a casual sense of our personal
ties and prepare us for those critical occasions when
we try to know them fully and freely. (And, Bomb or
no Bomb, we *are* possible for the foreseeable future, if
only because it is *we* who foresee it.) Such a culture
is possible so long as we are possible. If we are to survive our metamorphosis, such a culture—at least working in the living hope of such a culture—is imperative.

1962

4

ROBIN MOLINEUX
ON THE ANALYST'S COUCH:
A Note on the Limits of Psychoanalytic
Criticism

"For the individual's mastery over his neurosis begins where he is put in a position to accept the historical necessity which made him what he is. The
individual feels free when he can choose to identify
with his own ego identity and when he learns to
apply that which is given to him to that which must
be done. Only thus can he derive ego strength (for
his generation and the next) from the coincidence
of his one and only life cycle with a particular segment of history." ERIK H. ERIKSON, *"Ego Develop-*
ment and Historical Change"

IN OUR recent discovery that "My Kinsman, Major
Molineux" must be given a major place in the Hawthorne canon, we have inevitably come to look at the
tale through the eyes of psychoanalytic criticism. Inevitably, because not only is the critic in our time
armed, willy-nilly, with at least some of the forms of
psychoanalytic understanding, but also because the tale
itself seems to be explicitly a version of what is for
psychoanalysis the crucial segment of man's struggle
for adulthood, the Oedipal situation. Even the merest
amateur of psychoanalysis (and who among us is not
forced to be at least this?), armed with the latest paper-
back manual, cannot but discover (although he may
strive mightily to resist it) the fact that Robin Molineux (he *is* a Molineux, for in Major Molineux he

seeks his paternal uncle) is searching for a father-figure; that he has a difficult and confusing time finding him; that his search is charged with a sense of dream-work; that he finds him under deeply traumatic conditions; and that—without quite meaning to—he helps destroy him even as he finds him. Major Molineux is many things: as many things as we can fit into that primary psycho-cultural category in which the father is at once the loved and the hated, a teacher of the ways toward independence and a lord who denies the very goal he reveals—an Old Priest in a Grove, a Laius, a Hamlet Senior, a manifestation of the Old Order, etc., etc. This is, of course, because Hawthorne makes him who seeks Major Molineux first of all a richly human being in a richly human situation; and as in other magisterial works of art, that very humanity serves to define our understanding of the category in which we would place both the sought and the seeker, both teacher and pupil, both master and slave. If the polysemantic possibilities of all this astonish us, we have only to recall that it was the richly human Oedipus, in *his* richly human situation, who gave Freud a name for this primary category and so helped him finally define it. So it is only right that the critic who moves beyond the psychoanalytic amateurism of most of us should come to devote his study of "My Kinsman, Major Molineux" to what he claims to be an "interpretation" of the actual texture of the "poet's vision."

The words I have placed in quotation marks come from the epigraph to a chapter in Mr. Simon Lesser's recent *Fiction and the Unconscious*.[1] The chapter, called "Conscious and Unconscious Perception," is, I take it, a crucial one for Mr. Lesser's conception of the critic's job of work. It centers on analyses of two works of short fiction, "My Kinsman, Major Molineux" and

---

[1] (Boston, 1957), pp. 212-237. The chapter originally appeared in *Partisan Review*, XXII (1950), 370-390.

97

Sherwood Anderson's "I Want to Know Why." Mr. Lesser finds the two pieces to be variations on a single theme, the search for a father; and I think that I can make my point adequately by dealing only with his treatment of the Hawthorne tale. Mr. Lesser hopes, as he tells us at the end, that his discussion "will suggest not only how much may be unconsciously understood when we read fiction but the close bearing of what is unconsciously perceived upon our deepest and most tenacious concerns." In short, he would reveal to us the unconscious motivations in "My Kinsman, Major Molineux," so as to relate those motivations to our own private, secret ones—to make us conscious of the meaning of the tale and of a segment of our own experience, of each as it interpenetrates the other. The tale, that is to say, in its very artistic structure, in its very artistic integrity, would be a means for our further and deeper defining and articulating our own sense of ourselves. Such an intention is, I take it, a properly traditional one for the literary critic. But the usual problem arises: To what degree is the critic's analysis of the unconsciously motivated and motivating psychic structure of the tale valid in terms of the structure as a whole, as objectively, totally given? The one criterion for all criticism, psychoanalytic and otherwise, would be just this: the degree to which the critic has accounted for all that goes on in the tale, all that is there; and then, and only then, the degree to which he has related his total analysis to his sense of the tale's humanistic import.

Mr. Lesser's view of "My Kinsman, Major Molineux," is boldly and simply stated:

> To the conscious mind "My Kinsman, Major Molineux" is a story of an ambitious youth's thwarted search for an influential relative he wants to find. To the unconscious, it is a story of the youth's hostile and rebellious feelings for the relative—and for the father—

98

and his wish to be free of adult domination. To the conscious mind it is a story of a search which was unsuccessful because of external difficulties. To the unconscious . . . it is a story of a young man caught up in an enterprise for which he has no stomach and debarred from succeeding in it by internal inhibitions.

To reach this conclusion he emphasizes matters which, to my knowledge, have heretofore been inadequately attended to: the fact that the difficulties which Robin has are clearly made out to be difficulties of his own unconscious creating—that perhaps he does not want to find his kinsman, perhaps he is afraid to; the fact that he "does not pursue his [search] with any ardor"; the fact that there is something more-or-less ambiguously sexual about the search—particularly in the episode of the whore who assures him that his kinsman is inside her dwelling, asleep. All these facts are made to point to the now obvious conclusion: that if Robin does find his kinsman, he will have to submit to a kind of authority from which he seems to have wanted to escape when he left home. No wonder, Mr. Lesser would have us conclude, he is hesitant and confused. And no wonder that when he sits on the steps of the church, waiting to see his kinsman, "he has a fantasy in which he imagines that his kinsman is already dead." He is confused over what he really wants—or, as our experience of the story persuades us, what he unconsciously, therefore really, wants. And then when the crowd comes by, with Major Molineux a tormented loyalist prisoner in their midst, Robin (unconsciously) senses that the crowd also wants to free itself of the authority which this old man manifests.

> Without a voice being raised in protest, the crowd is acting out the youth's repressed impulses [to assert his freedom of his father] and in effect urging him to act on them also. The joy the crowd takes in asserting

99

its strength and the reappearance of the lady of the scarlet petticoat [the whore who had earlier invited Robin in to see his kinsman] provide him with incentives for letting himself go. . . . The relief he feels that he can vent his hostility for his kinsman and abandon his search for him is the ultimate source of his "riotous mirth." It is fueled by energy which until then was being expended in repression and inner conflict.

Mr. Lesser's Robin, then, is a youth who is finally freed to become an adult. The question remains: is this Robin, however unconsciously, also Hawthorne's. The answer is a curious one, I think—and the point of this note. It is: No. But not because this Robin is an untrue or distorted representation of Hawthorne's Robin; for so far as it goes, it is true to our sense of him. Rather, it is an incomplete representation of Hawthorne's Robin. Hawthorne's Robin is Mr. Lesser's and a good deal more. For Hawthorne's Robin is not merely freed to become an adult (perhaps he will, perhaps he won't; we aren't told at the end). As Hawthorne creates him for us, his freedom is not mere freedom, but rather freedom earned at the expense of guilt. And the guilt is explicitly the fundamental aspect of Robin's relation to his world, the world to which Mr. Lesser, in his psychoanalytic earnestness, pays little or no attention.

The kinsman whom Robin seeks out, tries to avoid finding, but finds only in the destroying—this kinsman, it should be remembered, is pictured as a noble, tragic figure, a loyalist caught up in Revolutionary anti-loyalist violence.[2] And those who destroy him—or torment him—are pictured as a crazy mob. Here the very pseudo-historicity of the tale must be taken into account. And whether or not Mr. Lesser knew that the name

[2] See "Hawthorne and the Sense of the Past; or, the Immortality of Major Molineux," pp. 137-174.

Molineux, being that of a famous radical leader in Revolutionary Boston, had a bitterly ambiguous meaning for Hawthorne, or that the disguised leader of the mob is a deliberate evocation of the figure well known as a wild and cowardly leader of Revolutionary Boston mobs—whether or not Mr. Lesser knew these facts, he should (and indeed does, casually) recognize that the story is ironically introduced by a paragraph rationalizing in a progressivist way the behavior of mobs (as we are told, one of the incidental prices for progress) and that the story recalls at the very least, as every red-blooded American should recognize, something like the Boston Tea Party. Hence, Robin in achieving his maturity is, unconsciously, an agent of progress; his coming to maturity, his struggles toward it, is that of the people for whom, as he helplessly identifies with them, he is a kind of surrogate, or icon. The concern of the story is not just Robin's struggles to free himself from authority, but also the implications of that struggle—with all its ambiguous, fearful, nightmarish quality and its hesitating doubt—for his future as a member of the society for whom he is surrogate and/or icon, and thus of the future of that society itself. The energy he takes from the crowd surely fuels Robin's mirth and enables him to free himself of kinsman-like, paternal authority by pushing him to participate in the tormenting of the old Major. But it is also—and we are not allowed to forget it, nor is Robin (witness his mood at the end of the tale)—an energy produced in good part by the destruction of another man: a man who, for all that we and Robin know, is totally innocent of the things for which he is tormented and destroyed. The crowd thus is guilty. Robin shares their guilt. Guilt is the price which Hawthorne makes Robin pay for his freedom.

Mr. Lesser will have nothing to do with such guilt. I think that this is because he is concerned only with Robin and not with the tale as a whole, because in

effect he has treated Robin as though he were a patient
visiting an analyst and Hawthorne as though he were
doing the work of an analyst by creating a situation in
which Robin's unconscious will work so as to free him
from what an analyst would take to be neurotic (or at
least, exacerbatedly normal) dependence. To a degree—
and Mr. Lesser shows this with remarkable precision—
Hawthorne is that analyst. But his responsibility is not
simply to "cure" his protagonist (as patient) and leave
him to his own (now refurbished, potentially more-or-
less autonomous) ego-centered devices. Rather it is the
responsibility of a creator, who must see to it that one
of his creations, his Robin, has an adequate and meaningful relationship with the world which, in the tale, is
also his creation. The tale, then, projects a created
world—not just a single figure, analyzed evocatively
and so remarked as being freed by means of a psychic
discharge arising out of his involved relations with his
world. That he is freed through that world does not
mean that he is freed from it; he is rather freed for
and with it. And his freedom—and, for Hawthorne I
daresay, all freedom—is dreadful. Its goal is a tragic
assertion of the inextricable relation of human freedom
and unfreedom in the world.

The imaginative writer makes whole worlds. Ana-
lyzable protagonist-patients are only part of these
worlds—significantly and integrally part of them, but
only part of them. And they have their fullest (which
is to say, their ultimate) meaning as they wend their
unconscious way through the world which they, as it
were, have been created into. Robin is taken off the
couch and put into his world; he works through his
nightmare and is left with the hard world of reality,
in which he discovers (or will discover) that he has
been all the time. Then, and only then, does (or will)
he become what he really is. Mr. Lesser cannot go this
far with him. He can only say:

102

From one point of view the unacknowledged forces playing upon the apparently simple and candid central character of "My Kinsman, Major Molineux" are deeply abhorrent. Our sympathy for the character should tell us, however, that there is another side to the matter. The tendencies which assert themselves in Robin exist in all men. What he is doing, unwittingly but flamboyantly, is something which every young man does and must do, however gradually, prudently and inconspicuously: he is destroying an image of paternal authority so that, freed from its restraining influence, he can begin life as an adult.

But an adult, Mr. Lesser in his hyperclinical role fails to say, for and in a world of other adults.

The danger of Mr. Lesser's approach is surely self-evident. It is one of inadequacy and partiality. But it is that kind of inadequacy and partiality which are so not by virtue of what they would forbid, forego, or supplant. Quite the contrary; for Mr. Lesser's approach takes us deeply into the heart of the tale. But he forgets that the heart has meaning only as it activates and is activated by a body. And psychoanalytic criticism would not seem necessarily to have to forget this fact and to stop where Mr. Lesser has stopped. The artist, we now grant, is gifted with a tendency to a kind of controlled regression. He can move deeply into the psyche and is able to evoke something quite close to those primary processes which man, in order to be man living with man, must resist, repress, or sublimate. But to a significant degree the artist *controls* his probing movement. And controlling it, he returns to the world, creates another world, an imaginative world, in which he reveals to us, with all the devices at his command, the forces, directions, and articulations, the meanings, of those unconscious processes—those instinctive powers which we must control and express so that we can live with them: which is to say, with ourselves. The element of control is managed through the creation of a world of men (akin to the world of the reader to whom Hawthorne addresses himself) in which the psyche lives and has its adventures. This element of control makes, *a fortiori*, for import, meaning, and significance. For it is the element whereby relationships are established and maintained. The artist's responsibility is, if not to the world for which he creates, at least to the world he does create. And he does not create his characters merely to be free to be themselves, as the analyst would free his patients. He creates them so that the selves which they may (or may not) freely become can be meaningful in relation to the world which he must create with, for, and through them.

The analyst, as I understand it, above all fights the temptation (one of the difficulties in counter-transference) to be a creator, a God. The artist cultivates it; it is his primary illusion, and that he knows it to be so makes it all the more available to him as a crucial factor in his motivation toward creativity. Hawthorne surely cultivated it. And no account of Robin Molineux which declares that his freedom was such as to give him that euphoria which marks the sense of release from neurotic pain and guilt—no such account is a just account of his tale. Mr. Lesser may well think (he implies it certainly) that Robin Molineux's initial disturbance and guilt, since they are like those of all men, are "normally" neurotic. But such traits are part of the objective, literary reality of Robin's character; and Hawthorne does not release him from them, as Mr. Lesser would have it that he does. It is within the power of psychoanalytic criticism to account for Robin's behavior. But that criticism cannot—if it will merely "analyze" protagonists like Robin—account for the meaning which Hawthorne imputes to it. Robin cannot be abstracted from the meaning of his guilt-laden world by being shown to be all-too-human in his neurotic confusion. That confusion, which Mr. Lesser expounds so well, is finally real only insofar as it gives us perspective on Robin's total situation, his total world, as Hawthorne would have us know and judge it.

It may be well that Hawthorne felt that what we call Oedipal guilt was inevitably an element of the growth toward adulthood; yet that nothing—not even the magic of a psychoanalysis of which he dreamed a wild dream in a sketch like "The Haunted Mind"—could free man from it, and that it was integrally part of an all-too-human reality principle. Then, on this score—*pace* Mr. Lesser—Hawthorne would have to be said not to have been even a latently complete Freudian. Moreover, recent developments in psychoanalytic theory itself—witness the words I have quoted as epigraph—would seem to indicate that a post- (not neo-) Freudian conception of growing-up is not altogether out of accord with the conception manifest in "My Kinsman, Major Molineux." But I gather that, on this score, Freud himself was, in his later life, not always a manifestly complete Freudian. Reading "My Kinsman, Major Molineux," translating it into Freudian terms, translating those terms back into the context of Robin Molineux's world (a step which Mr. Lesser will not take)—perhaps we could even say that Freud was a latent Puritan. We could settle the matter by looking only at the whole of Freud's text. And the psychoanalytic critic could settle corresponding matters likewise only by looking at the whole of Hawthorne's text—by taking Robin off the couch and putting him back into the tale.[3]

[3] [Since this essay was first published, I have seen a number of interpretations of "My Kinsman, Major Molineux" akin to Mr. Lesser's: Hyatt H. Waggoner, *Hawthorne: A Critical Study* (Cambridge, 1955, rev. ed., 1963), pp. 56-64; Franklin B. Newman, " 'My Kinsman, Major Molineux': An Interpretation," *University of Kansas City Review*, XXI (1955), 203-212; Louis Paul, "A Psychoanalytic Reading of Hawthorne's 'Major Molineux,' " *American Imago*,

XVIII (1961), 279-288; and Frederic C. Crews, *The Sins of the Fathers: Hawthorne's Psychological Themes* (New York, 1966), pp. 72-79. Mr. Crews' study is far and away the most sensitive and subtle of those I cite, yet he too is committed to the psychoanalytic critic's either/or as regards a "psychological" as against a moral-historical interpretation of the story. He concludes: "We may say that he [Robin] has cathartically rid himself of both filial depend-ence and filial resentment, and will now be free. . . . This emo-tional freedom is ignored by critics who want to draw a cautionary lesson from the tale" (p. 78). "Cautionary" is of course a reduc-tionist term when applied to the kind of historical understanding which Robin *seems* to have achieved at the end of the story. A condition of his "freedom" is the realization of what he has done, his degree of involvement—however inevitable and necessary. What Robin will do with his freedom, what his freedom will do to him—this we are not told. We know only that it is a freedom in, not from, history—Robin's history and also his culture's. In guilt—and in the righteousness inextricably bound up with it, as I point out elsewhere in these essays—begins responsibility, so Freud taught. Off the analyst's couch, back in the tale, Robin has a life to live. Simplifying the kind of freedom Robin achieves, Mr. Crews (and the others too) would in effect close off an issue which Hawthorne leaves open.]

1959/1968

II

Occasions

□□□□□□□□□□□□□□□

"—I WOULD TO GOD SHAKSPEARE HAD LIVED LATER, &
PROMENADED IN BROADWAY. NOT THAT I MIGHT HAVE
HAD THE PLEASURE OF LEAVING MY CARD FOR HIM
AT THE ASTOR, OR MADE MERRY WITH HIM OVER A
BOWL OF FINE DUYCKINCK PUNCH; BUT THAT THE
MUZZLE WHICH ALL MEN WORE ON THEIR SOULS IN
THE ELIZABETHAN DAY, MIGHT NOT HAVE INTER-
CEPTED SHAKSPERS FULL ARTICULATIONS. FOR I HOLD
IT A VERITY, THAT EVEN SHAKSPEARE, WAS NOT A
FRANK MAN TO THE UTTERMOST. AND, INDEED, WHO
IN THIS INTOLERANT UNIVERSE IS, OR CAN
BE? BUT THE DECLARATION OF
INDEPENDENCE MAKES A
DIFFERENCE."

Herman Melville to Evert A. Duyckinck
3 *March 1849*

5

THE METAPHYSICS OF INDIAN-HATING:
Leatherstocking Unmasked

> "He was a great, robust-souled man, all of whose
> merits are not even yet fully appreciated. But a
> grateful Posterity will take the best care of Fenni-
> more Cooper." HERMAN MELVILLE *to Rufus Wilmot*
> *Griswold, 19 December 1851*

1.

I TAKE my title from that of a climactic chapter in *The
Confidence-Man* (1857), the bitter novel with which
Herman Melville seems to have hoped to undermine
what he had come to judge were the crumbling foundations of nineteenth-century American culture. *The
Confidence-Man* is, in effect, the fantastic story of a
nineteenth-century shape-shifter, who, on a voyage on
a riverboat ironically called the *Fidele*, in various guises
plays on the naïve, optimistic trust of a body of representative Americans. The working motto of the novel
is, in fact, "No Trust," and its end is to project a vision
of ante-bellum American culture lost in its own manifest destiny—the crazy pursuit of the quick and easy
way to spiritual and material riches. The pursuer celebrated in the sequence which culminates in "The Metaphysics of Indian-Hating" is called Leatherstocking
Nemesis. Celebrating him, Melville bids hail-and-fare-
well to Cooper's Leatherstocking and to all those who
he knew would subsequently be created in Leatherstocking's image.

"The Metaphysics of Indian-Hating" comes after an
episode in which the Confidence-Man has, in one of

his many guises, got the best of a supposedly tough-minded Westerner. *Another* Westerner, having witnessed the episode, is reminded of a story of yet *another* Westerner: one who, so he says, would certainly have been tough enough to resist all claims on *his* confidence and trust. This is the famous Colonel John Moredock, a classic Indian-hater, whose story the teller says that he gives as it used to be told by Judge James Hall, known in Melville's time as a prime authority on the West. The confusion in point-of-view is of course deliberate; and it is made even more confused by the fact that he who tells Judge Hall's story of Moredock the Indian-hater tells it to a man whom he takes to be a cosmopolitan gentleman, but who actually is the Confidence-Man in yet another of his guises. Needless to say, modern critics of Melville's novel have often called it surrealistic or nightmarish, by way of indicating the maze of moral confusion through which its author takes his readers. Indeed, "The Metaphysics of Indian-hating" is given, so we can now see, as a way of understanding this moral confusion. I suggest that it may give us a way of understanding aspects of the general moral confusion of not only nineteenth- but twentieth-century American culture. Understanding Melville's Indian-hater is a means of understanding not only that archetypal figure Leatherstocking but also his continuing shape-shifting progeny. Too, it is a means of identifying them.

Let us begin by source-hunting, since in this exercise in interpretation knowledge of a source, *the* source, is crucial for our understanding. Melville is in fact working a careful variation on the traditional legend of the Indian-hater, one widely told and retold in his own time. (I have seen eleven novels in which Indian-haters figure prominently, and an even greater number of sketches and bits in historical works, all antedating

The Confidence-Man.)[1] The traditional legend of the Indian-hater has a natural form of its own. Almost inevitably and without exception, it tells of a young man whose family was treacherously massacred by Indians; who thereupon developed a monomania for vengeance; who dedicated his life to destroying Indians, left civilization and became a savage himself, and perhaps even went insane; who, in any case, was cut off by his monomania from all proper contact with family, home, and the good society.

Regularly an irony is remarked: it is this man who has made the frontier safe for civilization; yet, to do so, he has had to become one of the savages whom he would destroy. This is taken to be a mystery of progress; and if an Indian-hater is saved from savagery, his salvation is taken to be miraculous. Few Indian-haters are said to be saved thus. Most often the tellers of the story are forced to conclude with something like this: "the writer cannot attempt to palliate and excuse [the Indian-hater's] conduct, nor can he account for the admiration which his doings excited among the hardy pioneers, in any other way than by supposing that in the struggle for mastery between the aborigines and those who supplanted them, the refined and humane sentiments which are promoted by civilization and

---

1 The novels are James McHenry, *The Spectre of the Forest* (1823); N. W. Hentz, *Tadeuskund* (1825); James Kirke Paulding, *The Dutchman's Fireside* (1831); Robert Montgomery Bird, *Nick of the Woods* (1837); Anna L. Snelling, *Kabeasa* (1842); Samuel Young, *Tom Hanson, the Avenger* (1847); James W. Dallam, *The Deaf Spy* (1848); Emerson Bennett, *The Prairie Flower* (1840), *The Renegade* (1848), *Kate Clarendon* (1848); and James Quinlan, *Tom Quick, the Indian Slayer* (1851). The most interesting of the sketches are those of James Hall, which include—besides the sketch from *Sketches of History, Life and Manners in the West* (1834-35) which is Melville's immediate source for the Moredock story—"The Backwoodsman," collected in *Legends of the West* (1833), "The Pioneer," collected in *Tales of the Border* (1835), and "The Indian-Hater," collected in *The Wilderness and the War Path* (1846).

111

Christianity, were obliterated by the dark and unfeeling dogmas which obtain a lodgment in the human mind during perilous and bloody times."[2] Indian-hating, thus, is subsumed under the dogma of Christian, civilized progress.

In *The Confidence-Man* Melville, as I have noted, explicitly works with one of these Indian-hating stories, that of Colonel John Moredock, as it appears in James Hall's *Sketches of History, Life, and Manners in the West* (1834-35). In Chapter xxv, Melville introduces a stranger "with the bluff *abord* of the West."[3] Having overheard the affair of the ursine Missourian who has almost successfully resisted the Confidence-Man in one of his guises but who has fallen victim to him in another, the stranger is reminded of Judge James Hall on Moredock the Indian-hater; and he tells the story to the cosmopolitan gentleman.

At the outset, the cosmopolitan is shocked, says that he admires Indians, and goes into a paean to celebrated heroic chiefs—this, too, part of a tradition of writing on the Indian in Melville's time. As one would expect him to, the cosmopolitan as confidence-man endowing even the natural man with his kind of (false) confidence, can conceive of nothing but noble savages. But in spite of this pious interruption, the stranger will go on with his story. In Chapters xxvi and xxvii, he discusses first the "Metaphysics of Indian-hating" and then the life and work of that prime Indian-hater, Colonel Moredock. Both the story and the metaphysics are said to be quoted verbatim from Hall. And both fall into the traditional pattern, but with critical variations.

For Hall's brief, traditionally cautious and progressivist apologia for Indian-hating, Melville substitutes

[2] James Quinlan, *The Original Life and Adventures of Tom Quick, the Indian Slayer* [1st ptd. 1851 as *Tom Quick, the Indian Slayer*] (Deposit, N.Y., 1894), p. 101.

[3] I quote from Elizabeth Foster's edition of *The Confidence-Man* (New York, 1954).

(crediting it to Hall) one which is long, detailed, frank; one in which progress figures not at all: an analysis of the compulsively lonely, thoughtful, violent, self-willed, self-reliant, ungodly pathfinder who, even though he is a "provider of security to those who come after him, for himself asks nothing but hardship." In the *Sketches* Hall concludes simply: "It is not from a desire of conquest, or thirst of blood, or with any premeditated hostility against the savage, that the pioneer continues to follow him from forest to forest, ever disputing with him the right to the soil, and the privilege of hunting game."[4] In *The Confidence-Man* Melville, speaking through the Western stranger, makes Hall conclude: "Thus, though he keep moving on through life, he maintains with respect to nature much the same unaltered relation throughout; with her creatures, too, including panthers and Indians." The relation is one of single-minded hatred; the Indian-hater is a man who will have no contact with other men, who is compelled in his self-willed loneliness to face down nature and fight her to the death. So Melville's narrator (still nominally quoting Hall) fills out the rest of his introductory metaphysics with accounts of frontier hardships and savage villainy—all told from the point of view of the Indian-hater, and all serving to justify that point of view and to furnish it a metaphysics. What results is a definition of the "Indian-hater *par excellence*"—the Indian-hater of the tradition, with the regular biography, but now interpreted entirely in terms of the hatred and loneliness he embraces as positive goods: "Ever on the noiseless trail; cool, collected, patient; less seen than felt; sniffing, smelling—a Leatherstocking Nemesis." This is virtually (if, on the part of Melville's Hall, unconsciously) to make him into an animal, so that the conclusion comes naturally enough: " 'Terror' is his epitaph." The admiration of this Hall (and presumably of

[4] I quote from the *Sketches*, II (Philadelphia, 1835), 74-82.

the Western stranger who quotes him) for the Indian-hater is so extravagant as to force us to reject it. The irony is almost too heavy. For he is a kind of Holy Terror.

Whereas the actual Hall and the rest who wrote in the tradition had tried to rationalize the terror and loneliness of Indian-hating into part of some larger, glorious, progressivist scheme of things, Melville makes his Hall dwell only on terror and loneliness. This Hall is made to be caught up in the violence of the men whom he is describing; such violence clearly comes to be an end in itself. We are moved from the commonplace, quietly ordered, straightforward narrative of the Hall of the *Sketches* to the flamboyantly eruptive rhetoric of the pseudo-Hall of *The Confidence-Man*. The attempt is, I think, to make us know the terrors of hatred as directly and as fully as we have known and shall know those of false love and confidence.

Then, in Chapter XXVII the stranger, still largely quoting Melville's Hall, comes to the story of Moredock himself, and our knowledge of hatred is realized not as metaphysics but as action. And, as always, action is not quite so logically complete or extreme as metaphysics. For Moredock is not an Indian-hater *par excellence*; no man could be, as no man could be a real Leatherstocking out of Cooper—both being examples of the *beau idéal* of their types. But Moredock will do. At this point Melville makes his Hall follow most closely the Hall of the *Sketches*. Changes that are made from the original account are such that will make Moredock's action so palpable that the metaphysics which informs them cannot be denied. Moredock's mother in the *Sketches* has been married and widowed by the tomahawk "several times"; in *The Confidence-Man* it is "thrice." Her "large family" becomes a family of "nine children." The massacre of the family, John excepted, is told in more gruesomely concrete detail in

The Confidence-Man than it is in the *Sketches*. In general, what Melville does to Hall's account can best be illustrated by comparing a paragraph from the *Sketches* with its rendering in *The Confidence-Man*:

John Moredock was just entering upon the years of manhood, when he was thus left in a strange land, the sole survivor of his race. He resolved upon executing vengeance, and immediately took measures to discover the actual perpetrators of the massacre. It was ascertained that the outrage was committed by a party of twenty or thirty Indians, belonging to different tribes, who had formed themselves into a lawless, predatory band. Moredock watched the motions of this band for more than a year, before an opportunity suitable for his purpose occurred. At length he learned that they were hunting on the Missouri side of the river, nearly opposite to the recent settlements of the Americans. He raised a party of young men and pursued them; but that time they escaped. Shortly after, he sought them at the head of another party, and had the good fortune to discover them one evening, on an island, wither they had retired to encamp the more securely for the night. Moredock and his friends, about equal in numbers to the Indians, waited until the dead of night, and then landed upon the island, turning adrift their own canoes and those of the enemy, and determined to sacrifice their own lives, or to exterminate the savage band. They were completely successful. Three only of the Indians escaped, by throwing themselves into the river; the rest were slain, while the whites lost not a man.

. . .

He was just entering upon manhood, when thus left in nature sole survivor of his race. Other youngsters might have turned mourners; he turned avenger. His nerves were electric wires—sensitive, but steel. He was

115

one who, from self-possession, could be made neither to flush nor pale. It is said that when the tidings were brought him, he was ashore sitting beneath a hemlock eating his dinner of venison—and as the tidings were told him, after the first start he kept on eating, but slowly and deliberately, chewing the wild news with the wild meat, as if both together, turned to chyle, together would sinew him to his intent. From that meal he rose an Indian-hater. He rose; got his arms, prevailed upon some comrades to join him, and without delay started to discover who were the actual transgressors. They proved to belong to a band of twenty renegades from various tribes, outlaws even among Indians, and who had formed themselves into a marauding crew. No opportunity for action being at the time presented, he dismissed his friends; told them to go on, thanking them, and saying he would ask their aid at some future day. For upwards of a year, alone in the wilds, he watched the crew. Once, what he thought a favourable chance having occurred—it being midwinter, and the savages encamped, apparently to remain so—he anew mustered his friends, and marched against them; but getting wind of his coming, the enemy fled, and in such panic that everything was left behind but their weapons. During the winter, much the same thing happened upon two subsequent occasions. The next year he sought them at the head of a party pledged to serve him for forty days. At last the hour came. It was on the shore of the Mississippi. From their covert, Moredock and his men dimly descried the gang of Cains in the red dusk of evening, paddling over to a jungled island in midstream, there the more securely to lodge; for Moredock's retributive spirit in the wilderness spoke ever to their trepidations now, like the voice calling through the garden. Waiting until the dead of night, the whites swam the river, towing after them a raft laden with

116

their arms. On landing, Moredock cut the fastenings of the enemy's canoes, and turned them, with his own raft, adrift; resolved that there should be neither escape for the Indians, nor safety, except in victory, for the whites. Victorious the whites were; but three of the Indians saved themselves by taking to the stream. Moredock's band lost not a man.

Thus, following the Hall of the *Sketches*, Melville's Hall traces Moredock's career—emphasizing that Indian-hating did not completely destroy his civilized character, that he was, in spite of everything, a good family-man, a good storyteller, a good singer of songs. Yet he was also a good enough Indian-hater to make one think of the ideal, the hater *par excellence*. The Hall of the *Sketches* concludes with the simple statement that Moredock late in life once refused to be a candidate for the governorship of Illinois. Melville's Hall explains that Moredock refused because he realized that it would be improper for a governor, Indian-hater or not, to steal out now and then "for a few days' shooting at human beings. . . ." Further: "In short, he was not unaware that to be a consistent Indian-hater involves the renunciation of ambition, with its objects— the pomps and glories of the world; and since religion, pronouncing such things vanities, accounts it a merit to renounce them, therefore, so far as this goes, Indian-hating, whatever may be thought of it in other respects, may be regarded as not wholly without the efficacy of a devout sentiment."

2.

As Melville shows how Indian-hating and its metaphysics have been taken to be necessary in God's scheme of things American, his account, in all its satiric and parodic depth, is resonant with the deeply felt, totally committed nineteenth-century American sense of the special mission of American civilization as it moved ever westward. This was the American Idea of Progress. Much of the power of Melville's satire derives from the power of the idea, that is to say, of the metaphysics which it satirizes. And we must take that power into account if we are to understand and to judge that idea and the beliefs and actions which it generated. The idea of civilized mission, as Melville's satire lets us see, generated the idea of the tragic role of the Indian-hater, and thus of his heroic character. Moreover, it generated the idea of the equally tragic role of the Indian, and thus of his heroic character too. The Metaphysics of Indian-hating was postulated on an understanding of the destroyed as well as on an understanding of the destroyer.

American thinking about the Indian and his relation to White civilization was, until the middle of the eighteenth century, based on the notion that somehow the Indian would absorb, or be absorbed by, White civilization.[5] When the cruelty and rigor of events, White impatience and Indian stubbornness would not allow for such absorption, American thinking changed its emphasis and direction. It was based more and more on the notion that the gap between Indian and White society was too great to be closed; that corresponding to White civilization there was Indian "savagism"—for which we have no equivalent term now, at least consciously, since we tell ourselves that we no longer subscribe to the notion. As civilization had its high qualities—learning, cooperation, "pure" religion, the ability to proceed by and to learn from abstraction, so savagism had its high qualities too—practicality, individualism, "natural" religion, the ability to proceed by and learn from only the concrete and particular. The

[5] I summarize in what follows the argument of my *Savages of America: A Study of the Indian and the Idea of Civilization* (Baltimore, 1953, rev. ed., 1965).

118

qualities of civilization and savagism accordingly each derived from the form of the society which generated it. (This of course is Cooper's doctrine of "gifts.") The form of civilized society was agrarian and urban, marked by a system of private ownership and rule by law; the form of savage society was hunting, marked by a system of communal ownership and rule by custom. Moreover, the one way of life had evolved out of the other, and in so evolving had developed a newer and nobler kind of human being. Hypothetically, there should have been time for the various and varying savage Indian societies to develop into something close to civilized White society—American society. But these Indian societies had been isolated from Europe and from each other too long; and now time had run out, White Americans were moving westward, and Indians had to give way. True enough, they had their kind of virtues, as well as their kind of vices. But taken all in all, they were not up to the qualities demanded by the way of life which was sweeping over them. Maybe some of them might have been saved by any one of the many versions of the territory and reservation system which were introduced during the nineteenth century. But it seemed inevitable to many civilized men, on the Indian frontier and behind it, that savages, being savage, would resist savagely; that they would have to be beaten down savagely; that some civilized men would have to make the sacrifice of meeting savages on their own terms; and that savage Indian and proto-savage White man would be destroyed in the process. Yet: that civilization would prevail.

This understanding of the Indian was almost totally pervasive, a central element of the thinking of pioneering anthropologists and ethno-historians from Thomas Jefferson to Lewis Henry Morgan, as well as theorists of society, historians, and the like. However, most often it functioned not so much as an argument but as an assumption; not so much as a step in a logical chain leading to action as the very foundation of the logic itself. Even those who were genuinely concerned with the welfare of the Indian acted on this assumption and so became what we now call "gradualists." The situation could not have been otherwise, since this understanding proceeded from a prior understanding of the mission of civilization and of the self which would participate in that mission. I give an extreme, and therefore touching, example. In 1827, Charles Johnston published an account of his long captivity by the Shawnees, *A Narrative of Incidents Attending the Capture, Detention, and Ransom of Charles Johnston*, a document now prized by ethno-historians for its articulate and detailed description of Shawnee life. Yet having told his story, Johnston felt that it would not be necessary to discuss the character of the savages among whom he long lived. He explained why:

> Dr. Robertson, in the fourth book of his valuable *History of America*, has collected almost everything which, when his work was written, could be ascertained in relation to [the Indians]. Subsequent travellers and residents among them, have published facts and remarks, establishing the correctness of his general views. It may be questioned, whether any accession to those general views has been obtained, by later writers.

Now this Dr. Robertson is William Robertson, the eighteenth-century Scot, in whose *History* the view of savagism that I have outlined received one of its earliest full expositions. Yet many of his data, as Jefferson and others pointed out, were fantastic. Still Johnston accepted Robertson's general views. (And so, incidentally, did Jefferson and most others.) For Robertson believed, as Johnston must have, in the progress of Christian civilization; he could comprehend the Indian only in relation to that belief. And we may take John-ston as a type of the nineteenth-century American, so caught up in the necessity of belief in his Christian, civilized destiny that he must perforce subscribe to a general view of the Indian which, in sober ethno-his-torical fact, the very details of his captivity narrative show to be manifestly untrue. We may say, in sober historical-cultural fact, that for Johnston and his con-temporaries the "metaphysics" of Christian, civilized progress not only distorted the facts of Indian life but *made* them. In the process, certainly, it made them more bearable. Perhaps that metaphysics even con-tributed to making Johnston's captivity more bearable, was the ultimate means whereby he resisted becoming, in the nineteenth-century phrase, "completely Indian-ised." Certainly, as Melville's chapters and the tales from which they derive make clear, such a metaphysics made bearable the portion of guilt rising out of that hatred which drove the White man to destroy the In-dian. For that metaphysics revealed an Indian whose sacred destiny was to be destroyed. It followed neces-sarily that the destroyers themselves had a sacred destiny. Men between two worlds, those of savagism and civilization, absorbing some of the values of the first in order to advance those of the second, by virtue of this fact in good part cut off from the first while being unable or unwilling wholly to identify with the second, they in their fate could be comprehended only by a species of "metaphysics." To appreciate that meta-physics fully, in its pseudo-logic, its power, and its con-fidence—this indeed is to take it as something felt to be virtually sacred in its seriousness and significance. And taking it thus, if only in imagination, I should think, is the first step in understanding the history which it informs and those aspects of the American national character for which it supplied—and continues to supply—a rationale.

3.

It is also the first step in understanding the first, the *echt*, Leatherstocking as against Hall's Leatherstocking, and Melville's as he makes Hall's his. Francis Parkman's famous words epitomize the first Leatherstocking, who, as an agent of the power of American civilization, will be, when he has to, an Indian-destroyer, but never an Indian-hater:

> Civilization has a destroying as well as creating power. It is exterminating the buffalo and the Indian, over whose fate too many lamentations, real or affected, have been sounded for us to renew them here. It must . . . eventually sweep from before it a class of men, its own precursors and pioneers, so remarkable both in their virtues and their faults, that few will see their extinction without regret. Of these men Leatherstocking is the representative; and though in him the traits of the individual are quite as prominent as those of the class, yet his character is not on this account less interesting, or less worthy of permanent remembrance. His life conveys in some sort an epitome of American history, during one of its most busy and decisive periods.[6]

The Leatherstocking Tales then are to be read as essentially the story of Natty Bumppo—as the *beau idéal* of the frontiersman—in the context of the frontier, with what was for Cooper and his fellows a tension of civilization and noncivilization. Bumppo is the superman in a milieu in which such types could develop. But even this frontiersman in all his perfection—and this was Cooper's major insight—could not last; he was to be swept over by the very civilization for which he had cleared the way and to which in some respects he was

[6] The passage is from Parkman's review of the revised edition of Cooper's novels, *North American Review*, LXXIV (1852), 147-161.

superior. Hence his story is to be a kind of tragic story —made even more so by the essential rightness and necessity of it all. Cooper could never be on Bumppo's side: never would he intend to suggest that the civilization which sent Bumppo to a death on the prairie was thereby an evil force. Yet, for all his devotion to the idea that men must realize their social, civil qualities, Cooper could see "mythic" potentialities for good in a Bumppo. More important—and this is part of that major insight—he could see that westward expansion and progress in crushing such a man as Bumppo would crush something heroic in American life. If, as in the Preface to *The Pathfinder*, Cooper could speak of "the wonderful means by which Providence is clearing the way for the advancement of civilization across the whole American continent," still he knew too that Progress meant suffering as well as triumph.[7]

Significantly, the very first Bumppo whom Cooper portrayed was the Bumppo of *The Pioneers* (1823). Here Bumppo was to be defeated once and for all. We see him at the beginning of the novel with an "air of sullen dissatisfaction" complaining bitterly of Temple's "clearings and betterments," which have more and more restricted his freedom. He is gnarled and hardy; he lives with Chingachgook, no longer Big Serpent but Indian John, a chief whom liquor and the white man's ways have made old and useless. Over against them is set Judge Temple, the civilizer, who wishes to conserve the land for a better and richer life. He is clearing the wilderness, and Natty is part of it. Temple is all-powerful. He brings with him law, the law of societies, not of individuals. And, as Natty tells Grant, the minister, ". . . might makes right, and the law is stronger than an old man. . . ."

It is inevitable that Natty try to oppose might and

---

[7] Here and in what follows I quote from *Cooper's Novels*, Globe Edition (Boston, 1880).

the law. The poaching incident, Natty's resisting search and arrest, his conviction—these are symbolic of the more bitter aspects of the progress in which Temple (and Cooper) so dearly believed. That Temple should be indebted to Natty for saving his daughter's life points up only more the sad necessity of his sentencing Natty to the stocks and to prison. Hence Natty's speech at the ruins of the hut, which he has burned rather than allow it to be broken into, expresses the motif of *The Pioneers* and, indeed, of all the Tales:

> What would ye have with an old and helpless man?
> . . . You've driven God's creaters from the wilderness, where his providence had put them for his own pleasure; and you've brought in the troubles and divilties of the law, where no man was ever known to disturb another. You have driven me, that have lived forty long years of my appointed time in this very spot, from my home and the shelter of my head, lest you should put your wicked feet and wasty ways in my cabin. You've driven me to burn these logs, under which I've eaten and drunk—the first of Heaven's gifts, and the other of the pure springs—for the half of a hundred years; and to mourn the ashes under my feet, as a man would weep and mourn for the children of his body. . . .

If the rest of the novel is awkwardly and obviously managed, it is managed for a purpose—to set against Bumppo's heroic stand the power of the civilization which drives him westward. For westward he must go, even after the Temples and Effinghams have been united, even after the Judge has offered to care for him for the rest of his days. Cooper's civilization is a kindly, strength-giving force, if only one yields to it intelligently. But Natty can have none of civilization, as he can comprehend none of its ways. Being of the frontier, of an heroic age, he must perforce preserve himself in his own ways as long as he lives.

Around the motif set in *The Pioneers* Cooper built the rest of the Leatherstocking Tales. As he wrote them —*The Last of the Mohicans* (1826), *The Prairie* (1827), *The Pathfinder* (1840), and *The Deerslayer* (1841)— he described the stages of Natty Bumppo's mythic, heroic development, always setting him against persons and actions which represented the civilized world of which he could never be part. It is true that the particular details of Cooper's conception of Natty changed as he returned to him again and again. Most important, Natty became less and less the "real" frontiersman and more and more the *beau idéal*; the crudeness of the Natty of *The Pioneers* is hardly the freshness and naïveté of the Natty of *The Deerslayer*. However, these are strictly matters of detail, which condition the whole only incidentally. For Cooper was a busy man and— as is too patent to need demonstrating—an unsure and sadly insensitive artist. Yet, even if at times he might falter in detailed execution, he never faltered—if we read his novels with attention to their underlying ideology—in total conception.

To glance briefly at the Tales according to Bumppo's chronology: In *The Deerslayer*, Bumppo is young, uncertain of himself, not yet having killed his first Mingo. With him we see Hutter and Hurry Harry, "real" frontiersmen in all their crudity, and the young Chingachgook and his beloved. More important, there is Judith Hutter, drawn to Bumppo, who will have none of her. He must be free of the complexities of a kind of passion which he does not comprehend and therefore does not trust. For, while he does not have an Indian's "gifts," he also does not have those of White civilization.

And so it goes in *The Last of the Mohicans*, where Natty is entirely above the life of Alice and Cora Munro and young Heyward. Here it is Uncas, the son of Chingachgook, who, like his blood enemy, Magua, is brought to his death by his passion for Cora Munro. That the Indian and Cora should be united would be impossible in Cooper's world of civilization and progress; hence, temporizing the issue by making Cora's ancestry somewhat dubious, he must do away with them both. And so there remain only Bumppo and Chingachgook and their deep, heroic friendship.

In *The Pathfinder* Natty is in love, in love with a woman who represents the security and peace of the settler's cottage. He lives his adventurous life, killing Mingos, making rescues, winning victories; yet he cannot win Mabel. Realizing that this failure is only right, he tells Jasper Western (who is, as a matter of course, young and handsome and who does win Mabel) that he hasn't "idees enough" for her. She is of civilization, complex and thinking. He is of the frontier. Once more, it is the heroic concept which matters here. One can see in Cooper's picture of this and the other Bumppos all that contemporary historians and writers on society were saying about what the Indian (and the White man who might live an Indian life) should be as the product of a free, hunting, warring life—a man of action, not of "idees," a man whose hard life gave him time and means only to act and to intuit, not to think. And civilized men (Cooper, for example) thought.

Then there is *The Pioneers*, the first written and, as we have seen, the key volume in the series. And finally, *The Prairie*, with the end we have expected. Here is Natty Bumppo as spectator, as one whose age and accomplishments have set him above Ishmael Bush and his squatter family, Middleton, Paul, Inez, Ellen, and the naturalist, Obed Battius. Even though Natty is in the end to fight the Bushes, at the very first he realizes that he has something in common with them. When he tries to make Ishmael understand that the Sioux have attacked the squatter and his family because the Indians think of themselves as owners of the prairie, Ishmael cannot understand:

> "Owners!" echoed the squatter, "I am as rightful an owner of the land I stand on, as any governor in the States! Can you tell me, stranger, where the law or the reason, is to be found, which says, that one man shall have a section, or a town, or perhaps a county to his use, and another have to beg for earth to make his grave in? This is not nature, and I deny that it is law. That is, your legal law."
>
> "I cannot say that you are wrong," returned the trapper, whose opinions on this important topic, though drawn from very different premises, were in singular accordance with those of his companion, "and I have often thought and said as much, when and where I have believed my voice could be heard. . . ."

Here is a strange thing. The squatter, as Cooper had made abundantly clear in *The Pioneers* and was to make even clearer in *Home as Found* and in the Littlepage series, was an evil, non-civilizing force on the frontier. Yet he can make Natty agree with Ishmael, if on different grounds. Natty was to be as isolated as Ishmael. For, as Cooper points out *in propria persona* a few pages later, civil society was moving westward:

> The gradations of society, from that state which is called refined to that which approaches as near barbarity as connection with an intelligent people will readily allow, are to be traced from the bosom of the States, where wealth, luxury and the arts are beginning to seat themselves, to those distant, and ever-receding borders which mark the skirts, and announce the approach, of the nation, as moving mists precede the signs of day.

In *The Prairie* Natty is most of all Leatherstocking *philosophe*. Here more than in any of the other novels he comments on the evil of perverted man-made institutions and on the assurance of moral order which he finds self-evident in God's Nature. (If his early training among the Moravians is recalled here, as elsewhere, it is only as something auxiliary to this preorthodox natural religion.) Here he is set against the caricatured naturalist Battius and his hope that science can "eradicate the evil principle" from the world. This Bumppo is, once more, essentially the primitive man of the eighteenth-century rationalist historians and their nineteenth-century followers, who, even as they proclaimed the total superiority of civilized to savage institutions, insisted that the natural man could "philosophize," if only at a relatively low, intuitive level. Thus for Cooper and his fellows, Natty can partake in alarums and excursions and can face death with the contentment and complacency of one who serenely lives in the least complex and most directly comprehended of worlds, that untouched by civilized man. He has the best "gifts"—Cooper's repeated term for culture-bound traits—of both savagism and civilization.

Natty dies as he has lived. He is ready for death because there is nothing left for him in a world of Middletons. It is significant that Middleton is the grandson of Duncan Heyward, in whom Natty, in *The Last of the Mohicans*, had first found the strengths and weaknesses of the civilized life that was to give order to the frontier. The central motif of the Tales is stated explicitly. Middleton tells Natty just what his grandfather had said of the Leatherstocking of the fifties: "In short he was a noble shoot from the stock of human nature, which never could attain its proper elevation and importance, for no other reason, than because it grew in the forest." If there is to be a sorrow at Natty's death, it is sorrow at the inevitability of change, at the passing of one good, felt wholly, with the coming of another.

4.

Unhappily, we know too much—as Melville knew too much—to feel thus. The more "contextual" our perspective, the more difficult it is to take Leatherstocking at face value. Assenting to the heroic ritualism and the noble repudiations and self-sacrifices which give his life its immediate value, we must nonetheless see immanent in him, inevitable, the figure of the Indian-hater. Viewed in retrospect, his is an improvised life, a pseudo-myth, bodied forth in order that we may take refuge in it, and so avoid facing up to the facts of the metaphysics and the history in which it is grounded. For we now have a conspective view, perhaps achieved too easily after the fact, of Leatherstocking and his progeny: from Moredocks to Buffalo Bills and Dead-Eye Dicks, Nick Adamses, Nick Gatsbys, Sam Spades, Matt Dillons, Mike Hammers, and so on down the line—all of them revealing themselves, if we but look closely enough, as not only their own proper nemeses but ours.[8]

Surely the difference between the better and the worse among them is to be measured by the degree to which they are rather destroyers than haters. Artistically, the difference derives from the scope of their lives in the tales told of them. The lives of the better among them are clearly and intensely delimited by the range of beliefs and commitments possible to men in their situations; the lives of the worse among them partake, altogether falsely, of the range of beliefs and commitments possible only in the sort of society from

---

[8] Cf. Henry Nash Smith, "The Sons of Leatherstocking," *Virgin Land: The American West as Myth and Symbol* (Cambridge, 1950), pp. 51-120; and Henry Bamford Parkes, "Metamorphoses of Leatherstocking," in Philip Rahv, ed., *Literature in America* (New York, 1957), pp. 431-445.

which they have nominally been set apart. The difference is that between a Leatherstocking and a Moredock, a Nick Adams and a Mike Hammer, a reluctant celebrant of death and compulsive killer. But, so the record shows, the former seems always to have been a progenitor of the latter, since destruction, if it is conceived as necessary to a cultural mission, finally makes sense only as it is empowered by hatred. For better or worse, such figures have in common an attraction to violence, ritualized or raw, whereby they are invariably cut off from the society which, as willing or unwilling agents, they not only preserve but make possible. They supply a series of models, together they constitute an ideal type, for the American who is driven to dream of setting things right by taking the law into his own hands. Be they frontiersmen, mountain men, cowboys playing war games with Indians, big- and small-game hunters, formalists of the *corrida*, lonely sheriffs, or private eyes, they are all as tragic types at the least inadequate, at the most false. Still, as their worlds are ours, so are the tales told of them tales told of us—in effect communally composed versions of what Marianne Moore (in "New York") calls "the savage's romance,/ accreted where we need the space for commerce." Believing in one version or another of the romance, we become, like Cooper, our own confidence-men.

Leatherstocking—like all of them, the better or the worse—is so arbitrarily created, so much of his career is cut off from the world whose heroic exemplum it is intended to be, that, trying to accept him at face value, we must suspend our belief unwillingly if at all. Cooper summed him up in the Preface to the 1850 edition of the Tales:

> Removed from nearly all the temptations of civilized life, placed in the best associations of that which is deemed savage, and favorably disposed by nature to

improve such advantages, it appeared to the writer that his hero was a fit subject to represent the better qualities of both conditions, without pushing either to extremes.

But in a world whose prime expressive genre (be it romance or novel) is thickly and richly detailed prose fiction, the extremes are inevitably too much with us and must be explicitly and frankly taken into account, not just hypothetically accommodated to the whole. In the Leatherstocking Tales those extremes, of course, center on the intrinsic yet mutually exclusive rightness of both savagism and civilization. Integral to the rightness of the former is its disadvantages; to the rightness of the latter, its temptations. And if we read deeply enough into the context of the Tales, the heroic figure who is to mediate between the two is inconceivable except as he be fully expressive of the mixture of rightness, disadvantages, and temptations. By definition the mixture was fatal—but in the Leatherstocking Tales not fatal enough.

The richness of the rendering of Leatherstocking's career has for the most part led critics to insist that Cooper was secretly—or, in more modern terms, unconsciously—on his hero's side. And perhaps in biographical fact he was. But the Leatherstocking Tales are about Natty Bumppo, not James Fenimore Cooper; and Natty Bumppo is preeminently a creature of the fatal mixture of savagism and civilization. Cooper is repeatedly explicit about this. Still, for all his concern to see American culture for what it really is, he does not bring himself to see what it (or this aspect of it) essentially is—at once producer and product of the metaphysics of Indian-hating. Cooper's interpreters ever since the 1850's would appear to have felt it in the national interest to protect Leatherstocking from the temptations of civilization and the disadvantages

131

of savagism, as though to cling to a belief in a way of life which is denied by the very context (if we read it properly) in which it is set forth. Nonetheless, the real Leatherstocking, there for the beholding, is Leatherstocking Nemesis. D. H. Lawrence—in *Studies in Classic American Literature*—saw that he was the nemesis not only of savagism but of civilization, of life itself:

> He is a moralizer, but he always tries to moralize from actual experience, not from theory. He says: "Hurt nothing unless you're forced to." Yet he gets his deepest thrill of gratification, perhaps, when he puts a bullet through the heart of a beautiful buck, as it stoops to drink at the lake. Or when he brings the invisible bird fluttering down in death, out of the high blue. "Hurt nothing unless you're forced to." And yet he lives by death, by killing the wild things of the air and earth.
> It's not good enough.
> But you have there the myth of the essential white America.
> All the other stuff, the love, the democracy, the floundering into lust, is a sort of by-play. The essential American soul is hard, isolate, stoic, and a killer. It has never yet melted.

Ordinary readers, to be sure, do not have Lawrence's special perspective or insight. But they by now do (or can) have the requisite historical understanding whereby they may know the grand rationale of the Leatherstocking Tales and may further perceive those occasions between Cooper's time and ours at which again and again, in one form or another, Leatherstocking has reappeared. As Melville said in "The Metaphysics of Indian-hating": ". . . Indian-hating still exists; and no doubt, will continue to exist, so long as Indians do." We must then continue to take Indian-hating with high seriousness, must learn at once to respect and to fear it. We must learn to live with it—almost.

And of course we do live with it, only in different forms—forms as various as the progeny of Leather-stocking who project it for us. Our most obvious and extreme equivalent of Indian-hating is Negro-hating, or Negro-demeaning, which amounts to the same thing. This fact has been abundantly pointed out. I am here concerned to put this fact in the perspective of the tradition from which it derives and which it continues.

William Faulkner contributed a small article to the September 1956 issue of *Ebony* on the segregation controversy—addressing himself, in his role of major American sensibility, to the Negroes whose torment had long obsessed him. He denied, as he did so often, that he was looking forward to another War Between the States, and he went so far as to say that the Negro's primary institutional hope was the NAACP. He pleaded for flexibility and dignity, but above all for patience. Putting words into the mouths of Negroes, he wrote: "The white man has devoted three hundred years to teaching us to be patient; that is one thing at least in which we are his superiors. Let us turn it into a weapon against him." And how, practically, would this patience be expressed? In Faulkner's words:

> If I were a Negro in America today, [this] is the course I would advise the leaders of my race to follow: to send every day to a white school to which he was entitled by his ability and capacity to go, a student of my race, fresh and cleanly dressed, courteous, without threat of violence, to seek admission; when he was refused I would forget about him as an individual, but tomorrow I would send another one, still fresh and clean and courteous, to be refused in his turn, until at last the white man himself must recognize that there will be no peace for him until he himself has solved the dilemma.

Faulkner's rhetoric is of a kind with Cooper's and Parkman's, and, as it partakes of the traditional doctrine of "gifts" appropropriate to the White man and to the Negro, is if anything more deeply felt than theirs. It is in fact so deeply felt that it can lead him to play Melville to his own Cooper and so pass on his Leatherstocking a judgment of a sort beyond Cooper's ken. Faulkner's Leatherstocking is of the better kind, but still, in his final judgment, not good enough. His Leatherstocking is of course Ike McCaslin who, in the tales told of him, takes upon himself the burden of the violence and destructiveness inherent in the development of the Southern mode of civilization and, in so doing, isolates himself. In the *Go Down, Moses* sequence as a whole he is to the Indian Sam Fathers (who initiates him into the life of the wilderness even as it is being destroyed) as Leatherstocking is to Chingachgook. His burden is all the heavier than Leatherstocking's because of the historic role of the Negro, on whose exploitation and suffering much of the transformation of wilderness into civilization has been based. McCaslin comes to acknowledge that, willy-nilly, he has been involved in the destruction of the land and those who have lived in greatest harmony with it, even as he has been involved in the exploitation of those who have most suffered in that transformation. But he will not hate. Still, Faulkner will not let him, like Leatherstocking in *The Prairie*, take his burden with him and disappear into his own West. In "Delta Autumn," McCaslin—old, tired, and withdrawn— is to pay off a young Negro girl, so, on behalf of the young White man who had been having an affair with her, to get rid of her. He is ashamed, ashamed for his race, his people, and his society. He counsels patience:

"That's right. Go back North. Marry; a man in your own race. That's the only salvation for you—for a while yet, maybe a long while yet. We will have to wait. ..."

And she responds:

"Old man, have you lived so long and forgotten so much that you don't remember anything you ever knew or felt or even heard about love?"

McCaslin thus at the end must confront the fact of his own nemesis. Faulkner's explicit judgment of him, given in an interview, is this: "I think a man ought to do more than repudiate. He should have been more affirmative instead of shunning people."[9]

Leatherstocking and McCaslin succeed (if that is the proper word) in that they repudiate their own society rather than hate those who stand in its way, those whom they must help to destroy. But they cannot repudiate one thing their society has given them—the fact that their very being bears within it a potential for hatred, precisely as they have been the agents of a society which, even if repudiated, has made many of its advances through hatred, and also the violence and destructiveness which are concomitants of hatred. Understanding them, understanding their fatal inadequacies, we may understand their lesser analogues, who in their lives are made to realize the life-destroying values to which Leatherstocking and McCaslin are not allowed by their creators to commit themselves. It is inevitable that Leatherstocking and his progeny, including McCaslin, are almost all of them not allowed the fulfillment of love. *That* element of the metaphysics of Indian-hating (a price paid for repudiation) must abide, even for those who are heroic enough to resist its deepest self-destructive temptations. For the sort of heroes they are must above all contain within themselves the

9 Quoted in Arthur F. Kinney, " 'Delta Autumn': Postlude to 'The Bear,' " in F. L. Utley, L. Z. Bloom, A. F. Kinney, eds. *Bear, Man, and God* (New York, 1964), p. 393.

seeds of their own nemeses. Cooper's Leatherstocking is perfected in Melville's Indian-hater, as he is perfected in Ike McCaslin and the rest of his (for the most part sordid) progeny. Perfected, he is unmasked—perhaps one day to be undone, no longer necessary even as a figment of our national imagination.

1947/1952/1957/1968

6

HAWTHORNE AND THE SENSE OF THE PAST; OR, THE IMMORTALITY OF MAJOR MOLINEUX

"El pasado es indestructible; tarde o temprano
vuelven todas las cosas, y una de las cosas que
vuelven es el proyecto de abolir el pasado."
JORGE LUIS BORGES, *"Nathaniel Hawthorne"*

1.

IN THE "Prelude" to the *Tales of a Wayside Inn*, Longfellow has occasion to refer to some bibulous verses scratched on a window of the Inn by

the great Major Molineaux,
Whom Hawthorne has immortal made.

Longfellow thus identifies the tarred-and-feathered Loyalist of Hawthorne's "My Kinsman, Major Molineux" with another Molineux (the spelling of the name varies)—William Molineux, a well-to-do radical Boston trader, an organizer and leader of anti-Loyalist mobs, member of the Boston Revolutionary Committee of Correspondence, one of those who are said to have been at the Boston Tea Party. The excesses of this Molineux (after his death in 1774, ironically called "General" by those who thought he was too much of the mob) were celebrated in pre-Revolutionary Boston. In the opinion of one of his colleagues on the Committe of Correspondence, his career was one of "vigilance and industry"; in that of one of his Tory enemies, he led a "vicious life." According to the account of a Revolutionary contemporary, he was a "martyr" whose "distresses to promote the general interest produced an Inflammation of the bowels of which he perished"; according to that of a Tory historian, he was a "Pest to Society" who, frustrated in his attempts to urge the mob on to further violence, "retired to his House and finished his Life by Suicide." Somewhat confused contemporary accounts have Molineux an "agent" of a Loyalist whose property he had confiscated, or have the same Loyalist executor of Molineux's estate, which was confiscated after his death. By Longfellow's and Hawthorne's time, there seems to have been a Molineux legend; for in an 1829 *Token* story, the popular writer W. L. Stone uses the phrase "like another Mollineaux or Tom Crib" to point up a garish description of the violent twitching of a corpse.[1] In any case, it was obvi-

[1] I have gathered information on Molineux in William V. Wells, *Life and Public Services of Samuel Adams* (Boston, 1865), *passim*; Samuel Adams Drake, *Old Landmarks and Personages of Boston* (Boston, 1873), p. 358; Justin Winsor, ed., *The Memorial History of Boston* (Boston, 1886), II, xlvi; Arthur M. Schlesinger, *The Colonial Merchants and the American Revolution, 1763-1776* (New York, 1918), pp. 288-289; Annie Haven Thwing, *The Crooked and Narrow Streets of the Town of Boston: 1630-1822* (Boston, 1920), p. 219; Philip Davidson, *Propaganda and the American Revolution, 1763-1783* (Chapel Hill, 1941), pp. 27-28; R. S. Longley, "Mob Activities in Revolutionary Massachusetts," *New England Quarterly*, VI (1933), 99-130. The favorable opinions of Molineux which I quote are from a letter, 16 October 1774, from the merchant John Pitts to Samuel Adams, in Wells, *Life and Public Services of Samuel Adams*, II, 240, and from the MS diary of Thomas Newall, 22 October 1774 (Sparks MS 47, Houghton Library); the unfavorable opinions are from a Tory oration of 15 March 1775, in Wells, II, 138, and from Peter Oliver's *Origin and Progress of the American Revolution* (MS, 1781), p. 168 (Frederick L. Gay Transcripts, Massachusetts Historical Society). The two statements quoted from MS were discovered and transcribed by Mr. Leslie Thomas and sent to me by him through the good offices of Mrs. Kathryn Preyer. I owe great thanks to both. In general, the nature and occasion of such remarks indicate that they represent widely held opinion; thus I venture to posit a "Molineux legend." (The stone reference, called to my attention by Mr. Nolan Smith, is in "The Drowned Alive," *The Token* [Boston, 1829], p. 189.) It seems to me, for my purposes,

ous to Longfellow (and Hawthorne, in a letter ac-knowledging the salutation in the *Wayside Inn*, did not contradict him) that the two Molineuxes were one.[2] And if we are to understand the tale, its theme, and its bearing on Hawthorne's whole work, it should be made obvious to us. For "My Kinsman, Major Molineux" manifests fully that sense of the past which for Haw-thorne was not only a means to art and understanding, but one of their ends.

At William Molineux's death, his friend and collab-orator in Revolutionary matters, John Eliot, wrote, "Some are glad & some are sorry. *Nil nisi bonum de mortuis*. It's possible he may have been actuated by noble principles."[3] This, one comes to discover, is of a kind with other Revolutionary rationalizations of the excesses of mobs and their leaders. Crucially, it is of a kind with the rationale for such excesses which Haw-thorne makes the subject of the opening paragraph of "My Kinsman, Major Molineux."

The events of the story are said to have taken place "not far from a hundred years ago," and so are placed around 1730; yet the setting and actions are plainly of the immediately pre-Revolutionary period. And Haw-thorne makes it clear, in this opening paragraph, that he is dealing with a state of affairs which obtained generally in Massachusetts until the colonies broke

---

unnecessary to discover a particular source for Hawthorne's interest in Molineux, although such a discovery would be comforting. At any rate, it is worth noting that Molineux is mentioned (just that) three times in Caleb Hopkins Snow's *History of Boston* [1825] (Boston, 1828), pp. 281, 289, and 291, which Hawthorne withdrew from the Salem Athenaeum on 18 December 1827 and 17 Novem-ber 1829 (Marion L. Kesselring, "Hawthorne's Reading, 1828-1850," *Bulletin of the New York Public Library*, LIII [1949], 55-71, 121-138, 173-194). It may well be that a particular source will be turned up, as Hawthorne's known reading is more carefully studied.

[2] The letter is printed in Samuel Longfellow, *Life of Henry Wads-worth Longfellow* (Boston, 1886), II, 399-400.

[3] Quoted in Davidson, *Propaganda and the American Revolution*, p. 28.

away from Great Britain. He speaks briefly of colonial discontent with the empire system and of the difficulties of the British political officers in the face of that discontent, and then: "The reader, in order to avoid a long and dry detail of colonial affairs, is requested to dispense with an account of the train of circumstances that had caused much temporary inflammation of the popular mind." Excesses "actuated by noble principles" and "temporary inflammation of the popular mind"—these phrases, and many such like them, link Hawthorne's Molineux with the real one and force us to understand the fate of the first as an outcome of the actions of the second. As source-hunters, we can say that Hawthorne transforms the Revolutionary Molineux into the Loyalist Molineux. But the two in artistic fact are one. In the story, young Robin Molineux (for he is a Molineux, his father's father and Major Molineux's father having been brothers) finds his kinsman and helps hurt him and drive him away. Yet if we can put ourselves in Longfellow's position and connect the real Molineux with Hawthorne's, we can know that through Robin the two are one and that what he inevitably helps destroy and drive away is himself, or part of himself.

In effect, the tale defines phrases like "actuated by noble principles" and "temporary inflammation of the popular mind" in such a way that we must use them not as means of categorizing and putting away from us incidents out of our past, but rather as a means of knowing, identifying with, and accepting those incidents and that past. In the abuse and torture of such a one as Hawthorne's Major Molineux, William Molineux becomes immortal, but not precisely in the manner which he or his contemporaries would have expected. For to say of the abuse and torturing of Loyalists that it was owing to a "temporary inflammation of the popular mind," is to generalize the occurrence in such a way as to make it one of a class of occurrences; to explain it in terms of principles, not to understand it in terms of intentions, motives, and effects; literally to abstract it from our immediate attention. The net result is by rhetoric virtually to reduce to nothing the sense of personal responsibility and guilt. Yet at the same time all the good that flowed from the occurrence, and from all occurrences like it, is still with us. We may then, according to the rhetoric of this first paragraph, have our Revolution and forget it. Yet there is more to "My Kinsman, Major Molineux" than the first paragraph. The tale proper exists so that we cannot forget our Revolution, even as it grants the fact that we have it. Something like Original Sin becomes the prime fact of our political and social history. Adam's Fall and the Idea of Progress become not two myths but one. For—so the argument of the tale runs— if to become more than we are, we must destroy something in ourselves, then we cannot forget what it is we destroy. The tale exists to tell us. The two Molineuxes are one.

So, in the tale proper, young Robin, full of "nature's gifts," comes at night to Boston, seeking his kinsman and his fortune. He is all self-assurance; for his kinsman is wealthy and important, and all men will know him. Asking for guidance in his quest, Robin gets none. The first person he asks, a man who claims he has "authority," threatens him with the stocks. The next, an innkeeper, studiously avoids his question and chases him out of his inn into the street. The next, a pretty girl, peeping through a slightly open door, says she knows his kinsman and that he is in her house; taking her for his kinsman's housekeeper, Robin is about to go in, when the watchman comes and bids him begone. The girl disappears, and Robin asks for the watchman's guidance but still receives none. Once the watchman is gone, the girl reappears and beckons to Robin—only now

141

he is a little wiser and sees that she and her scarlet petticoat are not for a young son of a country minister. Robin continues to wander through the moonlit streets, now entirely confused in his quest in this strange place, which he knows mainly as a series of doors closing on rooms in which he does not belong. The atmosphere becomes more and more like that of an insane performance of *A Midsummer Night's Dream.* He encounters a man of extraordinary ugliness, whom he had first glimpsed in the inn, asks him his question, and at last gets an answer: "Watch here an hour, and Major Molineux will pass by." As the man leaves him, Robin observes that his face is curiously colored, one side red and the other black, "as if two individual devils, a fiend of fire and a fiend of darkness, had united themselves to form this infernal visage." His first positive communication is with one who figures Satan. Yet all that the questing youth can say is "Strange things we travellers see!"

Now he sits in front of a church and watches and waits. He muses on his past and on his hopes, and cheerfully talks over his plans with another stranger who, happening by, says he will sit and watch with him. He is once more all self-assurance, remarking to his new friend that "I have the name of being a shrewd youth." Soon they hear a noise, as if of merry-makers; as it comes nearer and nearer, Robin sees that it is some sort of parading celebration.

> A mighty stream of people now emptied into the street, and came rolling slowly towards the church. A single horseman wheeled the corner in the midst of them, and close behind him came a band of fearful wind instruments, sending forth a fresher discord now that no intervening buildings kept it from the ear. Then a redder light disturbed the moonbeams, and a dense multitude of torches showed along the street, concealing, by their glare, whatever object they

illuminated. The single horseman, clad in a military dress, and bearing a drawn sword, rode onward as the leader, and, by his fierce and variegated countenance, appeared like war personified; the red of one cheek was an emblem of fire and sword; the blackness of the other betokened the mourning that attends them. In his train were wild figures in the Indian dress, and many fantastic shapes without a model, giving the whole march a visionary air, as if a dream had broken forth from some feverish brain, and were sweeping visibly through the midnight streets. A mass of people, inactive, except as applauding spectators, hemmed the procession in. . . .

Robin too is a spectator, but not yet an applauding spectator. He says only, "The double-faced fellow has his eye upon me." And with that, could we, like Longfellow, immediately identify the two Molineuxes, we should also immediately note that the Satanic leader of this mob, he of the parti-color face, figures another celebrated Revolutionary personage. For the celebrated Boston mob-leader Joyce Jr., is described in contemporary accounts almost exactly as Hawthorne has Robin discover his mob-leader, parti-color face and all.[4] And

---

[4] See Albert Matthews, "Joyce Junior," *Publications of the Colonial Society of Massachusetts*, VIII (1906), 90-104. Matthews' principle source is an anonymous article in the Boston *Daily Advertiser*, 9 November 1821, which Hawthorne, of course, could have known. Moreover, Hawthorne could have known the *Advertiser* article as reprinted (wrongly attributed to the Boston *Gazette*) in Hezekiah Niles' *Principles and Acts of the Revolution* (Baltimore, 1822). Niles' volume, a loving collection of Revolutionary Americana "Dedicated to the Young Men of the United States," also contains a document mentioning Molineux as one hated by Tories and involved in mob action, and also an account neutrally critical of mobs (pp. 374 and 432). Since the *Principles and Acts of the Revolution* consists largely of speeches and documents whose rhetoric is analogous to that of the first paragraph of "My Kinsman, Major Molineux," it seems worthwhile to suggest the possibility that Hawthorne might well have known the volume. The volume in any case will supply the interested reader with a proper setting for the first paragraph of the tale.

we should have no trouble with or without the initial identification of the two Molineuxes, in identifying this kind of mob with the Mohawks who dumped tea in Boston Harbor in December 1773. At this point the historical texture of the story is at its richest, even as at this point the "temporary inflammation of the public mind" is at its highest. Yet Robin still only watches and waits.

But not for long. For in the center of the parade, sitting in an uncovered cart in his "tar-and-feathery dignity," is his kinsman, Major Molineux.

He was an elderly man, of large and majestic person, and strong, square features, betokening a steady soul, but steady as it was, his enemies had found means to shake it. His face was pale as death, and far more ghastly; the broad forehead was contracted in his agony, so that his eyebrows formed one grizzled line; his eyes were red and wild, and the foam hung white upon his quivering lip. His whole frame was agitated by a quick and continual tremor, which his pride strove to quell, even in those circumstances of overwhelming humiliation. But perhaps the bitterest pang of all was when his eyes met those of Robin; for he evidently knew him on the instant, as the youth stood witnessing the foul disgrace of a head grown gray in honor. They stared at each other in silence, and Robin's knees shook, and his hair bristled, with a mixture of pity and terror.

This, then, is the Recognition Scene. But it is as yet not enough. Robin hears, in turn, the laughter of each of the people whom he asked that night to help him find his kinsman, Major Molineux—the watchman, the whore, the innkeeper, the man of authority, the last standing on the balcony of his house opposite the church on whose steps Robin has waited to see his kinsman. "Then Robin seemed to hear the voices of

. . . all who had made sport of him that night. The contagion was spreading among the multitude, when all at once, it seized upon Robin, and he sent forth a shout of laughter that echoed through the streets,—every man shook his sides, every man emptied his lungs, but Robin's shout was the loudest there." Having committed himself (and us) to Robin's point of view, Hawthorne cannot comment in his own person; only a figure as comic and cosmic as the Man in the Moon can: " 'Oho,' quoth he, 'the old earth is frolicsome tonight!' " As indeed it was, in its temporary inflammation, with all of its nobleness of principle.

But for Robin there is only passion spent and a desire to go back to the country. His friend of the night, however, urges him to stay on. For perhaps, being a shrewd youth, he may rise in the world even without the help of his kinsman, Major Molineux. But can he, we ask. For through the William Molineux whose name they share, Robin and his kinsman are one, as through the history we share, or Hawthorne would make us share, we are one with them too. We can never again, except by cutting the living past out of ourselves, dismiss the violence of change, even change for the better, as a "temporary inflammation of the mind." For the public mind is first the mind of a William Molineux, then through him of a Robin Molineux, and finally through Robin of all Americans coming after him.

Such, it seems to me, is the reading one must give the story if he begins where Longfellow began. The story is meant to work in such a way as to manifest dramatically the burden of historical responsibility placed upon Robin. If the drama is adequate, as I think it is, then, by virtue of its working, the burden is not only Robin's but the reader's. To conceive that the story does all this is to conceive much for it, but surely not too much. It is only to bring ourselves to admit, in the words of Robert Penn Warren's prefatory

145

note to *Brother to Dragons*, itself one of his variations on what I shall venture to call the Molineux theme: ". . . if poetry is the little myth we make, history is the big myth we live, and in our living, constantly remake." More specifically, it is to discover that meaning of history which Jonathan Edwards epitomized toward the end of the *Doctrine of Original Sin Defended*:

> And I am persuaded, no solid reason can be given, why God, who constitutes all other created union or oneness, according to his pleasure, and for what purposes, communications, and effects, he pleases, may not establish a constitution whereby the natural posterity of Adam, proceeding from him, much as the buds and branches from the stock or root of a tree, should be treated as *one* with him, for the derivation, either of righteousness, and communion in rewards, or of the loss of righteousness, and consequent corruption and guilt.

Mr. Warren is a poet and novelist committed to deriving this meaning of history from the intractably dislocated facts of twentieth-century existence; Edwards was a theologian and philosopher committed to deriving a firmly ordered eighteenth-century view of existence from this same meaning. Halfway between them came Hawthorne, for whom at moments of creative illumination the facts of existence and this meaning of history were one.

2.

The theme of "My Kinsman, Major Molineux," the imputation simultaneously of guilt and righteousness through history, was a primary interest, perhaps *the* primary interest, of the young Hawthorne who was attempting "to open an intercourse with the world"— as he put it twenty years later in the preface of the third edition of *Twice-Told Tales*. In a forward-looking

146

Jacksonian America, he would do no less than define the sense in which all the good that descended from violence in the past was inextricably tied to the evil which that violence produced, so that insofar as one profited righteously from the good, one was guilty of the evil. According to this doctrine, as we can abstract it now, only through the discovery of historical responsibility (i.e. responsibility *in* history) could a man gain whatever of human freedom he might aspire to.

In 1829, Hawthorne was corresponding with the publisher Samuel Goodrich about a series of stories which he hoped to publish together as *Provincial Tales*.[5] Of the five surviving tales which can be more-or-less positively identified as belonging to the group, three besides "My Kinsman, Major Molineux" are variations on the Molineux theme. The least compelling of these is "Roger Malvin's Burial," in which the protagonist is made accidentally to kill his own son at the very place where he had long ago left a wounded companion to die alone. With the killing of his son, the protagonist's "sin" is said to be expiated, and he is free to pray and enter fully into the company of men. "Roger Malvin's Burial" is blurred in focus, however. On the one hand there is the sense of his own past which deadens the protagonist's life until he expiates the sin which made it; on the other hand there is the act of expiation and the events leading immediately up to it. In effect, Hawthorne cannot make up his mind which he is primarily interested in. At any rate, the tale itself is not of sufficient compass to let his interest in both, had he been able to develop it equally, achieve adequate expression.

Another of the *Provincial Tales*, "The Gentle Boy," in its original version (published in *The Token* in

[5] I follow the bibliographical analysis of Nelson F. Adkins, "The Early Projected Works of Nathaniel Hawthorne," *Papers of the Bibliographical Society of America*, xxxix (1945), 119-155.

1832), is much more clearly in intention a full-blown variation on the Molineux theme. It is important to note that we are here reading the original version of "The Gentle Boy"; for in revising the story for publication in *Twice-Told Tales*, Hawthorne was concerned to make it into something substantially new and different.[6] In the later, more familiar version, the Boy stands as victim at once of the Puritan drive for monolithic order and the Quaker zeal for enthusiastic individualism. If Ilbrahim is destroyed, it is as much by his mother's crazed religiosity as by the Puritans' fear of such religiosity; and to balance, as it were, the destruction of Ilbrahim, there is the destruction of the Puritan Tobias who befriends him. In the earlier version of the tale, however, Hawthorne again and again emphasizes the primary guilt of the Puritans for whose descendants (of whom he was one) he was writing. He does this, characteristically, by rationalizing Puritan persecution of Quakers in such a way as to suggest that the reader too would have acted Puritanically in the same situation.

This is a characteristic rationalization, deleted in the later version, whose effect is directly to draw a reader into the story and the history which descends from the killing of two Quakers in 1659:

> That those who were active in, or consenting to, this measure, made themselves responsible for innocent blood, is not to be denied; yet the extenuating circumstances of their conduct are more numerous than can generally be pleaded by persecutors. The inhabitants of New England were a people, whose original bond of union was their peculiar religious principles. For the peaceful exercise of their own mode of worship, an object, the very reverse of universal liberty of con-

[6] See Seymour L. Gross, "Hawthorne's Revisions of 'The Gentle Boy,'" *American Literature*, XXVI (1954), 196-208.

science, they had hewn themselves a home in the wilderness: they had exposed themselves to the peril of death, and to a life which rendered their accomplishment of that peril almost a blessing. They had found no city of refuge prepared for them, but, with Heaven's assistance, they had created one; and it would be hard to say whether justice did not authorize their determination, to guard its gate against all who were destitute of the prescribed title of admittance. The principle of their foundation was such, that to destroy the unity of religion, might have been to subvert the government, and break up the colony, especially at a period when the state of affairs in England had stopped the tide of emigration, and drawn back many of the pilgrims to their native homes. The magistrates of Massachusetts Bay were, moreover, most imperfectly informed respecting the real tenets and character of the Quaker sect. They had heard of them, from various parts of the earth, as opposers of every known opinion, and enemies of all established governments; they had beheld extravagances which seemed to justify these accusations; and the idea suggested by their own wisdom may be gathered from the fact, that the persons of many individuals were searched, in the expectation of discovering witch-marks. But after all allowances, it is to be feared that the death of the Quakers was principally owing to the polemic fierceness, that distinct passion of human nature, which has so often produced frightful guilt in the most sincere and zealous advocates of virtue and religion.

The whole passage, and particularly the last sentence, should remind us of the opening paragraph of "My Kinsman, Major Molineux," and particularly of that part centering on "temporary inflammation of the popular mind." We realize too that the Puritans of this "Gentle Boy," were just like the real Molineux, "actu-

149

ated by noble principles." But then, granting that "The Gentle Boy" has worked on us, we discover that our principles would have been just as noble, and no more. The method of this "Gentle Boy" clearly is analogous to that of "My Kinsman, Major Molineux"—the use of a tale to define a historical rationale in such a way as to explore its immediately, particularly, and individualistically human implications and possibilities. In the third of the *Provincial Tales* which can be taken as variations on the Molineux theme, the method is potentially more complex and actually less realized. In "Alice Doane's Appeal" Hawthorne tells the story of telling a story in order to draw us directly into the struggle to relate ourselves to our history and to assume the moral responsibilities, the guilt and righteousness, stemming from it. Sad to say, he cannot make the story work; and we must read only an unsuccessful trial.[7]

"On a pleasant afternoon in June" the author is walking with two young ladies—not in one of the usual places for summer promenades, however, but on Gallows Hill. Why? Because he has "often courted the historic influence of the spot." "We," he continues, "are not a people of legend or tradition. . . . We are a people of the present, and have no heartfelt interest in the olden time." Yet, on this calm day when all of the town's prosperity and riches, "healthfully distributed," seem so apparent, he will bring to his young ladies a

<hr/>

[7] I accept Professor Adkins' hypothesis, in the essay cited above, which is that "Alice Doane's Appeal" is a revision of a tale originally centering directly on Alice's story—the original tale being intended for *Seven Tales of My Native Land*, most of which Hawthorne destroyed. Randall Stewart (*Nathaniel Hawthorne: A Biography* [New Haven, 1948], p. 30) states that "Alice Doane's Appeal" is the same tale which was intended for the *Seven Tales*; therefore he does not include it in the putative contents of the *Provincial Tales*. The final bibliographical truth of the matter, however, is not relevant to the argument of this essay. What matters is that the story exists in its present form and was so written in Hawthorne's early years.

sense of their own history. He begins to read from a manuscript which he happens to have brought along. The story is that of a man who murders his sister's suitor, only to discover that the suitor is his twin brother and that he has been the victim of the machinations of a wizard. But curiously enough, as Hawthorne tells the story—regularly breaking off to remark to the reader on the effect he is immediately striving to create—it becomes unimportant, an incidental means to a large end. For the last scene of the story-within-the-story has Alice Doane apparently (it is not entirely clear) in the graveyard, addressing the specter of her brother's victim. It is the fact of the graveyard that is important. For being there, Hawthorne can summon up as horrifically as possible the specters of all dead criminals—and then can go on to Gallows Hill and summon up the specters of all those innocents accused of the worst of crimes, witchcraft, and then of those who accused, judged, and sentenced them. These last, the righteous who are guilty, are the true criminals; and we are their heirs.

This is the end of the tale: "I [the author is speaking in his own person] plunged into my imagination for a blacker horror, and a deeper woe, and pictured the scaffold—" He must stop just so: "But here my companions seized an arm on each side; their nerves were trembling; and, sweeter victory still, I had reached the seldom trodden places of their hearts, and found the well-spring of their tears. And now the past had done all it could."

But the past has not done all it can, since Hawthorne is uncertain—now sentimental, now stern—in bringing it to the young ladies who, as the auditors on whom he will make the past work, image his readers. The simple fact is that he could not manage the means whereby the young ladies and his larger reading audience could be brought together. Solution of the kind of technical problem he set himself in "Alice Doane's Appeal" was much beyond his ability. Portraying the audience *in* the story, he was so mindful of his real audience (genteel, female readers of *The Token*) that he could not free himself of the confusedly sentimental and stern manner in which he had perforce to address it. From the vantage point of "My Kinsman, Major Molineux," however, we can cut through the diffusion and vagueness in "Alice Doane's Appeal" to its implicit quality. We can interpret it as an experiment in the direct communication of a sense of the past. Hawthorne, in this interpretation, would confront his readers with the past out of which have come their character and their fortune. We can suppose, at least, how the past, properly summoned up in the manner of "Alice Doane's Appeal," might well have done all it could. Doing all it could, it would not have been the past of a "temporary inflammation of the public mind."

3.

To show the past doing, for good and for bad, all it could do. This is a way of describing the intention of a writer whose fiction would manifest that meaning of history which, adumbrating Hawthorne, I venture to call the Molineux theme. Saying this, however, we describe only one aspect of Hawthorne's art—and one, as it is perhaps evident by now, with which we are not too familiar. Certainly it might be termed a minor aspect, quantitatively considered; but it is nonetheless one which must be looked for in the whole of Hawthorne's work if we are to see its very wholeness. True enough, after the years in which he was composing the *Provincial Tales*, Hawthorne moved away from the Molineux theme into something else— something which, since he developed it so powerfully, we must admit to be altogether consonant with his true genius. His genius, as he discovered it, led him natu-

152

rally to what I shall call, for purposes of my analysis, a countertheme—not the imputation of guilt and righteousness through history, but rather the discovery and acceptance of guilt (and righteousness too) in the present. This countertheme—strictly speaking, Hawthorne's major theme—is the complement to the Molineux theme. Together they make the whole that is Hawthorne. Understanding one is a necessary condition of understanding the other.

In characteristic stories of the major theme, individuals come to see into their innermost selves as they hurt and are hurt. They come, in effect, to know what they really are; emphasis is not on the origin of the self they discover, but on its nature and its immediate quality. What, the question almost always is, is the outcome of a discovery of a self whose innocence and guilt are inextricably one? Some, Young Goodman Brown and Wakefield, for example, are completely destroyed—the one with his enjoying power atrophied, the other with his ability to go home lost. Some few survive; Hester in *The Scarlet Letter* is the great example. Hester's acknowledged guilt is humblingly educative, and she becomes—except for a moment when her dark passion reminds us of her essential nature— virtually an angel on earth. It is important for us to note, however, that once Hawthorne moved, in *The Scarlet Letter*, into the larger compass of the romance, this countertheme seemed to call, if only implicitly, for development of the very theme which it countered. So Little Pearl is brought to civilization, at the end is no longer just the child of nature, and her future looms nebulously on Hester's horizon. Hester is Little Pearl's history. When we have realized this, we have finished *The Scarlet Letter*.

We know what sin has done to Young Goodman Brown, Wakefield, Hester, and the many others in Hawthorne's great gallery of men and women whose lives project his major theme. But we do not know what it will do to their descendants. In most of the tales, of course, this is not an issue, and Hawthorne does not let it become one. And we recall that he revised "The Gentle Boy" so that it could not be an issue, so that the center of the story shifted from the Molineux theme to its countertheme. In a story of the compass of *The Scarlet Letter*, which deals with the complexities of relationship among three people whose very being is in a marked sense derived from the history of the Puritan community in which they live—in such a story, the issue must inevitably come up. Hawthorne lets it come up, and no more. All we know of Little Pearl is that now, because of her history, she has a chance of becoming a human being. How, and what kind, we do not know. Will she have, we wonder, a Sense of the Past?

4.

But we do know in *The House of the Seven Gables*. And it is here, I suggest, that Hawthorne wrote his fullest and potentially most comprehensive variation on the Molineux theme. Further, I suggest that unless we read the *Seven Gables* with the achievement of "My Kinsman, Major Molineux," and its kind in mind, we are likely to misread it and to see it either as an updated extension of *The Scarlet Letter* or as a genteel preadumbration of *Democratic Vistas*. These are, in fact, the alternatives we have generally set for ourselves. *The House of the Seven Gables* is neither of these. It is Hawthorne's most ambitious attempt to develop his theme of the imputation of guilt and righteousness through history. As such, it certainly lacks the power of "My Kinsman, Major Molineux" and of the first version of "The Gentle Boy." For Hawthorne could not focus his disparate materials so finely in the romance as in the tales. But the romance has a scope

154

and a possibility of development that the tales necessarily lack. If we admire "My Kinsman, Major Molineux" because it is what it is, we may admire *The
House of the Seven Gables* because it could have been
so much more than it is.

Hawthorne puts his understanding of the novel quite
blatantly and awkwardly in his Preface: "the truth . . .
that the wrong-doing of one generation lives into the
successive ones, and, divesting itself of every temporary advantage, becomes a pure and uncontrollable
mischief." He realizes, to be sure, that his romance is
not going to teach its lesson directly; but he hopes that
it will nonetheless do so through "some more subtle
process than the ostensible one." In any case, such
"high truth" as the story has must be implicit in it as
much in the beginning as at the end. Surely we are as
uncomfortable as Hawthorne is with such talk; but we
are not authorized on that account to disregard it.
Moreover, it comes often enough in the romance itself.
And then, because it comes integrally, we can take it
as in the nature of the story. For example, after Hawthorne has traced the history of the Pyncheons and
Maules in the first chapter, he can justifiably conclude
of the Pyncheon's legal tenure in the Seven Gables
property that:

> . . . there could be no question; but old Matthew
> Maule, it is to be feared, trode downward from his
> own age to a far later one, planting a heavy footstep,
> all the way, on the conscience of a Pyncheon. If so,
> we are left to dispose of the awful query, whether
> each inheritor of the property—conscious of wrong,
> and failing to rectify it—did not commit anew the
> great guilt of his ancestor, and incur all its original
> responsibilities. And supposing such to be the case,
> would it not be a far truer mode of expression to say
> of the Pyncheon family, that they inherited a great
> misfortune, than the reverse?

In the romance Hawthorne sets himself to answer the awful query. The world of Hepzibah and Clifford Pyncheon is dead. Something out of their past has contaminated it; yet something in their immediate present has actually killed it:

> In this Republican country, amid the fluctuating waves of our social life, somebody [Hawthorne is writing of Hepzibah's opening her shop] is always at the drowning-point. The tragedy is enacted with as continual a repetition as that of a popular drama on a holiday; and, nevertheless, is felt as deeply, perhaps, as when an hereditary noble sinks below his order. More deeply; since, with us, rank is the grosser substance of wealth and a splendid establishment, and has no spiritual existence after the death of these, but dies hopelessly along with them.

To say this is to discover an element of tragedy inherent in social progress. Moreover, since the original corruption is the Pyncheons', social progress would seem to be understood as the agent whereby that which is corrupt and contaminated is done away with. The tragedy is that of the person of good (if weak) will in whom that corruption and contamination is presently manifest. It would thus be exclusively Hepzibah's and Clifford's tragedy.

But, to extrapolate from the words of Hawthorne's Preface, all men inherit the wrong-doing of the past, so that, somehow, all men must be involved in this tragedy—and must be shown equally to share in whatever triumph may follow. Such, at any rate, seems to me to have been Hawthorne's intention in composing *The House of the Seven Gables* as he did. For the novel, considered thematically and in relation to its announced and reiterated intention, does not center on Hester and Clifford Pyncheon, but on Phoebe (who is only partly a Pyncheon) and on Holgrave-Maule. They

must be made to bear the imputation of guilt and righteousness as much as Hester and Clifford; only they
must be made, unlike Hester and Clifford, to come
through to some sense of triumph. That they are not
made to do so—this is the great failure of *The House of
the Seven Gables*. That they are intended to is its great
possibility.

In the romance, the history of the Pyncheon family
ends and begins again.[8] It ends because Maule's curse
descends on the family for (presumably) the last time;
it begins because the sin of the family is exposed, expiated, and the non-Pyncheon world is accepted for
what it is. Thus the crucial figures in the novel are
Phoebe and Holgrave. She is a prelapsarian Eve, a
Pyncheon who has enough non-Pyncheon blood in her
at once to love and reject her past. He is a post-lap-
sarian Adam, a Maule who is so deeply caught by the
injustice done to his family that he would reject his
past, all the past, and love no one; he is—or should be—
to Judge Pyncheon as Robin Molineux is to his paternal
uncle. In their union, Holgrave and Phoebe are to save
each other. Explicitly, Hawthorne makes Holgrave out
to be a young intellectual, like so many other young
intellectuals in nineteenth-century America, at once
mobile, unstable, rationalistic, disinterested, liberal,
and eager for change. And Phoebe is the little girl fresh
from the country, a little girl whose very freshness,
however delightful, must, in this post-Adamic age of
felix culpa, mark a certain inadequacy of character.
Her experience with the Pyncheons, her view of what
Maule's curse has done to Hepzibah, Clifford, and
Judge Pyncheon—these are said to mature her and
make her such a one as Holgrave, waiting disinterest-
edly (he thinks) for the destruction of the Pyncheons,

---

8 In this paradigmatic outline, I echo, with permission of the
publishers, my introduction to the new Everyman Edition of *The
House of the Seven Gables* (London, 1954).

needs so desperately. In their union, which is that of two young Americans who have borne the weight of their past while at the same time being touched by and drawn to the variegated life of the present, should lie their hope of the future. In them—as they make and are made by the life that surrounds them—should lie Hawthorne's expression of his sense at once of the burden of history and the hope of community.

For it is awareness of community that should issue from a fully expressive variation on the Molineux theme. In the end, Robin Molineux knows, at some level between that of consciousness and unconsciousness, how he is related to his past. He has achieved that knowledge by identifying with the community through which his sense of the past comes to him. In this case, to be sure, the community is only pathologically so, a mob of individuals abandoning themselves to what we might call *communitas adust*. But it is a community nonetheless, one with which Robin identifies, and one along with which presumably he will grow. (He may yet "rise in the world," so his friend of the night tells him.) We must say "presumably" because "My Kinsman, Major Molineux" centers upon the Recognition Scene; the rest will follow; it is to follow not only in Robin's life but in the lives of Hawthorne's readers. In *The House of the Seven Gables*, on the other hand, it is not enough for us simply to presume. For the romance ostensibly portrays not only its chief actors but the society out of which they come. To relate actors to society, so to discover the burden of righteousness and guilt they share—this would be to achieve for them and for readers of their story a sense of community, and through that, a sense of the past. It would be to move from seventeenth-century Pyncheons and Maules and their "temporary inflammation," through Holgrave and Phoebe and their inherited guilt and righteousness, to the community in which the reader participates equally

158

with them. Adam's guilt, after all, was imputed to all men; and a romance like *The House of the Seven Gables* must somehow deal with "all" the men who make up its society. Phoebe and Holgrave (in Hawthorne's scheme they are one) must be involved with their world, must identify with it, in a way which carries the power and authenticity of the Recognition Scene in "My Kinsman, Major Molineux," but must be larger and more inclusive than that scene is. That they are not so involved and do not so identify is a commonplace of our criticism, although not put in exactly this manner. Hawthorne cannot properly "relate" Holgrave and Judge Pyncheon. The story is too much Hepzibah's and Clifford's, too much a series of "romantic" sketches. The "change" worked on Phoebe and Holgrave by events out of their history is too much implicit to convince us of its necessity and reality. The paradigm, only, of the romance is theirs. The life of the romance is Clifford's and Hepzibah's—even Uncle Venner's. Hawthorne (and we with him) loses sight of the community in which Phoebe and Holgrave must live as Clifford and Hepzibah cannot. And the Molineux theme is not quite realized. Still, it is there—ineradicable.

5.

For Hawthorne, then, romance, even a "contemporary" romance like *The House of the Seven Gables*, entailed the study of history. If, as it is regularly claimed of him, he is a symbolist, he is in fact the symbolist as historian. And as such, he derives his symbols not from myth or exotic learning or Swedenborgianism or post-Kantianism, but from the facts of history itself —the factuality of the American historical experience as he studied and understood it. There are symbolic "correspondences" in his fiction, but, unlike the symbols of his great contemporaries, they are mysterious only for those people in his stories whose culture is at once bound to and strengthened by a central commitment to the mysterious. Hawthorne wants always to "explain" such correspondences, not to celebrate them, much less to lose himself in them. (Surely, he is the most "rational" of the writers of his period. I suspect that a source of his difficulty for us lies precisely in his insistent rationalism and that his discussions of the qualities of the "romance" are meant to bid us not to confuse the "strange" with the "mysterious." In an altogether American way, he would make the strange familiar without domesticating it.) Explaining such correspondences, Hawthorne would reveal a most humane mystery—that of the working of art. For in those of his stories which are studies of history, he repeatedly tries to discover a larger correspondence—that between past and present. He would demonstrate that this correspondence is a matter of the quite factual continuity of past into present. At his best, he is able to take his readers into the past, so to let them discover for themselves that knowing the past as it was—indeed, accepting the past as it was—is a necessary condition of living in the present as it is.

Like Poe, Emerson, Melville, and Whitman, he was for the most part not fond of the America in which he lived—a world in which individualism lacked the institutional constraints whereby it could be contained, shaped, and made part of a true community. In this world, Poe tried to establish the role of literature as a kind of overriding institution which guaranteed the freedom and autonomy of the self; Emerson and Whitman tried to work toward a poetry in which the self, through a renewed sense of its tie to nature and God, would transcend itself and establish a new religion; Melville sought for mythic understanding and ended late in his life, if I read *Billy Budd* correctly, with a Christian orthodoxy which he found second-best but

160

nonetheless inevitable. All, as we know, in effect took from the New England Puritan tradition the emphasis on the symbolic mode of understanding whereby man may know his fate. None of them, of course, could accept Puritan dogma. But all of them, except Hawthorne, looked beyond history, toward something larger than the human situation as given in the past and in the present. Unlike Hawthorne, they looked beyond the temporal and mundane for an authoritative guarantee of the veracity of such symbols as in their art they might discover.

Hawthorne not only took from the Puritan tradition its symbolic mode of understanding but accepted, if not the dogma of Puritanism, at least the conception of human nature, marked by an exacerbated and refined self-consciousness, which that dogma had been taken to confirm and account for. The very power in his rendering of a characteristically American consciousness derives initially from his awareness of its being specifically a form of Puritan consciousness. In one segment of his fiction, he did nothing less than use Puritanism to understand Puritanism, and thus worked toward an understanding—symbolic by virtue of being historical—of the American's Puritan origins. (This is what I have called his major theme, that of *The Scarlet Letter*, for example.) In another segment, he studied later American life, including that of his own time, and showed how it was trying to escape the burden—and was thus missing the rewards—of its heritage. (This is what I have called the Molineux theme, minor quantitatively but nonetheless a necessary complement to the major theme.) For him, then, Puritanism was, in fact, American history. The factuality of past life had to be transformed into the symbolism of present art and thereby be made part of the factuality of his readers' lives as they might live them. The task he set himself in his art was to make Puritanism "correspond"

161

to American history: through Puritanism and its conception of the nature and destiny of man, to find the means of making the American understand his own nature and destiny in the modern world. Hawthorne set out to make of American history not just a record of events, of successes and failures, much less a working out of a mystique, but a vital, indeed necessary and intrinsic, element in the American's consciousness of himself as American. History, the American's own, was to become a means to knowing and living with the self, the American's own. We are given a variation on Ortega's celebrated dictum, "Man has not a nature but a history." Hawthorne's variation is: "Man has no nature, except in his history."

Hawthorne was, as historian-romancer, more of a radical than he could bring himself to acknowledge. I use the word "radical" advisedly. For in his work Hawthorne is not only calling for, but forcing his readers—specifically his American readers—toward, a new and radical vision of history. The radical quality derives more from the process whereby the vision is to be achieved than from what is envisioned. But the two— process and substance—are not unrelated. In his fiction —by virtue of his technique as symbolist—Hawthorne would inculcate in his readers not just a sense of what history had been but a sense of what it was to be in history: by virtue of historical understanding to discover oneself once and for all inescapably paying the price for the rewards one reaped from the past. To know the past was not, for him, to view it from the heights of the present. It was to descend into the depths of the past—so to discover quite directly that one could get back to the heights, live in the present, only if he could bring himself to suffer symbolically that painful ascent which constituted the process of history. And the future? Today's heights, it would turn out, were tomorrow's depths.

It is true that Hawthorne wrote in an age obsessively conscious of history, above all, of its own history. But his historical consciousness, the kind he wanted to inculcate, was radically different from that of his contemporaries.

Historical understanding, for Hawthorne's contemporaries, generally entailed what philosophers call a metaphysical philosophy of history: that is, the discovery and elucidation of the laws of historical development whereby one could see how movement from past to present had *necessarily* occurred as in fact it had. There are a number of names for this particular metaphysical philosophy of history: among others, the Idea of Progress and Manifest Destiny. When, for example, one looks into the plans for the antiquarian societies which burgeoned in the first half of the nineteenth century, one finds stated again and again that the reason men collect historical data is that, when laid end to end, they will comprise a developmental pattern which in itself will guarantee that data-collecting is a meaningful activity. And I am sure that if one looked into the relationship between the sort of data collected and the informing reason for the collecting—the rationale for antiquarian curiosity—one would find operating a kind of preselective factor. The antiquarian found what he was looking for because he had known from the beginning that what he would look for would be "significant." In effect, he was carrying on an operation in deduction in a manner of which he was so sure that he could call it, without the least uneasiness, inductive. Such scientific history, such Baconian history, as it were, was in effect the product of an amateur operation in metaphysics.[9]

The example is perhaps trivial. But when one looks

[9] In this and what follows, I make use of my *Savages of America* (Baltimore, 1953, rev. ed. 1965), particularly pp. 112-114 and 160-168. [See also David D. Van Tassel, *Recording America's Past* (Chicago, 1960).]

into the establishment of many of the local history
societies in the period, one finds that the quantity of
such trivial enterprises has great qualitative significance for the period's sense of history. And the example is of a piece with others, surely not trivial.
There is, for example, Jared Sparks, whose general
statements of his aims as historian read like so many
versions of a Fourth of July oration. And at a more
sophisticated level, there are Hildreth and Bancroft,
whose politics are not exactly alike but whose notions
of historical process are essentially the same. There is
not yet an adequate history of American history: one
which will inquire into the relationship among a given
historian's historical commitment, his method as a
"researcher," and his style as a writer. If the multi-
volumed Bancroft is concrete, particular, at times a
powerful narrator, it is because he categorizes so well.
He renders everything and everyone "typical." And he
can do so only because his quite sophisticated metaphysical philosophy of history—charged as it is with the
power of post-Kantian ontological concepts—lets him
know in the second place exactly what he wanted to
know in the first place.

In the context of this essay, it is well to recall the
state of the American historical novel in Hawthorne's
time. Here is William Gilmore Simms in his Preface
to the 1853 edition of *The Yemassee*:

> What is the modern Romance itself? The reply is im-
> mediate. The modern Romance is the substitute which
> the people of the present day offer for the ancient
> epic. . . .
>
> When I say that our Romance is the substitute of
> modern times for the epic or the drama, I do not mean
> to say that they are exactly the same things, and yet,
> examined thoroughly, and [sic] the differences be-
> tween them are slight. The Romance is of loftier

origin than the novel. It approximates the poem. . . .
It does not confine itself to what is known, or even
what is probable. It grasps at the possible. . . .

And later, speaking of *The Yemassee* itself, "It is needless to add that the historical events are strictly true.
. . ." As Simms's words show, the historical romance
shares this with historical writing proper: that, like
the "ancient epic," it is based on "true" events. I suggest
that, as with the "ancient epic," it shares something
further: a metaphysical theory of history (in the case
of *The Yemassee*, the idea of progress as embodied in
the inevitable and necessary victory of civilization over
barbarism—or "savagism"). This is the sort of metaphysical philosophy of history that guarantees the significance of the events which, together, constitute the
past. The appeal to the pattern of the epic and to the
mode of poetry, and also the emphasis on the "possible—these are justifications for the way Simms
makes his version of the idea of progress create rather
than derive from the "truth" of the historical events
which *The Yemassee* recounts. Thus Simms's style as
writer is of the same order as Bancroft's—"better," but
of the same order.[10]

It is also of the same order as Cooper's and Parkman's—the romancer as historian and the historian as

[10] [Hawthorne, I have learned since writing this, was willing to
set himself against Simms's much reiterated conception of historical
fiction. He wrote in the *Salem Advertiser*, 2 May 1846, of Simms's
"series of picturesque and highly ornamented lectures on 'American
History, as suited to the purposes of Art' ": ". . . they abound in
brilliant paragraphs, and appear to bring out, as by a skilfully
applied varnish, all the lights and shades that lie upon the surface
of our history; but yet, we cannot help feeling that the real treas-
ures of his subject have escaped the author's notice. The themes
suggested by him, viewed as he views them, would produce nothing
but historical novels, cast in the same worn out mould that has
been in use these thirty years, and which it is time to break and
fling away." I take this example from David Levin's "Hawthorne's
Romances: The Value of Puritan History," *In Defense of Historical
Literature* (New York, 1967), p. 98.]

romancer. There is in them, above all, that quality of "typicality." Their "vividness" is not the vividness of richly particular details, to be known as such, but rather the vividness of the portraitist who composes according to an ideal which has become a necessary idea. The gain is a powerful sense of the meaning of the totality of events with which they deal. The loss is of a sense of complexity and involvement. All in all, Cooper and Parkman operate from the heights. They celebrate the struggle whereby the heights were gained. Because they understand so much, they often cannot see enough. But were they to see enough, they could not understand so much. Behind them, as source and inspiration, lies the work of the great eighteenth-century historiographers, and, most important, the work of Scott. And Scott, too, as recent study of his work has shown, brings to his great historical novels a metaphysical philosophy of history: an idea of progress whereby the past can be conceived, even celebrated, precisely as it has had necessarily to give way to the present.

In the *North American Review* in 1853, Parkman summed up the meaning of Cooper's work and, I think, of much of his own:

> Civilization has a destroying as well as a creating power. It is exterminating the buffalo and the Indian over whose fate too many lamentations, real or affected, have been sounded for us to renew them here. It must . . . eventually sweep from before it a class of men, its own precursors and pioneers, so remarkable both in their virtues and faults, that few will see their extinction without regret. Of these men Leatherstocking is the representative; and though in him the traits of the individual are quite as prominent as those of the class, yet his character is not on this account less interesting, or less worthy of permanent remembrance.

166

His life conveys in some sort an epitome of American history, during one of its most busy and decisive periods.

One notes the emphasis on Leatherstocking as representative, as "typical"—of his life as an "epitome." It is the inevitability of Leatherstocking's history (civilization "must" destroy if it is to create) which gives Parkman the means of comprehending Cooper's work—as it gave Cooper the means of doing it.

A more recent writer, himself at once master of and mastered by a metaphysical philosophy of history, puts the matter thus:

> As an explorer of the forest and prairies of the "New World" [Leatherstocking] blazes new trails in them for people who later condemn him as a criminal because he has infringed their mercenary and, to his sense of freedom, unintelligible laws. All his life he has unconsciously served the great cause of geographical expansion of material culture in a country of uncivilized people and found himself incapable of living in the conditions of this culture for which he had struck the first paths.

The writer I am quoting is Maxim Gorky. And I think it not surprising that a Marxist should clearly comprehend a work like Cooper's. Indeed, the one major book we have on the historical novel is the great Marxist critic Georg Lukacs' *Der Historische Roman*. Lukacs, from whose study I have taken the quotation from Gorky, is so sure in his own metaphysical philosophy of history (for dialectical materialism is a kind of metaphysics) that he can, in a sort of elective affinity, comprehend and elucidate Cooper, and with him Scott, in a fashion altogether consonant with that of Cooper's Manifest-Destiny-conscious contemporaries.

I cite Gorky and Lukacs to put my topic into a more

167

contemporary perspective. For the metaphysical philosophy of history in Cooper, Parkman, and the others is to Hawthorne's *critical* philosophy of history (so philosophers today would call it) as dialectical materialism is to what is now called existential historicism. (The sentence I have cited from Ortega and what I have called Hawthorne's variation on it are expressions of a central tenet of existential historicism.) The mode of historical understanding characteristic of Hawthorne's work—as a kind of critical philosophy of history—is as radically opposed to that of Parkman's, Cooper's, and the others' as the thought of an Ortega is to that of a Lukacs or a Gorky. This set of oppositions suggests that Hawthorne is "ours" precisely as his sense of history is ours—or, in his art, may become ours. Reading him, we may become more secure in his knowledge that our history has not only produced but includes us. Man has no nature, except in his history. For Hawthorne—the symbolist as historian—to know this, as he meditated upon Robin Molineux, Holgrave, and their American kind, was to know the imputation of guilt and righteousness through history.

6.

I have said that the Molineux theme is not quite realized in *The House of the Seven Gables* and have meant in the preceding section to indicate the conditions of Hawthorne's American culture which made its realization so difficult, and so important. The more contemporary the substance of his fiction, the more his world would be with him—and the more difficult to conceive of a Holgrave as a contemporary Robin Molineux. *The House of the Seven Gables*, wherein the Molineux theme is intended to be realized in the deep and extended, the dense, qualities of modern life, is perhaps too ambitious a romance—a romance striving to be a novel.

In point of fact, the Molineux theme went virtually unrealized—or was virtually unrealizable—for the rest of Hawthorne's life. Exactly why, we cannot say. Still, it is useful to remind ourselves of such likely reasons as his recent biographers have established. For those reasons show him acceding to the demands of a world which, so his fictions demonstrate, he could not have conceived of having made. Personally, he came more and more in the 1850's and after to accept uncritically the rather wide-eyed liberalism and equalitarianism of the Young America movement which supported his good friend and benefactor Franklin Pierce. Early in his career he had been suspicious of the doctrine that material things were primary instruments of political and moral progress. He came, in the 1850's, to terms with a world which accepted this doctrine, was appointed American Consul in Liverpool, and hoped (legally, since Consuls were given a certain percentage of all fees they collected) to secure the financial future of his family. His European experiences tended to make him see the differences between Europe and America as almost black and white. His latent provinciality—a means to control and assurance when he was writing of his own province—came to dominate his mind and his sensibility. If the Future was America's, then the Past was worth summoning up only as a bad example.[11]

Such was the character and opinion of the man into whom Hawthorne developed in the 1850's. *The House of the Seven Gables* marks the turning point in that development. In that romance, as we have seen, the world of Holgrave—the world, that is, of Young America—is ostensibly not the whole world. Hawthorne makes Holgrave say, "Shall we never, never get rid of this Past? . . . It lies upon the Present like a giant's dead body!" To find in Holgrave's words the meaning of the *Seven*

---

[11] See Lawrence Sargent Hall, *Hawthorne, Critic of Society* (New Haven, 1944), whose full account I here try to sum up.

Gables would be to wrench the passage out of context—
a temptation which the construction of the romance
makes it hard to resist. But in *The Ancestral Footstep*,
one of the abortive series of romances which Hawthorne tried to finish in his last years, the hero is made
to say, "Let the past alone: do not seek to renew it;
press on to higher and better things,—at all events, to
other things; and be assured that the right way can
never be that which leads you back to the identical
shapes that you long ago left behind. Onward, onward,
onward!" And in these words, so far as we can reconstruct this unfinished romance, is positively epitomized
the meaning that Hawthorne would have us discover.
After the unsuccess (artistic, to be sure—not commer-
cial) of *The House of the Seven Gables*, during the
later years in which the best he could do was *The
Marble Faun*, the Molineux theme was not just increasingly unrealizable for him. It was dead, having left little
or no positive trace of its existence.

One encounters in the Notebooks and reports of
travel of the last years, occasional meditations which
echo the Molineux theme. But they are, after all, just
Notebook passages and travel notes, and represent primarily humanitarian observations, not the moral and
metaphysical projections which such observations must
lead to if they are to be raised to the status of significant art. Here, for example, is Hawthorne's report, in
Our Old Home, of his understanding of the affection
directed toward him by a diseased boy whom he saw
in an English almshouse in 1856:

> [He concluded] that he was responsible, in this de-
> gree, for all the sufferings and misdemeanours of the
> world in which he lived, and was not entitled to look
> upon a particle of its dark calamity as if it were none
> of his concern: the offspring of a brother's iniquity

170

being his own blood-relation, and the guilt, likewise, a
burden on him, unless he expiated it by better deeds.[12]

Writing this, Hawthorne discovered that he was his
brother's keeper, something which Robin Molineux discovered and which Holgrave was supposed to discover.
But writing it, he did not discover either the complexities, the origins, the condition, or the history of
brotherliness.

At this stage in his life, Hawthorne was incapable
of the discovery, much less the revelation which for
the artist would have to follow it, if it were made. He
labored hard on a series of romances, really all attempts to write the same romance, in which an American (named variously Middleton, Etherege, and Red-
clyffe) would learn of a mysterious connection with
his past, would go to England to solve the mystery, and
would find that what he had inherited was the product
of only persecution and evil. At this point, apparently
having recognized the difference between Democrat
and Aristocrat, he would be able to break with the past
and so to face the world a new man, an American free
from all entangling alliances. Since Hawthorne never
could finish his romance, since all that we have are
abortive pieces, ranging from notes and scenarios to
whole sections, we cannot know truly what the romance (or romances) would have come to. Moreover,
in two of the unfinished romances this archetypal plot
is dominated by another one which moves in a somewhat different direction: this latter plot centers on the
discovery of an elixir which will guarantee immortality—all Future, that is, and no Past. Nonetheless, we do
have the fragments—*The Ancestral Footstep, Doctor
Grimshawe's Secret, Septimius Felton,* and *The Dol-*

[12] *Complete Works*, Riverside ed., VII, 353.

liver Romance.[13] And taking them at the least as the
record of a broken man's tired confusion and at the
most as the record of an artist's inadequate aspiration,
we may trace out some such archetypal plot as I have
ventured to outline, and see that it marks the death,
even the non-existence, of the Molineux theme. The
line from Robin through Holgrave to Middleton-Ether-
ege-Redclyffe is straight, if not always on the surface;
and it ends in death and denial. Also, it ends in artistic
failure.

What disturbed Hawthorne, so the final fragments
testify, was that he could not sufficiently motivate the
American's search for his ancestor. He had, in his quest
for symbols and ideas, to make that search compelling.
And he would not be satisfied with the search as an
end in itself, as something at the end of which his
protagonists would fearfully discover just themselves
as their past was making them. So he had them discover not just themselves, but just the past. And this
past was cut off from them entirely; it was alien—for
the Young American, nothing. Robin, we may recall at
this point, knows what he is and what he has done.
Even Holgrave-Maule is claimed to know what he is
and what he has almost done. (And in this sense
Hawthorne's minor Molineux theme becomes one with
its major countertheme.) But Middleton-Etherege-Red-
clyffe see what they are not and what they have not
done, and are grateful for the discovery—grateful, from
our point of view, for irresponsibility. In the process,
all possibility of social and thematic continuity is lost;
and the romances of which they are to be the heroes
are impossible. We can suggest all sorts of reasons, and
valid ones, for Hawthorne's failure as a writer in his

[13] My reconstruction of an archetypal plot for the last romances
primarily depends, of course, on the masterful editing of the outlines, trials, and scenarios for them by Edward Davidson, in his
Hawthorne's Last Phase (New Haven, 1949).

later years. But the one which forces awareness of itself as we trace his efforts with the Molineux theme into those years, is that his understanding of history failed him, or he failed it.

7.

We may call the Molineux theme by that name, because in the range of Hawthorne's work, it is in "My Kinsman, Major Molineux" that guilt and righteousness are most tellingly imputed to us through our history. If we have always known that Hawthorne is our prime example of a writer with a sense of the past, still we have not seen just how far he tried to make that sense carry him. In the stories centering on the Molineux theme, the sense of the past is made to reach out toward one of its possible limits. Only in "My Kinsman, Major Molineux" itself do we have any full feeling that a limit is reached and a certainty thus achieved. Only in this tale is Hawthorne's genius adequate to the task he sets himself and to the insight which directs his approach to that task.

The insight is one of considerable complexity, involving as it does a use of history both as object and subject. We may say of Hawthorne's historical fictions that they are of three main classes. There are those ("The Grey Champion" and its kind, for example) in which history is an object; their end accordingly is a recapturing of the past. There are those (*The Scarlet Letter* is the great example) in which history is subject; their end accordingly is through the past to achieve a perspective upon the present, or upon human nature taken as universally the same and therefore universally present. And there are those, finally, in which history is both subject and object. These last deal with historical themes in such a manner as to give us perspective upon our own involvement with those themes. They treat history as a continuum joining author, actor, and reader. Therefore, as they focus upon the quality of life as it exists at any given point on the continuum, they focus on the mutual involvement of the three parties in that continuum. The problem of composition in a work of this sort is complex and involved; for it entails at once portraying an historical episode, making the protagonist in the work come to see his relationship to the episode, and also making the reader aware of his relationship to the episode. The reader, that is to say, must be brought into some sort of direct relationship with the protagonist, so that what he takes from the story is, above all, an awareness of his own responsible involvement in the protagonist's actions.

Hawthorne more than once took upon himself the burden of creating the sort of composition in which history would be both subject and object. Since his understanding of history was of the kind ridden with guilt and righteousness, he took upon himself the burden of history itself, and hoped to share it with his readers. Writing about history, writing history, was to be a way of involving himself, his protagonists, and his readers in the pattern of guilt and righteousness which made history meaningful. The hope was in the end imperfectly realized, surely. But so has it been for many Americans—obsessed to realize it—after him. It might be that his age in America was not ready for the romance that *The House of the Seven Gables* or the last abortive pieces could have been. Certainly his age did little to enable him to write such a romance. "My Kinsman, Major Molineux" exists, as it were, in spite of the age. If we find it hard to read, and if we find the Molineux theme hard to trace in Hawthorne's whole work, it is perhaps because the tale and its theme exist in spite of our age too.

1954/1964/1968

174

7

HAWTHORNE AND THE TWILIGHT OF ROMANCE

"The disturbed eyes rise,
furtive, foiled, dissatisfied
from meditation on the true
and insignificant."
    ROBERT LOWELL, "Hawthorne"

READING through Hawthorne, one must come ultimately, in *The Marble Faun*, to inadequacy and failure. This judgment has become virtually a commonplace in our criticism. And, as such judgments so often are, this one is general enough to be valid. Yet the particular judgment remains to be made: why, how, and wherein failure and inadequacy in *The Marble Faun*? For it is not enough simply to say that Hawthorne's being an innocent abroad rendered him unable to put his Italian materials into any meaningful order. These are essentially qualities of the book itself—effects, not causes. The critical commonplace is still to be explored and thus justified, as are its implications for the development of American fiction in the second half of the nineteenth century and after.

In point of fact, inadequacy and failure in *The Marble Faun* result not from ignorance on Hawthorne's part, but from his at once knowing too much and his assuming the wrong things. Most important, what comes to be inadequate and to fail in *The Marble Faun* is Hawthorne's theory of romance, and also the practice which derives from and supports that theory. For in *The Marble Faun* the form of the romance as Haw-

175

thorne conceived of it is no longer capable of giving shape and meaning to the materials which it is to comprehend. Yet, as one recalls, *The Scarlet Letter*, the great tales, and the other long fictions succeed precisely as they are such romances; for in them, form, materials, and meaning cohere, each implicating and demanding the other. Indeed, as Hawthorne's earlier fictions may serve to indicate the limits to which the romance could be taken and still not lose contact with actuality, so *The Marble Faun*, understood integrally and interpreted historically, may serve to indicate just where the romance lost such contact, where the form began to lose its cultural strength and significance, where the romantic twilight set in. Thus the failure and inadequacy of *The Marble Faun* may be seen to reflect something more general, the failure and inadequacy of the American romance itself. And closer study of our critical commonplace may furnish at least a working basis for study of the romantic twilight of the mid-nineteenth century.

To put bluntly what we may take as given—Hawthorne was up to *The Scarlet Letter* as he was not up to *The Marble Faun*. Granting this, if only we can know how, why, and wherein, we can begin to know something of the gulf between the triumph of *The Scarlet Letter* and the failure of *The Marble Faun*, between the triumph of *The Scarlet Letter* and the triumph of, say, *The Ambassadors*.

1.

Notes on *The Marble Faun* must properly begin with and perhaps can be only a variation of this theme from Henry James' *Hawthorne*:

> Like all of Hawthorne's things it [*The Marble Faun*] contains a great many light threads of symbolism, which shimmer in the texture of the tale, but which are apt to break and remain in our fingers if we at-

tempt to handle them. These things are part of Haw-thorne's very manner—almost, as one might say, of his vocabulary; they belong much more to the surface of his work than to its stronger interest. The fault of *Transformation* [the English title of *The Marble Faun*] is that the element of the unreal is pushed too far, and that the book is neither positively of one category nor of another.

The symbolic threads are on the surface; the element of the unreal is pushed too far; this book is neither one thing (a romance) nor another (a piece of psycho-logical realism). So James.

The problem which remains is one of definition and judgment. Hawthorne conceived of *The Marble Faun* as he had of *The Scarlet Letter* and *The House of Seven Gables*. The relevant passages in the Preface to the *Seven Gables*, in which he had indicated the sort of fiction he was trying to work out, are worth quoting rather fully, for they define the American romance and its attributes:

> When a writer calls his work a Romance, it need hardly be observed that he wishes to claim a certain latitude, both as to its fashion and material, which he would not have felt himself entitled to assume, had he professed to be writing a Novel. The latter form of composition is presumed to aim at a very minute fidelity, not merely to the possible, but to the probable and ordinary course of man's experience. The former—while, as a work of art, it must rigidly subject itself to laws, and while it sins unpardonably so far as it may swerve aside from the truth of the human heart—has fairly a right to present that truth under circum-stances, to a great extent, of the writer's own choos-ing or creation. If he thinks fit, also, he may so man-age his atmospherical medium as to bring out or mel-low the lights and deepen and enrich the shadows of

the picture. He will be wise, no doubt, to make a very moderate use of the privileges here stated, and, especially, to mingle the Marvellous rather as a slight, delicate, and evanescent flavor, than as any portion of the actual substance of the dish offered to the Public. He can hardly be said, however, to commit a literary crime, even if he disregard this caution.

. . .

When romances do really teach anything, or produce any effective operation, it is usually through a far more subtile process than the ostensible one. The Author has considered it hardly worth his while, therefore, relentlessly to impale the story with its moral, as with an iron rod—or rather, as by sticking a pin through a butterfly—thus at once depriving it of life, and causing it to stiffen in an ungainly and unnatural attitude. A high truth, indeed, fairly, finely, and skillfully wrought out, brightening at every step, and crowning the final development of a work of fiction, may add an artistic glory, but is never any truer, and seldom any more evident, at the last page than at the first.

Here, in sum, is Hawthorne's theory of the romance. A romance is a moral work; it must be humanly true; it deals with experience in large. The "latitude" which the writer claims will enable him to move freely in his choice and use of materials, so long as they have bearing on his work. This definition, since it is certainly *ad hoc*, furnishes a rationale for Hawthorne's New England fictions and for the tales.[1]

For in these pieces Hawthorne moves impressively,

[1] This distinction between novel and romance was by no means original with Hawthorne. As Bertha Faust has shown (*Hawthorne's Contemporaneous Reputation* [Philadelphia, 1939], p. 69), the received distinction furnished the starting point for reviewers of Hawthorne's fictions. In other words, he was writing within a genre, with all the normative implications of the term and the act.

dealing with his materials freely—selecting, trimming, inventing, patterning—but never swerving aside from the truth of the human heart as he knows and has received it. Always there is an integral relationship among the larger elements of experience which he chooses to render symbolically or allegorically and the persons who have those experiences, the society in which those persons live, and the systematic morality of that society. In *The Scarlet Letter* Hester's sin is a particular sin for her community and a type of sin for the world; she bears her *A* as her society requires her to; and we may respond to the vision of Hester and her burden both for their particular (Hester's adultery—sin: seventeenth-century New England) and typical (sin—the fact of evil: the world of Hawthorne's readers) signification. Particular and typical are one in fact. Because the pattern is so clearly established, because the myth, the ideology, is there in historical fact, because Hawthorne knows it so thoroughly, he can seize upon its essentials and use them as he will—so long as he does not violate their order. For they express, in terms of the history, the *Erlebnis*, of a whole society, the truth of the human heart.

The problem here, however, is not to redefine the form and function of Hawthorne's greatest fictions but rather to see how he conceived of that form and function, thus how he conceived of the American romance. What is to be noted is that Hawthorne could write a romance and not be in any way vapid, loose, unrealistic, escapist, or pseudo-heroic. He conceived of his fiction simply as being concerned with reality taken in large; and such largeness did not entail vagueness or confusion. For working from received, traditionalized, historically valid patterns of thought and morality, he could look into the distant past and see it all the more clearly because he knew how and wherein that past bore on this present. The emotionality of his romance was an emotionality which developed out of knowledge, not lack of it, not as a substitute for it. Hence, assuming as they do a culturally verifiable and knowable pattern of reality, Hawthorne's great romances are the fictions of the New England man thinking, symbolizing, and allegorizing. They are romances not because of what they say but because of the way in which they say it. Here, for Hawthorne, in practice and in theory, romance is ultimately means, not matter.

2.

Precisely where Hawthorne succeeds in *The Scarlet Letter* and the rest, he fails in *The Marble Faun*. Once more, he writes what he calls a romance, and his *ad hoc* Preface serves as a guide to immediate theory and practice. Of his aim he says:

> The author proposed to himself merely to write a fanciful story, evolving a thoughtful moral, and did not purpose attempting a portraiture of Italian manners and character. He has lived too long abroad not to be aware that a foreigner seldom acquires that knowledge of a country at once flexible and profound, which may justify him in endeavoring to idealize its traits.

This last admission is frank enough. And, as if to assure himself, he goes on in the next paragraph:

> Italy, as the site of his Romance, was chiefly valuable to him as affording a sort of poetic or fairy precinct, where actualities would not be so terribly insisted upon as they are, and must needs be, in America. No author, without a trial, can conceive of the difficulty of writing a romance about a country where there is no shadow, no antiquity, no mystery, no picturesque and gloomy wrong, nor anything but a commonplace prosperity, in broad and simple daylight, as is happily the case with my dear native land.

It will be very long, I trust, before romance-writers may find congenial and easily handled themes, either in the annals of our stalwart republic, or in any characteristic and probable events in our individual lives. Romance and poetry, ivy, lichens, and wall-flowers, need ruin to make them grow.

Expressed in such genteelly theoretical language, the shift in emphasis between the *Seven Gables* Preface and this is somewhat subtle. But it is there, nevertheless; and it will be even more apparent in *The Marble Faun* itself. There is here still the assumption of "latitude," of stern moral purpose, and of concern for the truths of the human heart; but all are now taken to be properly observable only in a land of unlikeliness. The land, not the attitude or point of view of the writer, makes for romance—at least, at the outset. Recalling James' remarks on the bareness of Hawthorne's American culture, one realizes that, on the contrary, it was Hawthorne's knowing the special cultural richness of his New England that made for the latitude, the formal largeness in treatment, the romance, in *The Scarlet Letter*. And further, one realizes that James' remarks are applicable in a curiously inverted way: that if Hawthorne could see and feel only a vague mysteriousness in Italy, it was because in Italy he was entirely out of contact with such richly formalized and institutionalized elements in the culture of which he wrote. Being thus out of contact, being unable to find any formal basis for his romance, yet being able to think only in terms of such a romance—Hawthorne let content, matter, take the place of form, means.

The emphasis in *The Marble Faun* is upon a mysterious, half-known, deliciously felt content. Plunging his reader into a mass of guidebook detail, Hawthorne would make him live a life of safe and sane sensations. Taken together, the sensations would be focused on

181

events. Taken together, the events would have meaning. The meaning is that of a romancer who has fooled himself into believing that his romance is about people whom he knows, when it is about a land which he does not know. For if *The Scarlet Letter* is built out of a kind of historical, regionalist cultural certainty, then *The Marble Faun* is built out of a pseudo-historical, provincial cultural uncertainty—which returns us, perhaps, to our critical commonplace. So returning, we may note that this is not a sufficiently precise description of the situation: the point is not that it was impossible for Hawthorne to write adequately in some form about Italy (his *Notebook* remarks often show him to have been an eager, enthusiastic observer), but rather that it was impossible for him to write an adequate *romance* about Italy. And we must remember, finally, that the year was 1860, and *The Marble Faun* perhaps had to be written—if only to show that once it leaves home, romance, Hawthorne's kind of romance at any rate, travels in a twilight in which it can only feel its way along.

The theme—can one say the meaning?—of *The Marble Faun* is one which is central in all of Hawthorne's fiction: that coming into the world is coming into evil; that knowledge of the world is knowledge of evil; that knowledge is life; and that life is good, that ripeness is all. The form of the novel is tragic; at the end Miriam and Donatello must go forth like Milton's Adam and Eve, having asserted their free will, having lived fully, having sinned, ready for their punishment. This is the triumph in the tragedy. Hawthorne pictures them in their final joy at the carnival:

> To-day, Donatello was the sylvan Faun; to-day, Miriam was his fit companion, a Nymph of grove or fountain; tomorrow,—a remorseful man and woman, linked by a marriage-bond of crime,—they would set forth towards an inevitable goal.

182

Thus Hawthorne's Puritan vision. But this world of romance is not Hawthorne's; or at least he cannot make it his. The vision fades.

As the vision fades, so one's awareness of the theme fades. And Hawthorne, bringing himself up short again and again, must suddenly return to the theme and so make it comfortably explicit. The theme is not, as in *The Scarlet Letter*, to be seen growing inevitably out of materials of which it is to be part; rather it is moralized into the work, most often through Kenyon, whose person and observations taken together certainly show him to be one of the most perceptive muttonheads in our fiction. Repeatedly he points the moral, in his observations on art and/or life, in his comments on Donatello's and Miriam's situation, and even in his own unfinished bust of Donatello, of which Hawthorne says:

> Most spectators mistake it for an unsuccessful attempt towards copying the features of the Faun of Praxiteles. One observer in a thousand is conscious of something more, and lingers long over this mysterious face, departing from it reluctantly, and with many a glance thrown backward. What perplexes him is the riddle that he sees propounded there; the riddle of the soul's growth, taking its first impulse amid remorse and pain, and struggling through the incrustations of the senses. It was the contemplation of this imperfect portrait of Donatello that originally interested us in his history, and impelled us to elicit from Kenyon what he knew of his friend's adventures.

So it is throughout *The Marble Faun*.

In the last *omnium gatherum* chapter, Kenyon must explain everything ("with an inexpressible smile") to Hilda the pure and innocent:

> "It seems the moral of his story, that human beings of Donatello's character, compounded espe-

cially for happiness, have no longer any business on earth, or elsewhere. Life has grown so sadly serious, that such men must change their nature, or else perish, like the antediluvian creatures, that required, as the condition of their existence, a more summer-like atmosphere than ours."

"I will not accept your moral!" replied the hopeful and happy-natured Hilda.

"Then here is another; take your choice!" said the sculptor. . . "He perpetrated a great crime; and his remorse, gnawing into his soul, has awakened it; developing a thousand high capabilities, moral and intellectual, which we never should have dreamed of asking for, within the scanty compass of the Donatello whom we knew."

"I know not whether this is so," said Hilda. "But what then?"

"Here comes my perplexity," continued Kenyon. "Sin has educated Donatello, and elevated him. Is sin, then,—which we deem such a dreadful blackness in the universe,—is it, like sorrow, merely an element of human education, through which we struggle to a higher and purer state than we could otherwise have attained? Did Adam fall, that he might ultimately rise to a far loftier paradise than his?"

When Hilda cries out in terror at such blasphemy, Kenyon declares that he has never really believed this, that his mind has been wandering "wild and wide." Nevertheless, the fact remains and has been made crudely explicit throughout the whole of the story. It is, indeed, only through such explicit statements as these that the direction in which Hawthorne is moving becomes at all clear. The story proper will not offer up the meaning which he demands from it, which, in fact, he imputes to it. Thinking of *The Scarlet Letter* with its marvelous handling (Hawthorne's "latitude") of materials, we expect to come to realize the theme as those materials are arranged, evaluated, explored for us. We expect *The Marble Faun* to "mean" something because the incidents, the people, and the situations—each, as I have said, demanding and implicating the other—"mean" something in reality, something which we can know if only we can get close enough to the intensity and concreteness and immediacy of that reality. Whatever that something was, Hawthorne could not get at it directly. But he knew it was there; he felt it; he could show how this setting, this situation, and these people corresponded to something he knew already. And so he brought meaning, ready-made, to his fiction. Meaning, like method, is anterior to materials here. And meaning is also posterior—indeed, it is everywhere but *in* the materials. Thus the painful pointing of the moral does not adorn the tale.

The tale moves melodramatically from peak to peak; and each peak is made darkly mysterious. The four friends—world-wise Kenyon and innocent Hilda, Americans abroad, Miriam, the international figure, and Donatello, the simple Italian from a simple countryside—are thrown together in ruinous, decaying Rome. Kenyon's love for Hilda is undeclared but assuredly there and assuredly to be rewarded. Donatello's love for Miriam seems not to be rewarded; for she, carrying the weight of her mysterious past, is merely amused by him, as she is drawn to the pure Hilda, who is for her all the things she might have been. In the fourth chapter ("The Spectre of the Catacombs") Miriam's past, in the person of the hooded, monk-like figure, catches up with her; and she cannot rid herself of him or what he stands for. It is hinted that the crime of these two has been incest. But exactly what that crime, that past, is, what it means, what Miriam and he have done, we are never really to know. Even at the end we have been given only a few surface details of Miriam's story. And significantly Hawthorne gives us his most horrified hints in a chapter midway in the story, a chapter which he calls "Fragmentary Sentences"—as though even he cannot so conceive of the incest motif as to give Miriam's past the symbolic weight which it must carry. There is nothing to correspond in symbolic value and power to Hester's adultery, with the meaning that adultery had for her, her society, and for Hawthorne's (and our) morality. Hence there is no nexus, no wholeness here. There is only the wholeness of such emotion as mystery and melodrama might suggest.

If the fourth chapter is one melodramatic peak, then the eighteenth ("On the Edge of a Precipice") is another. Here Miriam and Donatello kill the man who has been haunting her; here Donatello loses his innocence and enters with Miriam into a "marriage-bond of crime"; here Hilda sees the crime and is held fast, forced into spiritual isolation, by what she has seen until she is able to tell it (she thinks of this as "confession") to a priest. From this eighteenth chapter the novel develops. Donatello, having lost his innocence, retreats to his Monte Beni to try to recover it; he fails, yet grows as he suffers. Miriam disappears. Hilda keeps her dreadful secret and finds that it isolates her too from man and art. And Kenyon observes. Finally he brings Miriam and Donatello together in final marriage-bonds. For they have come to see that they can achieve peace only by facing the fact of their sin; and they are ready to expiate their crime. In the gaiety of the carnival (the last melodramatic peak) they reappear in Rome, even as Hilda has been allowed to reveal what she has known of the crime.

Such events, and the figures involved in them, allow Hawthorne his proper latitude. And *The Marble Faun* is nominally constructed like the other romances—out

186

of large events and large characters moving symbolically in those events.

Yet once more Hawthorne fails. Donatello in his growth to wisdom and death is the central symbol in the story. We are told of his resemblance to a faun; the opening action concerns his friends playing with the idea that his ears must be like those of a faun. We see him as an unworldly, simple, earth-like creature, fascinated by the worldly and complex Miriam. But neither his conduct nor his growth can be kept fully in the focus of his value and function as a symbol. (We may think, once more, of *The Scarlet Letter* and of the coordination, even identification, of action, character, and symbolic value; and we remember that in the context of her society, Hester's actions, character, and behavior had a specific, socially knowable meaning—and that out of that meaning develops for us her significance and the significance of the story.) At times his faunness and innocence and growth are one. But we feel that Hawthorne, forcing the identification, does not discover it for us. His rendering of "inner psychology," as James called it, is of no avail, because there is little or no "outer psychology"—little or no structure of immediately grasped socio-cultural forms—in which to ground it.

Thus when Miriam, Hilda, and Kenyon are introduced playing with the notion of Donatello's resemblance to Praxiteles' faun, Hawthorne describes the statue in great detail, adumbrating upon the character of the faun, thus imputing that character to Donatello. Somehow, one feels that it should be the other way around; Donatello's character should gradually be imputed to the idea of a faun—if there can be discovered in an actual Donatello such a character. Hawthorne seems to feel this too; for he ends the passage, speaking in his own person:

And, after all, the idea may have been no dream, but rather a poet's reminiscence of a period when man's affinity with nature was more strict, and his fellowship with every living thing more intimate and dear.

Thus too, Hawthorne later invents the fanciful story of the Monte Beni pedigree (that Donatello's long line had originated with the union of a human and a nymph) in order fancifully to explain his Donatello. It would seem that here he was unable to see very deeply into the fact that, as he observed (once more, in his own person), "mankind are getting so far beyond the childhood of their race that they scorn to be happy any longer." Specifically, he could not discover the possibility of genuinely symbolic force in the figure of Donatello.

Hilda's innocence seems also to be intended as a symbolic force. Her "white shining purity" is noted as "a thing apart." Yet she is merely hypostatized into this. Her purity we are to know by her excellence as a copyist, her living apart in her tower, her keeping a candle burning for the Virgin, her resisting (half-heartedly?) the temptations of Catholicism, and so on. But we know really little of the how and why of these things. They are not overtly related to any known past or to each other; she calls herself a Puritan; and we look in vain for serious adumbration of a Puritan-Catholic conflict. Once we are told of Donatello's faunness, at least we can see how his actions embody that quality. But once we are told of Hilda's purity, what does it come to?

We look too in this romance for a rigorous handling of the action and of the leading symbols; we look for a web of life in the multitudinous complexities of action and situation. But such meaningfulness exists only in the largest, almost scattered, details of the story—in

Donatello's resemblance to the faun, in his life at rustically innocent Monte Beni, in Hilda's lonely tower, in her resisting (if she does) the smothering richness of the cathedral, in seemingly accidental resemblances between paintings and protagonists (Miriam and Beatrice Cenci, Miriam's tormenter and the dragon in a painting by Guido). Such meaningfulness, thus, is seldom felt wholly, for it is not worked out systematically. As often as not it is made a matter of accident. Hawthorne cannot capitalize on the "latitude" of his form. One suspects it is because Hawthorne is lost. And one remembers the ending, which had to be added to editions after the first, in which Kenyon, questioned as to whether or not Donatello's ears *really* resembled those of the faun of Praxiteles, says ("smiling mysteriously"), "I know, but may not tell. On that point, at all events, there shall not be one word of explanation." One doesn't want a word of explanation; one wants to know without benefit of explanation. In such a romance one wants it to be so only if it has to be so.

If action, characterization, and symbolization fail, Hawthorne assumes that their place is taken by setting. Rome is the past bearing down corruptly on the present. Miriam's and Donatello's corruption is felt to be Rome's; but the corruption, in the story, is originally Rome's, not theirs. One is meant to feel Rome, and through Rome, Miriam and Donatello. Whereas in *The Scarlet Letter* one had come to feel New England (and the world at large) through Hester, Dimmesdale, and Chillingworth.

Here we are forced to return to Hawthorne's own conception of the special sort of romance he was writing in *The Marble Faun*: "Romance and poetry, ivy, lichens, and wall-flowers, need ruin to make them grow." And Rome was ruin. Of "that state of feeling which is experienced oftenest at Rome" he writes in the first chapter:

Viewed through this medium, our narrative–into which are woven some airy and unsubstantial threads, intermixed with others, twisted out of the commonest stuff of human existence–may seem not widely different from the texture of all our lives.

This last hope is at once wistful and pathetic. Reduced to it lowest common denominator, it is the hope of the ante-bellum American abroad, discovering that foreigners are, after all, just folks. But more than this, it is the hope of a romancer whose romance is to be rootless and thus decayed–to be felt, not known.

The Marble Faun is like Miriam's studio, which Hawthorne describes so lovingly in his fifth chapter:

. . . one of those delightful spots that hardly seem to belong to the actual world, but rather to be the outward type of a poet's haunted imagination, where there are glimpses, sketches, and half-developed hints of being and objects grander and more beautiful than we can anywhere find in reality.

One wonders if Hawthorne was aware of the implications of such a statement. For, as he had seen and demonstrated clearly elsewhere, the romancer must return to a reality he knows, whence cometh his strength. He had done just this in the great New England novels and in the great tales; in these pieces the principle of moral reality had been so firmly grasped, so familiar, so intensely *there*, as to allow him his special "latitude." Here, in *The Marble Faun*, the reality is unfamiliar; yet it is for him emotionally so charged and his desire to know it so strong, that he tricks himself into believing that he can treat it just as though it were familiar. In doing so, in thus preserving that "latitude," he misconceives, or reconceives, of his romance. Perhaps we may say that he was trying to break free from his "regional" limitations. If this is

so, then he did not realize that he would have to prepare himself to make a genuine break and not try to
work himself and his artistic practice into still another
romance. In any case, he ends in Italy in *The Marble
Faun* with "half-developed hints"—apparently the more
desirable because half-developed. This is romantic twilight.

3.

Nevertheless it is impossible simply to say that if
Hawthorne had stayed in New England, all would have
been well for his art. For one can see that such a work
as *The Marble Faun* was always imminent in Hawthorne's fiction, as it must be in the work of any
romancer such as he. Once received, integrated, local-
ized, firmly grasped values and value patterns are lost,
feeling takes the place of comprehending, grandiosity
the place of grandeur, pathos the place of understanding, a *Marble Faun* the place of a *Scarlet Letter.*

For Hawthorne this was always the danger—a danger
which we can see from the beginning of his career
until the end—this in the form of his sketches. In the
sketches the habit (the method) of thinking and understanding in symbolic patterns became the habit (the
method) of feeling in what the New Englander could
easily persuade himself were symbolic patterns. Hawthorne's sketches are to the tales as *The Marble Faun*
is to *The Scarlet Letter.* Reading them, one can see
how *The Marble Faun* was forever in the making in
Hawthorne's mind. Effortlessly, as it were, he moved
into the romantic twilight.

The form of the prose sketch—the genre, as F. O.
Matthiessen has noted in *American Renaissance* that
so charmed Hawthorne's age—is relatively simple. The
sketch consists essentially of a descriptive and/or historical essay grounded on what may be called scenic
pathos. That is, the writer describes in detail some-

thing he has or might have seen or reconstructs a segment of the past in a narrative of slight dimensions,
and draws from his description or reconstruction a
mood, or even a vaguely philosophical conclusion. The
important thing is the end-product, which is always of
an indefinite texture—general wistfulness, polite awe,
a shudder at the mysteriousness of life, resignation to
mutability, and the like. The writer takes no definite
stand; he realizes the past not in terms which still
specifically focus his own and his reader's life-view,
but in terms which can give rise often only to what
Irving Babbitt called "the unrelated thrill." Thus Hawthorne in "Sights from a Steeple" (collected in *Twice-
Told Tales*), perhaps his best-known sketch, pictures
himself as looking over the city, cuts down his field of
vision in a kind of geometrical pattern, and puzzles
over the activity of those townspeople whom he observes. A storm is about to break, and he must descend.
Yet

> A little speck of azure has widened in the western
> heavens; the sunbeams find a passage, and go rejoic-
> ing through the tempest; and on yonder cloud, born,
> like hallowed hopes, of the glory of another world
> and the trouble and tears of this, brightens forth the
> Rainbow.

Here there is only mood and quasi-philosophy.

The general attitude from which the sketch develops
is as significant as the genre itself. Thus the sketch
grows out of the intellectual milieu of the conventional
mid-nineteenth-century literary New Englander. For
him the sketch represents a weakened symbolic pattern in which emotionality has been substituted for
specific meaning. The Puritan faculty for seeing physical objects primarily as figurations of spiritual states has
survived. But emphasis has been shifted from that
spirituality and one's deep humility and self-abasement

in the face of it, to the satisfying yet "safe" emotional experience which is part of seeing figured in one's surroundings the values by which he has been brought to believe he should live. Hawthorne's sketches all fit into this pattern, with its quasi-philosophic mood and scenic pathos; and he produced them steadily and it would seem easily throughout his career. The majority of the entries in the *Notebooks*, as Randall Stewart has pointed out, are sketches in embryo. And as late as 1852, in the Preface to *The Snow Image*, Hawthorne insisted that the early sketches which he was including in the volume disturbed him because they came so nearly up to his best. (As we learn more of his professional career, we discover that *ex post facto* he was too often fond of pieces written for the gift-book trade, pieces which in fact he had originally driven himself to write. They perhaps came more naturally to mind than he liked to admit.) His hope might be, as Austin Warren concludes,[2] that "by the reduction of material objects to the status of tokens shadowing forth to the senses the spiritual states of men, he might effect a moralization of the natural world whereby the Beautiful became the vehicle for the True and the Good." Yet his large-scale and steady production of sketches makes it apparent that he always found it was very easy for him to feel instead of to think, to see vaguely instead of clearly, to suggest rather than to say, to emotionalize rather than to moralize the natural world.

All this can be demonstrated briefly. The sketches, for the most part, are like "Sights from a Steeple." In "Footprints on the Sea-Shore" (collected in *Twice-Told Tales*), the thoughtful man seeks solitude, having bid his troubles farewell. He explores the beach, learns much of life in general, and ends by observing sadly that the verses which he traces in the wet sand

2 *Nathaniel Hawthorne* (New York, 1934), p. lxiv.

are erased by the waves—as all things human are erased by some great power. Then he returns to the busy world, as all men must. In "The Procession of Life" (collected in *Mosses from an Old Manse*), there is a detailed account of attempts to organize a great procession according to social position, disease, intellectual powers, degree of sorrow, crimes, love, and social maladjustment. The materials of the sketch are interesting as adumbrations of ideas which elsewhere concern Hawthorne deeply, but the whole treatment is semi-melodramatic and conventional. The Chief Marshal of the procession, Hawthorne writes, can only be Death; "but God, who made us, knows, and will not leave us on our toilsome and doubtful march, either to wander in infinite uncertainty, or perish by the way." And finally, there are in "Main Street" (collected in *The Snow Image*) Hawthorne's portraits of types of New Englanders, preceded by what is for all intents and purposes an analysis of method and procedure in the historical sketches:

> In my daily walks along the principal street of my native town, it has often occurred to me, that, if its growth from infancy upward, and the vicissitudes of characteristic scenes that have passed along this thoroughfare during the more than two centuries of its existence, could be presented to the eye in a shifting panorama; it would be an exceedingly effective method of illustrating the march of time. Acting on this idea, I have contrived a certain pictorial exhibition, somewhat in the nature of a puppet-show, by means of which I propose to call up the multiform and many-colored Past before the spectator. . . .

It is true that Hawthorne can achieve at times, in "Buds and Bird Voices" (collected in *Mosses*), for example, something that approximates intensity. But, reading the sketches in their entirety, one comes to feel

194

that this quality is almost fortuitous. What remains is an unhappy sense that the sketches are conceived in a desire, perhaps so unconscious as to represent merely a habit, to evoke general mood, scenic pathos, and quasi-philosophy. For Hawthorne this would seem always to have been the easy way.

4.

It is significant, moreover, that the sketch as such enters progressively more and more into Hawthorne's larger fictions after *The Scarlet Letter*. In *The Scarlet Letter* itself only the curious "Custom House" Preface can be taken simply as a sketch. But not too simply, since Hawthorne, in setting his historical perspective, is virtually parodying that too popular, too easy form— as though to take advantage of his readers' expectations and, as it were, deliberately to turn the genre to the advantage of his romance. In *The House of Seven Gables*, at any rate, the sketch has become a part (but not too great a part) of the stuff of the novel itself, especially in the important chapters which contain the account of Hepzibah's little shop. Such bits are scattered throughout *The Blithedale Romance*—in the seventeenth chapter, for example, in which Coverdale looks from his window at "all the nooks and crannies, where Nature, like a stray partridge, hides her head mong the long-established haunts of men. . . ." But it is in *The Marble Faun* that the sketch becomes the structural core of the novel itself and dominates its form.

Rome is ruin—"a vague sense of ponderous remembrances." Thus Chapters v, vi, viii, x, xii, xiii, xv, xxxii, and xlviii are primarily sketches and derive their meaning as they serve to develop scenic pathos. In Chapter xxxii (called "Scenes by the Way"), for example, Hawthorne writes a series of somewhat pleasing descriptions of the Italian countryside, its people, and their religion and churches; he is concerned mainly with comparing the happy indolence of the Italians with the happier activity of his own New Englanders. He concludes the sketch, however, with a picture of poor Donatello going from shrine to shrine kneeling, hoping to be helped "towards a higher penitence." There is indicated or derivable no adequate relationship between the lengthy description and its tone and the slight narrative portion of the chapter. Hawthorne leaves his readers to shift for themselves. Essentially, he confuses his own feelings (however tenuous)—what he feels must be the self-evident integration of background, action, and moral signification —with the response he desires from his readers. In short, he thinks and writes in terms of the sketch.

In the sketch, then, one sees another aspect of the failure of Hawthorne's mind and art to comprehend matters removed from the New England milieu in which he could work so well. Yet although it is important to note that Hawthorne used the sketch as such in his novels, it is more important to see how the sketch is the product of the same sort of intellectual set that produced *The Marble Faun*. Specifically, Hawthorne tries to deal with an area of experience in terms and in ways which are alien to that area, since the terms and the ways derive from another area and are integral with it. That is to say, the sort of Puritan values that he could discover in the New England past (as past, or as past bearing down on present) or in exotically conceived lands and situations—such values he could not discover in the day-to-day nineteenth-century reality of New England or Italy. Hence, the sketches are to the tales as *The Marble Faun* is to the Preface of *The House of Seven Gables*, as the genteel tradition is to high Puritanism, as twilight is to burning daylight. The prime fact is inadequacy.

It is, of course, the inadequacy of the romance. We

may say that, as a whole, this American romance succeeds insofar as it satisfies Hawthorne's prescription for it in *The House of Seven Gables*. For the truth of this romance is meant to be general and operative; and the characters, situations, and settings in and through which we come to know that truth must be seen in large. Thus the romance is extravagant; thus, as Hawthorne wrote, there is available to the writer a certain "latitude" in fashion and material. But always, truth, characters, situations, settings, extravagancies, and materials must be grounded in local fact—in fact, that is, which however distant, however much in the past, however exotically received, must be felt and known immediately. (In Hawthorne the immediacy is characteristically historical, a past sensed powerfully enough to be known in the present.) Only thus can the romancer derive his symbols.

For Hawthorne, in *The Scarlet Letter* and the best long fictions and tales, general operative truth was to be located immediately in the symbol, in a character's symbolic situation, growing out of a kind of milieu in which that symbol would have real existence—in fact, historical existence. When he sought such general operative truth outside that kind of milieu—as in *The Marble Faun*—he could not find a proper basis for it. But the habit, the seeking, was there, deep in him, in his New England mind. And he let the habit trick him into believing that a symbolic romance was possible in an alien milieu, in the world outside, in a realm whose history he could feel but not understand.

Certainly Hawthorne was trying to widen the scope of his fiction. But he demanded of his materials in *The Marble Faun*, as in the sketches, a kind of meaning which for him was not there. From where we read him it would seem that an "outside" world could best be portrayed in what he called a novel—with its minute fidelity to the probable and ordinary course of man's

197

experience, with no demand for settled symbolic sig-
nifications if they are not there to be had in their lived-
through present or past. Hawthorne's enormous fond-
ness for the realism of Trollope's novels—with, as he
said, all "inhabitants going about their daily business
and not suspecting that they were being made a show
of"—indicates that he had at least an inkling of what
it would be to deal novelistically with the present. And
his unfinished pieces—*Septimius Felton, The Dolliver
Romance*, and *The Ancestral Footstep*—show him working hard at finding large historical symbols in the flux
of the probable and ordinary course of man's experience, trying to superimpose the form of a historical
romance on the materials of a historical novel. The
point is that he was no Trollope and that the last historical pieces are unfinished.

5.

Taken both for itself and for the cultural situation
which it bodies forth, *The Marble Faun* is of major significance for the course of our letters. For it was not
only for Hawthorne that the romance was to fail. I
suggest that, working out from *The Marble Faun*, beginning with Hawthorne's theory and practice, one can
look at other failures of other romances and come to a
larger understanding of the romantic twilight. For example, as Willard Thorp has abundantly shown, Melville too had theorized (in *The Confidence-Man*) that
"reality" in fiction had best dealt with in large: "It is
with fiction as with religion, it should present another
world, and yet one to which we feel the tie." In *Moby-
Dick* there is that other world, a world to which we feel
the tie because action, characterization, and symbolization are somehow one, a world in which meanings are
organically to be discovered, not contrived. Yet Melville
moved later to *Pierre*, in which he also attempted to
widen the scope of his art. And *Pierre* is contrived, as

The Marble Faun is contrived; Melville forces arbitrary symbolic values onto situations, settings, and characters; he extemporizes, philosophizes, religionizes, satirizes, writes melodrama, pastoral, and naturalistic fiction all at once; and he tries to superimpose the pattern of the romance on a world which he cannot know well enough to comprehend totally. In *Pierre* Melville does not go abroad; yet he is utterly lost, as utterly lost as Hawthorne in *The Marble Faun*. For Melville takes to *Pierre* assumptions about artistic form which play him false.

In 1860, when the publication of *The Marble Faun* was just one event among many, the twilight of romance was fast setting in. Later James could understand the nature of this romantic twilight and put his understanding in stories written with tragic awareness of ante-bellum adequacy and inadequacy—an adequacy and inadequacy, we must remember, explored essentially in terms of the probable and ordinary course of man's experience. The principle of reality, of morals, and of values, was not one to be understood in large, in the context of an integrated, regionalized American culture. There was, in fact, to be no fixed principle— just experience, flux, change, and ever-widening horizons, the world of the novel. To paraphrase Lambert Strether—one cultivated the illusion of principles, and lived. The American abroad was to be figured as a Strether—or even a Christopher Newman or an Isabel Archer—an innocent looking for the world of the romance and finding that of the novel.

1948/1968

8

WHITMAN:
The Poet in 1860

"Was der Mensch sei, sagt
ihm nur seine Geschichte."
WILHELM DILTHEY, *"Der Traum"*

1.

As EARLY as February 1857, Walt Whitman was planning a new edition of *Leaves of Grass*. He wanted to give the collection a scope, a range, a quality of completeness which it so far had lacked. By June or July 1857 he had some seventy new poems ready. We presume he could not make arrangements to publish them. Then, from March 1857 to June 1859, he was caught up in the day-to-day busyness of editing the Brooklyn *Daily Times*, meanwhile relaxing as best he could in the pleasures of being a celebrated, or notorious, young Bohemian. He wrote few poems during this period. Once freed from his editorial duties, he began again to write poems. And sometime between April and December 1859, he had a series of poems set up and printed—with the intention of making revision on the proof sheets, much as writers in our time use faircopy typescript. Once more he was ready to publish a new, enlarged *Leaves of Grass*. He intended merely to fill out and give substance to the 1856 *Leaves of Grass*, not to reorder and reconstruct the volume—so, as it turned out, to initiate the series of transformations which mark its subsequent history.

That he did actually transform the volume is owing

200

to an unexpected opportunity offered him in a letter, February 10, 1860, he received from a new publishing firm in Boston:

DR SIR. We want to be the publishers of Walt. Whitman's Poems—Leaves of Grass.—When the book was first issued we were clerks in the establishment we now own. We read the book with profit and pleasure. It is a true poem and writ by a *true* man.

When a man dares to speak his thought in this day of refinement—so called—it is difficult to find his mates to act amen to it. Now *we* want to be known as the publishers of Walt. Whitman's books, and put our name as such under his, on title-pages.—If you will allow it we can and will put your books into good form, and style attractive to the eye; we can and will sell a large number of copies; we have great facilities by and through numberless Agents in selling. We can dispose of more books than most publishing houses (we do not "puff" here but speak *truth*).

We are young men. We "celebrate" ourselves by acts. Try us. You can do us good. We can do you good—pecuniarily.

Now Sir, if you wish to make acquaintance with us, and accept us as your publishers, we will offer to either buy the stereo type plates of Leaves of Grass, or pay you for the use of them, in addition to regular copy right.

Are you writing other poems? Are they ready for the press? Will you let us read them? Will you write us? Please give us your residence

Yours Fraternally
THAYER & ELDRIDGE.[1]

---

[1] My account of the publication of the 1860 *Leaves of Grass* derives primarily from Fredson Bowers' Introduction to his *Whitman's Manuscripts: Leaves of Grass (1860)* (Chicago, 1955); secondarily from Gay Wilson Allen, *The Solitary Singer: A Critical Biography of Walt Whitman* (New York, 1955). The text of the Thayer and

A month later Whitman was in Boston with his manuscript. (He visited Emerson, who, so he recalled in his old age, tried to dissuade him from putting the "Enfans d'Adam"—later "Children of Adam"—sequence into the new *Leaves of Grass*.) By late April the volume was announced as about to be published; and it was issued in mid-May—the work of Whitman in what I should call his "humanist" phase, a true poem writ by a man who knew that he had, at whatever cost, to be true to his sense of himself as man.

2.

This is a Whitman whom we know but little. By now we know well the Whitman of the 1855 *Leaves of Grass*, who is too much shaken by his triumphant discovery of his sense of himself to need to know what he has discovered. And of course we know even better the Whitman of the 1892 *Leaves of Grass* (the last edition), who has moved beyond discovery and knowledge to

---

Eldridge letter is taken from Professor Bowers' Introduction, p. xxxii.

The Thayer and Eldridge edition, dated 1860-1861, was issued in various bindings: at least twelve are known. In later issues the portrait of Whitman was sharpened by being set against a tinted background. As in the 1855 and 1856 editions, Whitman's name appears on the copyright page but not the title page. Perhaps two or three thousand copies were issued before Thayer and Eldridge's bankruptcy in 1861; but this, according to Whitman's bibliographers, is a sheer guess. In any case, there are in existence many more copies of the 1860 edition than those issued by Thayer and Eldridge. For, apparently in 1876, a New York printer named Richard Worthington somehow secured the 1860 plates and began printing copies from them. In 1880 he offered Whitman $250 to authorize such an edition, was refused, but continued to print copies from the plates, striving to make the books he published increasingly like the authentic edition in paper and binding. Eventually he was forced to pay Whitman $50 for use of the plates. Worthington's pirated editions may be distinguished from the authentic 1860 edition by the absence on the verso of the title page of the words "Electrotyped at the Boston Stereotype Foundry" and "Printed by George C. Rand & Avery."

that stage of prophetic insight and expression wherein the hard truths of merely human existence are so often catalogued and filed away in cosmic consciousness. These introductory notes are intended to suggest how we may come to know the Whitman of the 1860 *Leaves of Grass*. He too can be read "with profit and pleasure," perhaps with higher profit and greater pleasure than our abiding images of Whitman have so far allowed. For this is a Whitman who confronts us on a ground neither of his nor our choosing, the ground of our lives lived through day to day. He is a Whitman who, however briefly, rests satisfied—because there is no alternative to being satisfied—with the fact that the poet, like the rest of us, is always in the middle of his journey.

He looks forward, of course. But at this stage of his career he is overwhelmingly, poignantly, even tragically, aware of the difference between past, present, and future. He freely predicts what is to come, while yet declining to guarantee its coming. Thus in the fourteenth of the "Chants Democratic" (a version of the poem we best know as "Poets to Come"):

Poets to come!
Not to-day is to justify me, and Democracy, and what
    we are for,
But you, a new brood, native, athletic, continental,
    greater than before known,
You must justify me.

Indeed, if it were not for you, what would I be?
What is the little I have done, except to arouse you?

Whitman is, he concludes, "the bard" of a "future" for which he writes only "one or two indicative words."

The vision is utopian, of course, and became increasingly so in the 1870's and 1880's, when he was not only calling for but guaranteeing a state of things whereby poems would work so as eventually to make for the withering away of poetry. In a preface of 1872 he could claim:

> The people, especially the young men and women of America, must begin to learn that Religion, (like Poetry,) is something far, far different from what they supposed. It is, indeed, too important to the power and perpetuity of the New World to be consigned any longer to the churches, old or new, Catholic or Protestant—Saint this, or Saint that. . . . It must be consigned henceforth to Democracy *en masse*, and to Literature. It must enter into the Poems of the Nation. It must make the Nation.

And by 1888 (in "A Backward Glance O'er Travel'd Roads") he could claim that, contrary to European critical opinion, verse was not a dying technique:

> Only a firmer, vastly broader, new area begins to exist—nay, is already form'd—to which the poetic genius must emigrate. Whatever may have been the case in years gone by, the true use for the imaginative faculty of modern times is to give ultimate vivification to facts, to science, and to common lives, endowing them with glows and glories and final illustriousness which belong to every real thing, and to real things only. Without that ultimate vivification—which the poet or other artists alone can give—reality would seem to be incomplete, and science, democracy, and life itself, finally in vain.

These two statements (and they are quite typical) sum up Whitman's growing sense of the power of poetry, and thus of the poet: religion, operating as poetry—and only as poetry—can make the nation, vivify it, or, in the language of a late poem like "Passage to India," "eclaircise" it.

"In the prophetic literature of these states," he had

written in 1871 (in "Democratic Vistas"), ". . . Nature, true Nature, and the true idea of Nature, long absent, must, above all, become fully restored, enlarged, and must furnish the pervading atmosphere to poems." And later in the same essay: "The poems of life are great, but there must be the poems of the purports of life, not only in itself, but beyond itself." Life beyond life, poetry beyond poetry: This idea came to count for more and more in Whitman's conception of his vocation and, accordingly, of that of the poets who were to come. The last edition of *Leaves of Grass* is surely the testament of the sort of "divine literatus" whom he had earlier prophesied. Indeed, he had not only prophesied himself but made the prophecy come true. But, as he acknowledged, this was not the only form of his testament. For, when he wrote of the last edition, "I am determined to have the world know what *I* was pleased to do," he yet recognized: "In the long run the world will do as it pleases with the book." The question remains: how may we use the book so as to know what we please to do with it? And more: what does the book, in is structure and function, in its growth, teach us about the vocation of poet in the modern world? And more: how may it help the poets who are yet to come discover, and so define, their vocation?

The hard fact—my sense of which, I must admit, derives from my admiration for the 1860 *Leaves of Grass*—is that Whitman fails as prophetic poet precisely because he is such a powerfully humane poet. The adjective makes us flinch, perhaps, but only because, like Whitman, we have found the beliefs it implies so difficult to hold to that we have come, if not to seek for the prophetic utterances which will offer us something in their stead, then to discount them as disruptive of the high sense of our private selves on which we ground our hopes for the lives we must live.

Still, it might be that a close reading of Whitman, the poet of 1860—for it is he whose advocate I am being —will teach us what it might be like once more to hold to them.

Be that as it may, the record of Whitman's life would suggest that his own power, his own humanity, was in the long run too much for him. When, hoping to look beyond the end of his journey, he tried to write prophetic poetry, he came eventually to sacrifice man —that finite creature, locked in time and history, at once agonized and exalted by his humanity—for what he has encouraged some of his advocates again to call cosmic man, the cosmic man of, say, these final lines from "Passage to India":

> Passage, immediate passage! the blood burns in my
> veins!
> Away O soul! hoist instantly the anchor!
> Cut the hawsers—haul out—shake every sail!
> Have we not stood here like trees in the ground long
> enough?
> Have we not grovel'd here long enough, eating and
> drinking like mere brutes?
> Have we not darken'd and dazed ourselves with books
> long enough?
>
> Sail forth—steer for the deep waters only,
> Reckless O soul, exploring, I with thee, and thou with
> me,
> For we are bound where mariner has not yet dared to
> go,
> And we will risk the ship, ourselves and all.
>
> O my brave soul!
> O farther farther sail!
> O daring joy, but safe! are they not all the seas of God?
> O farther, farther, farther sail!

It is the idea of that "daring joy, but safe"—everywhere in the poem—which prevents one from assenting to this passage and all that comes before it. The passage of the soul, whether it is everyman's or a saint's, is not "safe," however "joyful." Whitman cannot focus the poem on the sort of human experience to which one might assent because one could acknowledge its essential humanity. The figures in the passage proliferate farther and farther out from whatever center in which they have originated, until one wonders if there ever was a center. Probably not, because the experience of the protagonist in this poem is that of cosmic man, who, because he is everywhere, is nowhere; who, because he can be everything, is nothing. This Whitman, I believe, mistakes vivification for creation, the ecstasy of cadence for the ecstasy of belief, efficient cause for final cause, poet for prophet. Which is not, I emphasize, the same as conceiving of the poet as prophet.

Whitman's genius was such as to render him incapable of the kind of discipline of the imagination which would make for the genuine sort of prophetic poetry we find in, say, Blake and Yeats: of whom we can say that they were poets as prophets, for whom we can observe that poetry is the vehicle for prophecy, not its tenor. Whitman is at best, at his best, visionary and sees beyond his world to what it might be. Blake and Yeats are at best, at their best, prophetic and see through their world to what it really is. Visionary poetry projects a world which the poet would teach us to learn to acknowledge as our own; it comes to have the uncanniness of the terribly familiar. Prophetic poetry projects a world which the poet would teach us is alien to our own yet central to our seeing it as it really is, a world built upon truths we have hoped in vain to forget. As the characteristic manner of visionary poems makes us feel, we say of the visionary world that we could have made it, at least in dream-work.

We say of the prophetic world that we could not possibly have made it; for, as the characteristic manner of prophetic poems drives us to assent, it was there already. The ground of visionary poetry is indeed dream-work and magical thought; the ground of prophetic poetry, revelation and mythical thought. Thus the special language of prophetic poetry—one of its most marked formal characteristics—must, by the definition of its purpose, be foreign to us (for it reveals a world, and the strange things in it, hidden from us); yet, by the paradox of prophecy, it is a language native to us (for the things it reveals, being universal, out of the realm of day-to-day time, space, and conception, put all of us, all of our "actual" world, under their aegis). That language we can "understand" because its grammar and syntax are analogous to our own; understanding it, we assent to—and perhaps believe in—the metaphysical system which its structure and vocabulary entail; trying to account for its origin, we must grant the justness of the poet's reporting to us that he has been, in some quite literal sense, "inspired." Rob the visionary of his poetry, and only he remains. Rob the prophet of his poetry, and the stuff of his prophecy remains, perhaps as the stuff of philosophy.

When the mood came over him, as it did increasingly, Whitman did claim to have been "inspired" in this literal sense. But even so, his later work fails as prophetic poetry (for that is what it is meant to be) precisely because, like the earlier work, it projects not a world to which the poet stands as witness, but one to which he stands as maker. Without him, without his voice and his vision, it could not exist. But he asks of the world projected in the later work that, in accordance with the requirements of prophetic poetry, it have the effect of revelation given by a source beyond himself, that its language be at once of and not of our workaday world, that it imply what in "Democratic

Vistas" he called a "New World metaphysics." Yet the editions of *Leaves of Grass* from 1867 on fail of the centrality and integrity of properly prophetic poetry—fail, I think, because the poet mistakenly assumes that poetry, when it is made to deal with the universe at large, becomes prophecy. For all his revisions and manipulations of his text, for all his enlargement of his themes, the later Whitman is but a visionary poet. And, since he asks more of it than it can properly yield, the vision, and consequently the poetry, even the conception of the poet, get increasingly tenuous. A certain strength is there, of course, but it is the strength of an earlier Whitman, who perhaps prophesied, but could not bring about, his own metamorphosis from poet to prophet. His genius was too great to let him forget that, after all, it was poets who were to come.

True enough, he wrote toward the end of "A Backward Glance O'er Travel'd Roads":

> But it is not on "Leaves of Grass" distinctively as *literature*, or a specimen thereof, that I feel to dwell, or advance claims. No one will get at my verses who insist upon viewing them as a literary performance, or attempt at such performance, or as aiming mainly toward art or aestheticism.

One says: how right, how sad, how wasteful! For, ironically enough, Whitman's words characterize the failure of the 1892 *Leaves of Grass*. And one turns to the earlier Whitman, I daresay the authentic Whitman, whose verses did aim mainly toward art and aestheticism, toward a definition of the vocation of the poet in that part of the modern world which was the United States.

3.

The 1855, 1856, and 1860 editions of *Leaves of Grass* make a complete sequence—in which the poet invents modern poetry, explores its possibility as an instrument for studying his role in the world at large, and comes finally to define, expound, and exemplify his vocation. The sequence, in brief, is from language to argument; and it is controlled at all points by a powerful sense of the ego which is struggling to make the move—thereby to realize the limits of its own humanity, which are the limits of argument. If, as we well know, the vocation of poet envisaged in the 1855 and 1856 editions is to be explicated by Emerson's "The Poet" (1844), that envisaged in the 1860 *Leaves of Grass* is to be explicated by Emerson's account of Goethe in *Representative Men* (1850): not Shakespeare, not Plato, not Swedenborg—so Emerson was sure—would do for the modern world, which yet "wants its poet-priest, a reconciler." Goethe was one such: "the writer or secretary, who is to report the doings of the miraculous spirit of life that everywhere throbs and works. His office is a reception of the facts into the mind, and then a selection of the eminent and characteristic experiences." Note: just a "writer"— what John Holloway in an important book of a few years ago called the Victorian Sage, a philosopher of a kind, but one who constructs his argument according to a grammar of assent. Emerson had concluded:

> The world is young: the former great men call to us affectionately. We too must write Bibles, to unite again the heavens and the earthly world. The secret of genius is to suffer no fiction to exist for us; to realize all that we know; in the high refinement of modern life, in arts, in sciences, in books, in men, to exact good faith, reality and a purpose; and first, last, midst and without end, to honor every truth by use.

The 1860 *Leaves of Grass*, as one of Whitman's notebook entries indicates, was to be a Bible too: "The Great Construction of the New Bible. . . . It ought to be ready in 1859." It was to offer a "third religion," Whitman wrote. And in a way it does; but, for well and for ill, that religion is a religion of man—man as he is, locked in his humanity and needing a religion, yet not claiming to have it by virtue of needing it, not hypnotizing himself into declaring that he has it. (For Whitman a little cadence was a dangerous, if exciting, thing, much cadence, disastrous.) The Whitman of the 1860 *Leaves of Grass* is, par excellence, Emerson's "secretary," reporting "the doings of the miraculous spirit of life that everywhere throbs and works." To accept a miracle, to live in its presence, even to try to comprehend it, this is not the same as trying to work a miracle, even claiming to have worked one. And, as the poets who have come after him have variously testified in the puzzled, ambiguous relation to him, Whitman's way with the language of poetry, going against the grain of mass communications and "positivism," may well teach us how to recognize and acknowledge miracles. It cannot teach us how to work them, or even how to earn them. One can well imagine how hard it must be for a poet to go so far with language, only to discover that he can go no farther. Such a discovery constitutes the principal element of greatness in the 1860 *Leaves of Grass*. I suggest that it is at least worth entertaining the notion that such a discovery constitutes the principal element of greatness in Whitman's poetry as a whole.

I have said that in 1855 Whitman "invented" modern poetry. By this I mean only that, along with other major poets of the middle of the century, he participated, but in a strangely isolated way, in the development of romanticist poetics toward and beyond its symbolist phase. ("To invent" may mean, among other things, "to stumble upon.") I do not mean to claim too much for the word "symbolist" here; I use it only generally to indicate that Whitman too came to realize that a poet's vocation was fatefully tied to the state of the language which constituted his medium. He discovered with Baudelaire—although without Baudelaire's (and incidentally Emerson's) overwhelming sense of the problem of "correspondences"—that as regards language "tout vit, tout agit, tout se correspond." The medium thus had a "life" of its own, and so might generate "life," the "life" of poetry. Poetry on this view thus became *sui generis*, a unique mode of discourse; and the role of the poet became more and more explicitly to be that of the creator, one who might "free" language to "mean," a creator in a medium, pure and simple. We have in Whitman's early work a version of that conception of poet and poetry with which we are now so familiar: to whom was the poet responsible? Not to whom, the reply ran, but to what? And the answer: to language. Language as such was seen to be the sole, overriding means to establish, or re-establish, community. The perhaps inevitable drift—not only in Whitman's work but in that of his contemporaries and of the poets who have come—was toward an idea of poetry as a means of communion, perhaps modern man's sole means of communion, his religion. Professor Meyer Abrams (in *The Mirror and the Lamp*) concludes his account of these developments thus:

> It was only in the early Victorian period, when all discourse was explicitly or tacitly thrown into the two exhaustive modes of imaginative and rational, expressive and assertive, that religion fell together with poetry in opposition to science, and that religion, as a consequence, was converted into poetry, and poetry into a kind of religion.

Professor Abrams is speaking about developments in England. In the United States conditions were somewhat simpler and, withal, more extreme. From the beginning, that is to say, Whitman was sure that the imaginative and rational might well be subsumed under a "higher" category, which was poetry. So that—as I have indicated in my remarks on Whitman and prophetic poetry—for him there was eventually entailed the idea that the New Bible might be just that, a total and inclusive account of cosmic man, of man as one of an infinitude of gods bound up in Nature. It is a nice question whether or not the "symbolist" dedication to the idea of language-as-communion must inevitably lead to a search for a metalinguistic structure of analogies and correspondences and then to an idea of poetry as religion and religion as poetry. And it is a nicer question whether or not "symbolist" poetics—with its emphasis on medium as against matrix, language per se as against language-in-culture—is characterized by a certain weakness in linguistic theory. Whitman's work raises these questions; and a full critique of his work would entail a critique of his theory of poetry, thus of his theory of language, thus of his theory of culture. We will not have that until we begin to read seriously the 1860 *Leaves of Grass*.

In any case, we must grant Whitman his special kind of "unmediated vision." (I am inclined to avoid the phrase "mystical experience" here, for it serves only to raise questions so as to make them unanswerable. Moreover, it is a too-easy means to legitimizing, particularly in terms of the earlier poems, Whitman's later claims to being a prophet.) We are made aware above all that the poet is "in" the world, that if he leaves it he will perforce have to take it with him. His power over language has taught him—and us too, if we can bear the knowledge—that, in a quite naturalistic sense, the world is "in" him. The shock of discovery is terrific: so many presences, so much experience, in a little room! According to the common sense of his culture, it should not have been possible. And the poet, properly grown mistrustful of orthodox principles of selecting and ordering all that he has come to know, will try to contain it all; for he knows that in containing it all he is containing himself, as he is part of it. The means to the containing is the visionary power. At its most telling, Whitman's earlier poetry manifests what has been called (by Erich Kahler) an "existential consciousness," but of a mid-nineteenth-century American sort—its key term, its center of strength and weakness, being not anguish but joy. Or rather, the key term is "triumph"—as suffering, the poet endures, and rejoices, seeing that it is his vocation as poet to teach men that they can endure. The freedom which ensues is wonderful, not dreadful.

Thus I take the 1855 and 1856 editions of *Leaves of Grass*, which most freshly project this mode of consciousness, as stages on the way to the 1860 edition. In 1855 and 1856 Whitman shows that he has learned to report truthfully, and to contain, what he has seen; in 1860, that he has learned to measure its significance for the poet taken as "secretary"—the archetypal "writer." The form of the 1855 and 1856 editions is that of a diary; the form of the 1860 edition, that of an autobiography. Whitman strove to go beyond autobiography, but in vain. The movement from the 1855 to the 1856 editions is the movement from the first "Song of Myself" and the first "The Sleepers" (both originally untitled) to the first "Crossing Brooklyn Ferry" (called in 1856 "Sun-Down Poem"). The poet first learns, as we would put it now, to discipline himself into regressing deeply into his own pre-conscious; then, with his new-found sense of himself as at once subject and object in his world, he learns to conceive in a new way of the world at large; he is, as though for the first time, "in" the world, even as he discovers that it is "in" him. The crucial factor is a restoration of the poet's vital relationship to language. A good, powerfully naïve account of this discovery is that in Whitman's prose *American Primer*, written in the 1850's but not published until after his death:

> What do you think words are? Do you think words are positive and original things in themselves?—No: Words are not original and arbitrary in themselves.— Words are a result—they are the progeny of what has been or is in vogue.—If iron architecture comes in vogue, as it seems to be coming, words are wanted to stand for all about iron architecture, for the work it causes, for the different branches of work and of the workman. . . .
>
> A perfect user of words uses things—they exude in power and beauty from him—miracles in his hands— miracles from his mouth. . . .
>
> A perfect writer would make words sing, dance, kiss, do the male and female act, bear children, weep, bleed, rage, stab, steal, fire cannon, steer ships, sack cities, charge with cavalry or infantry, or do any thing, that man or woman or the natural powers can do. . . . [Note the insistence on "natural," not "supernatural," powers.]
>
> Likely there are other words wanted.—Of words wanted, the matter is summed up in this: When the time comes for them to represent any thing or any state of things, the words will surely follow. The lack of any words, I say again, is as historical as the exist- ence of words. As for me, I feel a hundred realities, clearly determined in me, that words are not yet formed to represent. . . .

These sentiments generally, and some of these phrases particularly, got into Whitman's prose medi- tations. More important, from the beginning they in- form the poems. They derive much from Emerson's "The Poet," of course; but they are not tied to even Emerson's modestly transcendental balloon. The power

215

which Whitman discovers is the power of language, fueled by the imagination, to break through the categories of time, space, and matter and to "vivify" (a word, as I have said, he used late in his life—so close to Pound's "Make it new") the persons, places, and things of his world, and so make them available to his readers. In the process, since the readers would, as it were, be using words for the first time, he would make them available to themselves, as poets in spite of themselves.

It is as regards this last claim, that the reader is a poet in spite of himself, that the 1860 *Leaves of Grass* is all-important. For there Whitman most clearly saw that the poet's power to break through the limiting categories of day-to-day existence is just that: a poet's power, obtaining only insofar as the poem obtains and limited as the poem is limited. In 1860, that is to say, Whitman saw that his Bible was to be a poet's Bible, and had to be built around a conception of the poet's life: his origins, experience, and end; his relation with the persons, places, and things of his world. The 1855 and 1856 volumes are but collections of poems—their organization as rushed and chaotic as is the sensibility of the writer of the *American Primer*. Within individual poems there is form, a form which centers on the moment in the poet's life which they project. But the 1860 *Leaves of Grass* is an articulated whole, with an argument. The argument is that of the poet's life as it furnishes a beginning, middle, and end to an account of his vocation. As I have said, the 1860 volume is, for all its imperfections, one of the great works in that romantic mode, the autobiography. Or, let us give the genre to which it belongs a more specific name: archetypal autobiography. The 1860 volume is autobiographical as, say, *Moby-Dick* and *Walden* are autobiographical; for its hero is a man in the process of writing a book, of writing himself, of making himself, of discovering that the powers of the self are the stronger for being limited. The hero who can say "No!" in thunder discovers that he can say "Yes!" in thunder too, but that the thunderation is his own and no one else's.

To say that the 1860 *Leaves of Grass* is quintessentially autobiographical is to say what has been said before, most notably by Frederik Schyberg, Roger Asselineau, and Gay Wilson Allen. But I mean to say it somewhat differently than they do. For they see in the volume a sign of a crisis in Whitman's personal life; and this is most likely so. Yet I think it is wrong to read the volume as, in this literal sense, personal, that is, "private." (The Bowers edition of the surviving manuscript of the 1860 edition clearly shows that Whitman—naturally enough, most often in the "Calamus" poems—wanted to keep the book clear of too insistently and privately personal allusions. He was, I think, not trying to "conceal," much less "mask," his private personality, but to transmute it into an archetypal personality. It is a mistake to look so hard, as some critics do, for the "private" I.) Thus I should read the volume as not personal but archetypal autobiography, as yet another version of that compulsively brought-forth nineteenth-century poem which dealt with the growth of the poet's mind. (Well instructed by our forebears, we now have a variety of names for the form, all demonstrating how deeply, and from what a variety of non-literary perspectives, we have had to deal with the issues which it raises for us: *rite de passage*, quest for identity, search for community, and the like.) Whitman's problem, the poet's problem, was to show that integral to the poet's vocation was his life cycle; that, having discovered his gifts, the poet might now use them to discover the relevance of his life, his lived life, his *Erlebnis*, his career, to the lives of his fellows. It is the fact that his newly discovered use of poetry is grounded in his sense of a life

217

lived-through: it is this fact that evidences Whitman's ability here, more than in any other version of *Leaves of Grass*, to contain his gift and use it, rather than be used by it. Of this volume Whitman said:

> I am satisfied with *Leaves of Grass*, (by far the most of it) as expressing what was intended, namely, to express by sharp-cut self assertion, One's Self and also, or may be still more, to map out, to throw together for American use, a gigantic embryo or skeleton of Personality,—fit for the West, for native models.

Later, of course, he wanted more. But, so it seems to me, he never had the means beyond those in the 1860 edition to get what he wanted. And that has made all the difference. Since a reader who comes fresh to the 1860 edition must take that difference into account, I shall venture an outline of the argument and at the end shall give special emphasis to "A Word Out of the Sea"—an early version of "Out of the Cradle Endlessly Rocking"—which marks its turning point.

4.

The 1860 *Leaves of Grass* opens with "Proto-Leaf" (later, much revised, "Starting from Paumanok"). Here Whitman announces his themes and, as he had done before, calls for his new religion; but he gives no indication that it is to be a religion of anything else but the poet's universalized vocation. (My misuse of the word "religion" is his. The nature of the 1860 *Leaves of Grass* is such that one is to be neither victimized nor saved by following him here.) It might yet, on this account, be a precursor to a religion, in the more usual (and I think proper) sense, as well as a substitute for it. "Whoever you are! to you endless announcements," he says. There follows "Walt Whitman," a somewhat modified version of the 1855 poem which became "Song of Myself." It is still close to the fluid

version of 1855; strangely enough, it is so overarticu-
lated (with some 372 sections) that it does not have
the rather massive, and therefore relatively dogmatic,
articulation of the final version. In all, it gives us an
account of the poet's overwhelming discovery of his
native powers. Then in the numbered (but not separately titled) series of poems called "Chants Democratic," the poet, after an apostrophic salutation to his
fellows (it ends "O poets to come, I depend upon
you!"), celebrates himself again, but now as he conceives of himself in the act of celebrating his world.
The chief among these poems—as usual, much modified
later—became "By Blue Ontario's Shore," "Song of the
Broad-Axe," "A Song for Occupations," "Me Imperturbe," "I Was Looking a Long While," and "I Hear
America Singing." Following upon "Walt Whitman,"
the "Chants Democratic" sequence successfully establishes the dialectical tension between the poet and his
world, the tension being sustained as one is made to
realize again and again that out of the discovery of his
power for making words "do the male and female act"
in "Walt Whitman" has come his power to "vivify" his
world in the "Chants Democratic."

The transition to the next sequence "Leaves of Grass"
—again the poems are numbered but not separately
titled—is natural and necessary. For the poet now asks
what it is to make poems in the language which has
been precipitated out of the communal experience of
his age. The mood throughout is one of a mixture of
hope and doubt, and at the end it reaches a certitude
strengthened by a sense of the very limitations which
initially gave rise to the doubt. The first poem opens
with two lines expressing doubt; later, when the prophetic Whitman willed himself not to doubt, the lines
were dropped, and the poem became the "positive" "As
I Ebb'd with the Ocean of Life." The second poem is
a version of an 1855 poem, "Great Are the Myths";

and it was finally rejected by Whitman as being, one guesses, too certain in its dismissal of the "mythic" mode toward which he later found himself aspiring. The third poem, which, combined with the sixth, later became "Song of the Answerer," opens up the issue of communication as such. The fourth, a version of an 1856 poem which eventually became "This Compost," conceives of poetry as a kind of naturalistic resurrection. It moves from "Something startles me where I thought I was safest"—"safest," that is, in his relation to the materials of poetry—to a simple acknowledgment at the end that the earth "gives such divine materials to men, and accepts such leavings from them at last." The fifth (later "Song of Prudence") considers the insight central to the poet's vocation. To the categories of "time, space, reality," the poet would add that of "prudence"—which teaches that the "consummations" of poetry must finally entail the necessary relationship of all other "consummations": the imagination's law of the conservation of energy. The sixth (which, as I have said, later became part of "Song of the Answerer") develops an aspect of the theme of the fourth and fifth; but now that theme is interpreted as it is bound up exclusively in the problem of language: "The words of poems give you more than poems, / They give you to form for yourself poems, religions, politics, war, peace, behavior, histories, essays, romances, and everything else." At this depth of discovery there is no possibility of any kind of logically continuous catalogue of what words "give you to form for yourself." Poetry is a means of exhausting man's powers to know the world, and himself in it, as it is. Beyond this, poems

> . . . prepare for death—yet are they not the finish, but rather the outset,
> They bring none to his or her terminus, or to be content and full;

Whom they take, they take into space, to behold the
   birth of stars, to learn one of the meanings,
To launch off with absolute faith—to sweep through
   the ceaseless rings, and never be quiet again.

In the seventh poem (later "Faith Poem") the poet
discovers that he needs "no assurances"; for he is
(as he says in the eighth poem, later "Miracles") a
realist and for him the real (by which he here means
phenomena) constitute "miracles." The poet is led in
the ninth poem (later "There Was a Child Went
Forth") to a recollection of his first discovery of the
miraculousness of the real, a discovery he only now
understands; this poem, taken in relation to the rest
of the sequence, properly anticipates "A Word Out of
the Sea," in which Whitman makes so much of the
word "now." The tenth poem opens with a passage
dropped from the later version, "Myself and Mine,"
but one which is essential as a transition in the sequence:

It is ended—I dally no more,
After to-day I inure myself to run, leap, swim, wrestle,
   fight. . . .

Simply enough, the poet, having accepted his vocation
and its constraints, is now free, free through it, and
he must now teach this freedom to others:

I charge that there be no theory or school founded out
   of me,
I charge you to leave all free, as I have left all free.

The rest of the sequence, fourteen more poems, celebrate aspects of the poet's new freedom as it might be
the freedom of all men. It is the freedom to rejoice in
the miraculousness of the real, and has its own costs.
The greatest is a terrible passivity, as though in order
to achieve his freedom man has to offer himself up as

221

the victim of his own newly vivified sensibility. Being as he is, the poet sees (in 12) "A vast similitude [which] interlocks all"; yet he must admit (in 15) "that life cannot exhibit all to me" and "that I am to wait for what will be exhibited by death." He is (in 17) the man who must "sit and look out upon all the sorrows of the world, and upon all oppression and shame"; and he must "See, hear, and [be] silent," only then to speak. He declares (in 20): "whether I continue beyond this book, to maturity, / . . . / Depends . . . upon you, / . . . / . . . you, contemporary America." Poem 24, wherein the poet completes his archetypal act and so is compelled to give himself over to his readers, tells us:

> Lift me close to your face till I whisper,
> What you are holding is in reality no book, nor part
>   of a book,
> It is a man, flushed and full-blooded—it is I—*So long!*
> We must separate—Here! take from my lips this kiss,
> Whoever you are, I give it especially to you;
> *So long*—and I hope we shall meet again.

I quote this last poem entire, because I want to make it clear that the lapses into desperate sentimentality—and this poem is a prime example—are intrinsically a part of Whitman's autobiographical mode in the 1860 *Leaves of Grass*, as they are of the mode, or genre, which they represent. It will not do to explain them away by putting them in a larger context, or considering them somehow as masked verses, evidences of Whitman the shape-shifter. (Speaking through a persona, Whitman too often hides behind it.) Caught up in the agonies and ambiguities of his conception of the poet, Whitman too often fell into bathos or sentimentalism. Yet bathos and sentimentalism, I would suggest, are but unsuccessful means—to be set against evidence of successful means—of solving the archetypal autobiographer's central problem, of at once being and seeing himself, of bearing witness to his own deeds. If what he is, as he sees it, is too much to bear, if he is incapable of bearing it, if his genius is such as not to have prepared him to bear it—then his miraculism will fail him precisely because he cannot stand too much reality.

Bathos and sentimentalism—and also anxious, premonitory yearnings for something beyond mere poetry —inevitably mar the rest of the 1860 *Leaves of Grass*, but not fatally, since they are the by-products of its total argument. At some point most foxes want to be hedgehogs. Whitman, in this *Leaves of Grass* as in the others, is a poet who must be read at large. But I suggest that he can be best read at large in the 1860 *Leaves of Grass*. When he can be read in smaller compass, as in "A Word Out of the Sea," it is because in a single poem he realizes that he has come to a turning point in what he is developing at large. Presently I shall consider in detail this poem, which became "Out of the Cradle Endlessly Rocking," and I shall want to suggest that the earlier version, set in its earlier context, is even greater than the later. At this point, I note only that it comes as one of a loosely related series of poems, following the "Leaves of Grass" sequence, in which the poet meditates the sheer givenness of the world his poems have discovered, as though for the first time. In these poems he is even capable of seeing himself as one of the givens. But then he must specify in detail the nature of his kind of givenness, which includes the power to give, to bring the given to a new life.

After "Salut au Monde!" "Poem of Joys," "A Word Out of the Sea," "A Leaf of Faces," and "Europe," there is first the "Enfans d'Adam" sequence; and then, after an interlude of generally celebrative poems, the "Calamus" sequence. These two sequences are passionate in a curiously objective fashion. I have suggested that the proper word for their mood and tone is neither personal nor impersonal, but archetypal. They furnish contrasting analogues—directly libidinal analogues, as it were—for the poet's role, seen now not (as in the earlier sequences) from the point of view of a man telling us how he had discovered his gift, put it to use, and measured the cost of using it properly, but seen rather from the point of view of the reader. The explicit sexuality of the poems surely is Whitman's; and we cannot but be troubled by its frank ambivalence. But there are enough times when, ambivalent or not, it is rendered so as to make it virtually anonymous, so that the reader can acknowledge it at least as potentially his. Libidinal *analogues*, not *metaphors*, I have said; for the only way in which Whitman can teach his readers what it means to participate in "making" something is, through a directly applicable analogue, to evoke in them a response which articulates and thus generalizes all that is involved in moving from sexuality to love. At times in these two sequences Whitman seems driven to conceive of sexuality and love in terms of the making of poems—as though, for whatever reason, he were confused, even frustrated, by his own "procreant urge" (as he calls it in "Walt Whitman" / "Song of Myself"). It is, on the one hand, a matter of so trivial a thing as "poetic diction"; and, on the other, of so all-consuming a thing as the simple acknowledgment of "the pent up rivers of myself" and "the hungry gnaw that eats me night and day." Too often the effect is of protesting too much; but then, it is always so in writing which is directly, not metaphorically, libidinal. As Whitman knew too well for our comfort, the final discrimination has to be ours. The important point is that not only the place of the "Enfans d'Adam" and "Calamus" sequence in the 1860 *Leaves of Grass* but also the generalizing directives that Whitman puts in many of the poems—that place and directives at the very least bid us entertain the possibility of their analogizing function.

Since the problem is great, we might well be justified in looking for outside help in solving it. Such help is at hand in the manuscript versions of many of the 1860 "Enfans d'Adam" and "Calamus" poems, which Professor Bowers has edited. The beginning of the twelfth of the "Calamus" poems reads:

> Are you the new person drawn toward me, and asking
>   something significant from me?
> To begin with, take warning—I am probably far different from what you suppose;
> Do you suppose you will find in me your ideal?
> Do you think it so easy to have me become your lover?

The manuscript version begins, however:

> Be careful—I am perhaps different from what you
>   suppose;
> Do you suppose you will find in me your ideal?
> Do you suppose you can easily be my lover, and I
>   yours?

And the thirty-sixth poem of the sequence begins:

> Earth! my likeness!
> Though you look so impassive, ample and spheric there,
> I now suspect that is not all.

The manuscript version of this poem begins:

> Earth! Though you look so impassive, ample and
>   spheric there—I suspect that is not all.

The crucial revisions are: in the twelfth poem, the addition of the first two lines, centering on "asking something significant . . ."; and in the thirty-sixth, that of "my likeness" in the first line. The tendency here, and throughout the poems of which we have manuscript versions, is to call our attention to the poet's relation to the "other" which he addresses—thus to the reader as he is asked to imagine himself as caught up in the experience of making poems and inquiring what the making might mean.

The "I" of these poems is meant to include the reader, as at once potential poet and reader of poems. The "Enfans d'Adam" sequence tells us how it is, what it means, what it costs, to be a maker of poems; and the "Calamus" sequence, how it is to be a reader of poems. In the first instance the analogue is procreation; in the second it is community. If Whitman's homosexuality led him to write more powerfully in the second vein than in the first, we can well afford to be grateful for the fact that we can learn from these poems as from few others, to understand everyman's potential for "alienation" as Whitman has the power to evoke and define it for us. That understanding is carried through to the end, as we are told in the next to last of the "Calamus" sequence that we are to be ready for the poet's most "baffling" words, and then as we are given those words in the last poem of the sequence:

> When you read these, I, that was visible, am become
> invisible;
> Now it is you, compact, visible, realizing my poems,
> seeking me,
> Fancying how happy you were, if I could be with you,
> and become your lover;
> Be it as if I were with you. Be not too certain but I am
> with you now.

Later Whitman changed "lover" to "comrade"—mistakenly, I think; for, as their function in the 1860 volume shows, the "Calamus" poems were to carry through to completion the poet's conception of his painfully loving relation with his readers.

Having, in the "Enfans d'Adam" and "Calamus" sequences, defined the poetic process itself, as he had earlier defined the poet's discovery of that process, Whitman proceeds variously to celebrate himself and his readers at once under the aegis of the "Enfans d'Adam" and the "Calamus" analogues. Much of the power of the poems, new and old, derives from their place in the sequence. In "Crossing Brooklyn Ferry" and the series of "Messenger Leaves" there are addresses to all and sundry who inhabit Whitman's world, assurances to them that now he can love them for what they are, because now he knows them for what they are. There is then an address to Mannahatta, which returns to the problem of naming, but now with an assurance that the problem has disappeared in the solving: "I was asking for something specific and perfect for my city, and behold! here is the aboriginal name!" Then, a little farther on, there is in "Kosmos" an address to the simple, separate persons, to each of his readers who is "constructing the house of himself or herself." Then, after a series of apothegm-poems, there is "Sleep-Chasings" (a version of the 1855 "The Sleepers"), now a sublime poem, in which the poet can freely acknowledge that the source of his strength is in the relation of his nighttime to his daytime life, the unconscious and the conscious. The last stanza reads:

> I will stop only a time with the night, and rise betimes,
> I will duly pass the day, O my mother, and duly return
> to you.

"Sleep-Chasings" is the more telling for being followed by "Burial" (originally an 1855 poem which eventually became "To Think of Time"). For in his incessant moving between night and day, the poet manages to make poems and so proves immortal. He makes men immortal in his poems, as he teaches them to make themselves immortal in their acts:

To think that you and I did not see, feel, think, nor
    bear our part!
To think that we are now here, and bear our part!

This poem comes virtually at the end of the 1860
volume. Only an address to his soul—immortal, but in
a strictly "poetic" sense—and "So long!" follow. In the
latter we are reminded once again:

This is no book,
Who touches this, touches a man,
(Is it night? Are we here alone?)
It is I you hold, and who holds you,
I spring from the pages into your arms—decease calls
    me forth.

We are reminded thus, to paraphrase a recent Whitmanian, that in the flesh of art we are immortal—which
is a commonplace. We are reminded also that in our
age, the role of art, of poetry, is to keep us alive enough
to be capable of this kind of immortality—which is not
quite a commonplace.

5.

The central terms in the argument of the 1860
Leaves of Grass run something like this: first, in the
poems which lead up to "A Word Out of the Sea," self-
discovery, self-love, rebirth, diffusion-of-self, art; and
second, in the poems which follow "A Word Out of
the Sea," love of others, death, rebirth, reintegration
of self, art, immortality. The sequence is that of an
ordinary life, extraordinarily lived through; the claims
are strictly humanistic. The child manages somehow
to achieve adulthood; the movement is from a poetry
of diffusion to a poetry of integration. Immortality
is the result of art, not its origin, nor its cause. The
humanism is painful, because one of its crucial elements (centering on "death" as a "clew" in "A Word Out

of the Sea") is an acknowledgment of all-too-human limitations and constraints. So long as Whitman lived with that acknowledgment, lived in that acknowledgment—even when living with it drove him (as it too often did) toward bathos and sentimentalism—he managed to be a poet, a "secretary," a "sage," a seer, a visionary. His religion was the religion of humanity, the only religion that a work of art can directly express, whatever other religion it may confront and acknowledge. Indirectly, it can confront religion in the more usual, and more proper, sense; for it can treat of man in his aspiration for something beyond manhood, even if it cannot claim—since its materials are ineluctably those of manhood—to treat directly of that something-beyond. The burden—someone has called it the burden of incertitude; Keats called it "negative capability"— is a hard one to bear. Whitman, I am suggesting, bore it most successfully, bore it most successfully for us, in the 1860 *Leaves of Grass*.

This brings me to the most important of the poems first collected in this volume, "A Word Out of the Sea." (It was originally published separately in 1859, as "A Child's Reminiscence.") Thus far I have tried to suggest the proper context in which the poem should be read, as part of the volume for which it was originally written, as a turning point in the argument of that book. Note that "A Word Out of the Sea" comes about midway in the book, after "Walt Whitman," the "Chants Democratic," "Leaves of Grass," "Salut au Monde!" and "Poem of Joys"—that is, after those poems which tell us of the poet's discovery of his powers as poet and of his ability to use them to "vivify" his world and himself in it, after his discovery that it is man's special delight and his special agony to be at once the subject and object of his meditations, after his discovery that consciousness inevitably entails self-consciousness and a sense of the strengths and weaknesses of self-consciousness. Moreover, "A Word Out of the Sea" comes shortly before the "Enfans d'Adam" and "Calamus" sequences—that is, shortly before those poems which work out the dialectic of the subject-object relationship under the analogue of the sexuality of man as creator of his world and of persons, places, and things as its creatures. I cannot but think that Whitman knew what he was doing when he placed "A Word Out of the Sea" thus. For he was obliged, in all his autobiographical honesty, to treat directly of man's fallibilities as well as his powers, to try to discover the binding relationship between fallibilities and powers—to estimate the capacity of man to be himself and the cost he would have to pay. The poems which come before "A Word Out of the Sea" have little to do with fallibilities. They develop the central terms of the whole argument only this far: self-discovery, self-love, rebirth, art. Theirs is the polymorph perverse world of the child. In them, death only threatens, does not promise; power is what counts. The turning point in the poet's life can come only with the "adult" sense of love and death, the beginning and the end of things —out of which issues art, now a mode of immortality. In "A Word Out of the Sea" the 1860 volume has its vital center. Beyond this poem, we must remember, are the "Enfans d'Adam" and "Calamus" sequences, and also "Crossing Brooklyn Ferry" and the "Messenger Leaves" sequence.

The 1860 poem begins harshly: "Out of the rocked cradle." The past participle, unlike the present participle in the later versions, implies no continuing agent for the rocking. The sea here is too inclusive to be a symbol; it is just a fact of life—life's factuality. Then comes the melange of elements associated with the sea. They are among the realities whose miraculousness the poet is on his way to understanding. Note the third line (omitted in later versions) which clearly establishes the autobiographical tone and makes the boy at once the product of nature at large and a particular nature: "Out of the boy's mother's womb, and from the nipples of her breasts." All this leads to a clear split in point of view, so that we know that the poet-as-adult is making a poem which will be his means to understanding a childhood experience. Initially we are told of the range of experiences out of which this poem comes. The sea as rocked cradle seems at once literally (to the boy) and metaphorically (to the poet) to "contain" the song of the bird, the boy's mother, the place, the time, the memory of the brother, and the as yet unnamed "word stronger and more delicious than any" which marks a limit to the meaning of the whole. This is quite explicitly an introduction. For what follows is given a separate title, "Reminiscence," as though the poet wanted to make quite plain the division between his sense of himself as child and as adult. Then we are presented with the story of the birds, the loss of the beloved, and the song sung (as only *now* the poet knows it) to objectify this loss, thus make it bearable, thus assure that it can, in this life, be transcended. Always we are aware that the poet-as-adult, the creative center of the poem, seeks that "word stronger and more delicious" which will be his means finally to understand his reminiscences and—in the context of *this* volume—serve to define his vocation as poet, at once powerful and fallible. The points of view of bird, child and adult are kept separate until the passage which reads:

Bird! (then said the boy's Soul,)
Is it indeed toward your mate you sing? or is it mostly
    to me?
For I that was a child, my tongue's use sleeping,
Now that I have heard you,
Now in a moment I know what I am for—I awake,

And already a thousand singers—a thousand songs,
    clearer, louder, more sorrowful than yours,
A thousand warbling echoes have started to life within
    me,
Never to die.

The boy, even as a man recalling his boyhood, does
not, as in later versions, at first address the bird as
"Demon." He is at this stage incapable of that "or"—in
the later reading "Demon or bird." Even though his soul
speaks, he is to discover some lines later his special
"poetic" relation to the bird. Moreover, as "boy" he
holds toward death an attitude halfway between that
of the bird, who is merely "instinctive," and that of
the man, who is "reflective," capable of "reminiscence."
Yet the points of view begin to be hypnotically merged
—after the fact. In the boy's "soul" the poet discovers
a child's potentiality for adult knowledge; but he keeps
it as a potentiality, and he never assigns it to the bird,
who (or which) is an occasion merely. Yet having seen
that potentiality as such, he can "now," in the adult
present, work toward its realization. He can ask for
"the clew," "The word final, superior to all," the word
which "now" he can "conquer." I cannot emphasize
too much that it is a "word" which he seeks—that the
poet is translating the sea (and all it embodies) as
prelinguistic fact into a word, knowledge of which will
signify his coming to maturity. "Out of," in the original title, is meant quite literally to indicate a linguistic
transformation. In the record of the growth of his
mind, he sees *now* that the word will once and for all
precipitate the meaning he has willed himself to create,
and in the creating to discover. And it comes as he recalls that time when the sea, manifesting the rhythm
of life and death itself,

Delaying not, hurrying not,
Whispered me through the night, and very plainly be-
    fore daybreak,

Lisped to me constantly the low and delicious word
   DEATH,
And again Death—ever Death, Death, Death. . . .

(Not "Death," merely repeated four times as in later versions—but "ever," beyond counting. The prophetic Whitman was bound to drop that "ever," since for him nothing was beyond counting.)

The merging of the points of view occurs as not only past and present, child and adult, but subject and object (i.e. "The sea . . . whispered me," not "*to* me") are fused. The poet now knows the word, because he has contrived a situation in which he can control its use; he has discovered (to recall the language of the *American Primer* notes) another reality, one that words until *now* had not been formed to represent. He has, as only a poet can, *made* a word out of the sea, for the duration of the poem understood "sea" as it may be translated into "death," "ever death." His achievement is to have enabled us to put those quotation marks around the word—guided by him, to have "bracketed" with language this portion of our experience. We discover that as language binds us in the poet's time, so it is bound in human time.

If the end of the poem is to understand cosmic process as a continual loss of the beloved through death and a consequent gain of death-in-life and life-in-death, nonetheless it is an end gained through a creative act, an assertion of life in the face of death, and a discovery and acknowledgment of the limits of such an assertion. This act is that of the very person, the poet, whom death would deprive of all that is beloved in life. Moreover, the deprivation is quite literally that, and shows the poet moving, in high honesty, from the "Enfans d'Adam" sequence to "Calamus." In the 1860 volume, "A Word Out of the Sea" entails the "Calamus" sequence.

In any case, at this stage of his career Whitman

would not yield to his longing for such comfort as would scant the facts of life and death. There is, I repeat, that opening "rocked," not "rocking," cradle; there is the quite naturalistic acknowledgment of the "boy's mother's womb." And there is stanza 31 (the stanzas in the 1860 poem are numbered, as the stanzas of the final version are not):

O give me some clew!
O if I am to have so much, let me have more!
O a word! O what is my destination?
O I fear it is henceforth chaos!
O how joys, dreads, convolutions, human shapes, and
all shapes, spring as from graves around me!
O phantoms! you cover all the land, and all the sea!
O I cannot see in the dimness whether you smile or
frown upon me;
O vapor, a look, a word! O well-beloved!
O you dear women's and men's phantoms!

In the final version, the equivalent stanza reads only:

O give me the clew (it lurks in the night here somewhere,)
O if I am to have so much, let me have more!

The difference between "some clew" and "the clew" marks the difference between a poet for whom questions are real and one for whom questions are rhetorical, as does the confrontation of "chaos." The later Whitman was convinced that the lurking clew would find him, and to that degree, whatever else he was, was not a poet. The earlier Whitman, in all humility, feared that what might issue out of this experience was "phantoms"—a good enough word for aborted poems. And often, but not too often, he was right.

Finally, there is not in "A Word Out of the Sea" the falsely (and, in the context of the poem, undeservedly) comforting note of "Or like some old crone rocking the cradle, swathed in sweet garments, bending aside."

The sentimentality and bathos of this too-much-celebrated line, as I think, is given away by the fact that it is the only simile, the only "like" clause, in the poem. And, in relation to the total effect of the poem, the strategic withdrawal of the "Or" which introduces the line and of the parentheses which enclose it is at least unfortunate, at most disastrous.

6.

I make so much of the kind of disaster, as I think it is, because it became increasingly characteristic of Whitman's way with poetry after the 1860 *Leaves of Grass*. The facts, as I interpret them, show that Whitman, for whatever reason, after 1860 moved away from the mode of archetypal autobiography toward that of prophecy. He worked hard to make, as he said, a cathedral out of *Leaves of Grass*. He broke up the beautifully wrought sequence of the 1860 volume, so that, even when he let poems stand unrevised, they appear in contexts which too often take from them their life-giving mixture of tentativeness and assurance, of aspiration, and render them dogmatic, tendentious, and overweening.

In D. H. Lawrence's word, Whitman "mentalized" his poems. In order, by contrast, to fix the mode of the 1860 *Leaves of Grass* in the mind of a reader coming to it for the first time, I give a few examples of "mentalizing" revisions of 1860 poems. The opening of the third "Enfans d'Adam" poem reads in the 1860 text:

O my children! O mates!
O the bodies of you, and of all men and women, engirth
me, and I engirth them.

In the 1867 version the lines read:

I sing the body electric,
The armies of those I love engirth me and I engirth
them.

235

Another example: the opening line of the fourteenth poem of the same sequence reads in the 1860 version, "I am he that aches with love," and becomes in 1867, "I am he that aches with amorous love." (This is the "amorous" which so infuriated Lawrence.) And another example: the opening lines of the fifteenth poem in the sequence read in the 1860 version, "Early in the morning, / Walking . . . ," and became in 1867, "As Adam early in the morning, / Walking. . . ." Small examples surely. But note the unsupported and unsupportable claims of "body electric," "armies," "amorous," and the Old Testament "Adam."

A larger, but still characteristic, example is Whitman's revision of the first of the 1860 "Leaves of Grass" sequence, which became "As I Ebb'd with the Ocean of Life." The 1860 poem opens thus:

> have just been impressing me.
>
> Elemental drifts!
> O I wish I could impress others as you and the waves
>
> As I ebbed with an ebb of the ocean of life,
> As I wended the shores I know.

In the poem as it appears in the 1892 edition of *Leaves of Grass*, the first two lines (expressing doubt, as I have pointed out) are missing; the third has been simplified to "As I ebb'd with the ocean of life." In effect the poet is no longer conceived as part of an "ebb." The fourth line stands as we have it now. Later, in the seventh line of the 1892 version, the poet says that he is "Held by this electric self out of the pride of which I utter poems." In the 1860 version he says that he is "Alone, held by the eternal self of me that threatens to get the better of me, and stifle me." And so it goes —with all passion beyond spending (unless vivified by a kind of cosmic electroshock), all poetry beyond the mere writing, all life beyond the mere living. The

236

poet's tactic, however unconscious, is to claim to have transcended that which must have been hard to live with, his extraordinarily ordinary self and the ordinarily extraordinary death that awaits him. Granting the mood and movement of the later editions of *Leaves of Grass*, it is only proper that Whitman would have rejected the eighth poem in the 1860 "Calamus" sequence, which begins "Long I thought that knowledge alone would suffice me—O if I could but obtain knowledge!" and ends, as the poet is brought to confront the readers to whom he would offer his poems, "I am indifferent to my own songs—I will go with him I love. . . ."

One more example, this one not of a revision but of an addition to a sequence originating in the 1860 volume. In the 1871 *Leaves of Grass*, Whitman, now wholly committed to making of his poem a series of prophetic books, placed in the "Calamus" sequence the woolly "Base of All Metaphysics," the last stanza of which reads:

Having studied the new and antique, the Greek and
    Germanic systems,
Kant having studied and stated, Fichte and Schelling
    and Hegel,
Stated the lore of Plato, and Socrates greater than
    Plato,
And greater than Socrates sought and stated, Christ
    divine having studied long,
I see reminiscent to-day those Greek and Germanic
    systems,
See the philosophies all, Christian churches and tenets
    see,
Yet underneath Socrates clearly see, and underneath
    Christ the divine I see,
The dear love of man for his comrade, the attraction of
    friend to friend.

Of the well-married husband and wife, of children and
  parents,
Of city for city and land for land.

Whitman stuck by this poem until the end, and it went
unchanged into the 1892 edition, contributing its bit
to the "mentalizing" of the whole. And it is only too
typical of additions to the book made from 1867 on.

My comparative observations here derive, of course,
from a strong conviction, or prejudice, in favor of the
1860 *Leaves of Grass.* I offer them with a certain diffidence. But, without diffidence, I suggest that the 1860
Leaves of Grass, in and of itself, is a great *book*—so I
am persuaded, Whitman's greatest.

In any case, the prophetic Whitman begins to take
over *Leaves of Grass* in the 1867 edition and is fully
in command by the time of the 1871 edition. (We shall
know more of the take-over when we are given an edition of Whitman's own copy of the 1860 edition—
marked heavily for revision.[2] I have seen a microfilm
copy of it and have noted that it manifests a Whitman
by 1865, a date given in some of the marginalia, quite
conscious of his need to make his poems confirm the
redefinition of his role which seems to have been a consequence of his Civil War experiences.) It is, unhappily,
still the later Whitman whom we know best. It is he
with whom our poets have had to make their pacts and
truces—so that during the uneasy peace they may come
to know another (and in fact an earlier) Whitman,
whose way with poetry they seem to sense but can never
quite get to. The way to that Whitman, who emerged
in 1855 and came to maturity in 1860, is not impossible, although working with the Inclusive Edition
(upon whose variant readings I have depended) is

2 [Such an edition has recently been prepared by Arthur Golden,
and published by the New York Public Library.]

tedious. But there is a yet more direct way—reading not only the 1855 edition (which we should by now know well enough) but the 1860 edition, "a true poem," as his publishers knew it would be, "writ by a *true* man."

1961

9

HENRY JAMES AND HIS *AMERICAN*

"Oh, how it must not be too good and how very bad
it must be!"   James' Notebook entry on
The American as a play.

IN SEPTEMBER 1913 an American lady wrote to Henry
James on behalf of a "young man from Texas" who
needed guidance into the study of James' fiction. (The
young man was Stark Young, who became a man of
letters in his own right.) James was seventy, famous, in
his own way an Olympian. Yet he replied promptly,
with graciousness and good humor. He sent two introductory reading lists, noting in both cases the order in
which the books were to be read. The second list, he
wrote, was the "more advanced"; and it went thus—1.
The American, 2. *The Tragic Muse*, 3. *The Wings of the
Dove*, 4. *The Ambassadors*, and 5. *The Golden Bowl.*
Further, he insisted that all the novels should be read
only as revised for the New York Edition of his fiction.
Nowadays, we are not at all surprised that at this stage
in his life James should have preferred the final version
of *The American*. (It was first serialized, 1876-1877, in
The Atlantic Monthly; then published in Boston in
1877; slightly revised for an English edition of 1879;
drastically revised for inclusion in the New York Edition in 1907.) For in the New York Edition, James
strove to give his earlier fiction a finish which would
make it consistent with the image of his life work which
he had long struggled to set for himself.

We tend to be a little surprised, however, that James
should have put *The American* on an "advanced" list—

especially in the light of the results, on the whole unfortunate, which came from his attempt to make it somehow consonant with the manner of his later fiction. We had nonetheless best begin with his advice. If we do so, we shall find that *The American* is indeed the best introduction to the "advanced" James, one of his masterpieces. But in looking closely at the kind of mastery it exhibits, we shall be forced to gainsay James a little and decide that the earlier version of *The American* is distinctly superior to the later. In the earlier version James advances into the first full treatment of his great international theme; and his technique as novelist is one with the degree and quality of his understanding of the theme. He tells us no more than we are sure he knows, than he *convinces* us he knows; and so we can let ourselves know it too. Revising *The American*, he failed, because by the time of the revision he had come to know more than he could with conviction make his old story tell. Moreover, he was too honest to his sense of what he had known when he first wrote the novel to be able successfully to make us believe that he had known more all along. James was too great an artist, too great a man, to be—in spite of himself—a good second-guesser. *The American* is a young man's novel, exuberant rather than profound in its wisdom. The James who revised *The American* for the New York Edition made the mistake of trying to convert exuberance into profundity.

James, it is said, "invented" the international novel. And this is so—if we take the word "invent" in a solidly etymological sense. James lived in a culture—that of nineteenth-century America—in which the international novel was there for the inventing, the coming-upon. There was required for the inventor a man whose sense of things was, by heritage and education, large enough to see what was there to be invented and brave enough to do the inventing. (There also was required genius;

but that we can only take note of, acknowledge, so to pass on to our inquiry into its exercise.)

One phase of American life from the very beginning has involved a continuing attempt to absorb into our own all that is "best" in foreign cultures. The impulse behind this attempt has not necessarily been imperialistic. But it has entailed a conviction that American culture is capacious enough to transform into an ever larger version of itself whatever is brought to it from abroad. Consonant with this phase, there has been another, assiduously nativist in tone, whereby Americans are said to be, if not totally sufficient unto themselves, at least in no need of advice from abroad unless they happen to ask for it—which they seldom are likely to do. Since the second phase has been called "Know-Nothingism," we might call the first "Know-Everything-ism." The record of his life shows that James was almost from the cradle acutely sensitive to both phases, and as acutely certain that in their extreme forms both were products of ignorantly utopian ways of thinking about American culture. He was a very practical man. And he was able to see that, practically speaking, when the American should come of age and feel secure enough to renounce both the know-everything and the know-nothing components of his heritage, he would indeed, in ways he could hardly suspect, find himself made into a new man. Having in America discovered the power of the self, the new man might in Europe discover its forms. His American experience would empower his sense of life's possibilities; his European experience would define them. Only through definition, he would have somehow to learn, could there be at once wholeness and enlargement. James' principal scene therefore had to be Europe. He wrote in his notebook, 25 November 1881:

My choice is the old world—my choice, my need, my life. There is no need for me today to argue about this; it is an inestimable blessing to me, and a rare good fortune, that the problem was settled long ago, and that I have now nothing to do but to act on the settlement.— My impressions here [Boston] are exactly what I expected they would be, and I scarcely see the place, and feel the manners, the race, the tone of things, now that I am on the spot, more vividly than I did while I was still in Europe. My work lies there—and with this vast new world, *je n'ai que faire.* One can't do both—one must choose. No European writer is called upon to assume that terrible burden, and it seems hard that I should be. The burden is necessarily greater for an American—for he *must* deal, more or less, even if only by implication, with Europe. . . .[1]

The irony, of course—and it is the increasing bite of the irony which marks James' growth as a novelist—is that he makes his characteristic Americans come to Europe intending to discover . . . Europe! Thus the international theme. We read of the adventures of an American at last sensitive enough to realize that his New World has neither incorporated nor transcended the Old. He is sensitive enough because his situation in his culture, now beyond its self-consciously pioneering days, has made him so. He has earned the right, because he feels the need, to go adventuring in the Old World. And he finds that he is not prepared to face up to what he encounters: a world whose ways are not just more complex than his own, but more rewardingly complex, and in super-subtle ways. He has known the rewards of living fully—but known them in simple, straightforward forms. Yet he has not known how

[1] *The Notebooks of Henry James*, ed. F. O. Matthiessen and Kenneth B. Murdock (New York, 1947), pp. 23-24.

subtle and complex the forms could be, and in their subtlety and complexity how much more rewarding than those he has previously known. He has not known much about styles, manners, institutions, customs, traditions, history. Above all, he has not known that the subtlety and complexity of such forms are at bottom moral qualities. But then he discovers that, even if he is unprepared, he has not lost out entirely. For he learns that he has discovered in his European adventures an enlarged capacity within himself to know, to understand, maybe to grow. And so, as he learns that he may give as much as he takes, his defeat is a victory. His defeat manifests the possibility—only that—of *our* victory.

The end of his story is to teach us—under the narrative of the encounter of the American with Europe and Europeans—that it is of the essence of a full life to give and to take; that, as it has rather surprisingly turned out, this is the meaning of the New World's re-encounter with the Old; that the life of the human spirit at its most powerful and rich must express the reciprocal dynamism of the Old and the New, of past and present, of constraint and freedom. The stages in the history of the development of an American character are these: first the freedom not to be done to; then the freedom to do; then, *now*, the freedom not to do. James' internationalized Americans discover, but not too late, that they do in fact have a history. In them, as in their suffering they must learn, history is not ended, or begun again, but rather summed up.

The international novel, then, is one written for Europeans as well as Americans. As an American—dare one say *only* as an American—James discovered the international novel: which was no more, and no less, than a discovery (beyond European cosmopolitanism as well as beyond American provincialism) of international life. In a way, the vital center of James' internationalism is his fecundating sense of what is traditionally called humanism. In effect, James succeeded in reinventing humanism for the modern world. Or rather, in his "advanced" novels—successively, and from successively differing perspectives—he succeeded in elucidating the necessary conditions of a modern world in which humanism would be possible: that there had to be people like his Americans in it, but that they now had to learn to be *wholly* in it, and to pay for what they must learn.

Thus it is essential that a man like Christopher Newman, the hero of *The American*, be altogether *in* Europe. Only thus may he come to know that Europe, as well as America, is vitally constitutive of that larger world in which, in order to realize his full capacities as American, he must henceforth live. To say this is to overread a little, perhaps—and to see in Newman the first full-blown sign of James' discovery of the American as International Hero. One is at least justified in saying it by James' designation of *The American* as one of his "more advanced" novels, albeit the simplest one. In the novels which come after *The American*, the central figure tends most often to be an American girl—one of a series of young women increasingly conscious of their capacity for the total humanism into which their European adventures lead them. James was eloquent witness of the transformation of the American Adam into an American Eve. When a man is the central figure, as in *The Ambassadors*, he is made out to be more passive than is Newman of *The American*, and also considerably less heroic, precisely because he is capable of *knowing* more.

As Constance Rourke long ago pointed out, Newman is James' version of a traditional hero of American fiction, the Westerner. James early reports:

> It was our friend's eye that chiefly told his story; an eye in which innocence and experience were singularly

blended. It was full of contradictory suggestions; and though it was by no means the glowing orb of a hero of romance, you could find in it almost anything you looked for. Frigid yet friendly, frank yet cautious, shrewd yet credulous, positive yet sceptical, confident yet shy, extremely intelligent and extremely good-humoured, there was something vaguely defiant in its concessions, and something profoundly reassuring in its reserve.

His is "an intensely Western story," we are told a little later; and a few salient details are supplied as the story develops—that Newman has made much of his money in the West; that he has known frontier life and lived it fully; that his frontier energies have made him enormously successful in business and in the Civil War too; and more. When we are told that his was "the instinct of the practical man, who had made up his mind what he wanted, and was now beginning to take active steps to obtain it"—when we are told this mid-way in the novel, we have already a sense of the origins of that instinct. Hence we are prepared better than Newman for the revelation of its limitations. Newman does in fact have what one of the Bellegarde's friends calls his "légende"; but it is, in an America fast coming of age, a "plain prose version of the legend of El Dorado."

Life for Newman, when he first comes on to the international scene, is a pretty simple affair. And he has a way of relating himself simply to others and so of making it appropriate that James' rendering of the character of the others is also simple—too simple, we may say after the fact. It is here most clearly that James' art in *The American* is of a different order from his art in some of the later "advanced" novels. For there is a kind of unrelieved super-subtle air of corruption about Urbain de Bellegarde and his mother. Young Valentin de Bellegarde is thereby made out to be singular—

too singular—to the degree that he does not carry this air. And Madame de Cintré, Madame de Bellegarde's daughter, is by the same token a saint—as indeed she is claimed to be. So too with the others—Nioche and his daughter and Lord Deepmere—who at times seem to be living parodies of what, when we consider the facts of the case realistically, they might well have been. Together, they comprise a world that Newman never made but one which nevertheless comports well with that American world which has in fact made him. They are projections not so much of Newman's sensibility, but of the sensibility of the culture which made him. Did James not know so much about Newman and tell it to us, we might have a right to carry out all the way our realistic consideration of the facts of the case. Then we would have only Newman's sensibility, stripped of its antecedents, completely there; and we would be obliged to learn to read James in such a way as to discriminate between Newman's world as it forces itself into his waiting consciousness and what we can infer about the facts of the case. But this is the method of the later novels of the "advanced" class. In *The American* the method is of a different kind.

When toward the end of the novel, Newman goes for his last glimpse of Claire de Cintré, now "safe" among the Carmelite nuns, he feels that his situation is "too strange and too mocking to be real; it [is] like a page torn out of a romance, with no context in his own experience." In short, it partakes of melodrama; and in the rest of the novel he must see the melodrama all the way through. Suffering it, he rises above it. Newman's American character has led him into an essentially melodramatic situation, as it has made of him a naïf for whom the constitution of any world beyond his own must be by necessity melodramatic. In melodrama probable cause and effect are relatively inoperative; and passions, ideas, and actions are everywhere "unreasonably" exaggerated. Even the laws of "romance" no longer hold; for, to paraphrase James' words, melodrama is romance out of context. And Newman is a character most appropriate to a romance—to a story by Hawthorne or Melville or Mark Twain. But he *is* out of context, and his view of things will not hold. The hero of a romance lives in a world in which meaningfulness is guaranteed not by manners or morals or institutions but by a shared assurance that men move according to instincts which everyone can know, understand, and depend upon. Out of context, the instincts become meaningless—unless, as is the case with Newman, he whose instincts they are can will them into a means of transcending his new context and so perhaps of understanding it. In any event, *The American* is a melodrama because Newman's view of life is melodramatic; and our need for a satisfactory sense of "probability" in art is satisfied, because a man like Newman might instinctively—we can say unconsciously—design his adventures thus. What he fails to take into account is the fact that his native view of life will not necessarily obtain in other contexts, specifically in the international context. That he acts in such a way as to enlarge his view and make it obtain—if only in defeat: thereby hangs James' tale.

Perhaps it is safer to say that in *The American* James has designed a story which is appropriate to Newman's view of life. The plot has a symmetry which is wholly appropriate to melodrama. Newman is at the center. The Bellegardes are ranged around him, each answering to an aspect of his melodramatic vision: Claire, the ideal woman, his "dream realised," as he says; Valentin, virtually one of the Three Musketeers; Urbain de Bellegarde and his mother, embodiments of an impulse toward preservation of old institutions grown so strong as to evolve an instinct exactly contrary to that which dominates Newman. The Nioches, father and daughter, are lower-class analogues of the Bellegardes—only they are, necessarily, more "realistic." They have to climb, and it amuses Newman to see them climbing. He can cope with the Nioches as he can't with the Belle-gardes, The Bellegardes are dominated by the past; the Nioches, by the future. Newman is above all a person of the here and now. Mlle. Nioche is to Valentin de Bellegarde as Mme. de Cintré is to Newman; as Valen-tin helps Newman for the good—by encouraging him in his suit for Mme. de Cintré's hand, so Newman helps Valentin for the bad—by being, however unwilling, an agent for bringing Valentin and Mlle. de Nioche to-gether. The novel really begins with Newman's asking Mlle. de Nioche about the price of one of her "copies" of paintings in the Louvre: "Combien?"—which is vir-tually the only French word he knows. And it comes to the beginning of the end with Mme. de Belle-garde's asking Newman, "How rich?"—which are vir-tually the only English (or American) words which mean anything to her. And Mrs. Bread's revelation of the guilt of Mme. de Bellegarde and Urbain—this too, with its aura of secret meetings and dying words, is of a piece with the melodrama. Everything seems to fit, as in melodrama it should.

However, the point is that in the end something does not fit—that Newman discovers what it is to be out of context. And so the melodrama becomes a means of transcending melodrama and achieving the under-standing of art—in which finally everything once more seems necessary and fitting, in context. But almost from the very beginning of the novel, we are urged to believe that Newman has the capacity to transcend his melodramatic adventures, that he has strong defenses against his instincts for melodrama. This is his gift for what at one point James explicitly calls "American humour." Again and again we are reminded that he can joke, that he can often enough see the grotesque and absurd sides of his new as well as of his old life. At another point, James gives details:

> Newman had sat with Western humorists in knots, round castiron stoves, and seen "tall" stories grow taller without toppling over, and his own imagination had learned the trick of piling up consistent wonders.

In some deep, almost unconscious way Newman realizes that his affair with the Bellegardes is a "consistent wonder," therefore a "tall" story.

A famous passage from James' study of Hawthorne (published in England the same year as the first English edition of *The American*) furnishes a crucial gloss here. It is the passage in which James, wondering how it was possible for a man to be a novelist in a culture which furnished him so little to write about, begins by citing all the institutions of high society which America lacks: "No state, in the European sense of the word, and indeed barely a specific national name. No sovereign, no court, no personal loyalty, no aristocracy, no church. . . ." The passage goes on at length in this way, until:

> The natural remark, in the almost lurid light of such an indictment, would be that if these things are left out, everything is left out. The American knows that a good deal remains; what it is that remains—that is his secret, his joke, as one may say. It would be cruel, in this terrible denudation, to deny him the consolation of his natural gift, that "American humour" of which of late years we have heard so much.

James' Notebooks show that he originally intended the passage for a "story"—as a summary comment on one such as Newman? In any case, along with Newman's instinct for melodrama goes an instinct for humor; and the latter makes the former possible for art. That is, until that point in *The American* when the Bellegardes have forced Mme. de Cintré to withdraw her pledge to marry Newman, and James writes:

> All that he understood, in his deep and simple indigna-
> tion, was that the matter was not a violent joke, and
> that the people before him were perfectly serious.

From this point on, "American humour" cannot be much of a consolation, and Newman must summon up from its deepest sources within himself that integrity which will in the end force him to see that any venge- ance on the Bellegardes would be meaningless. Still, it might well be that such integrity—whereby the Ameri- can can measure the meaningfulness of things—is also the source of "American humour." It is the integrity of the hero of the romance, in context or out.

And James himself is something of a humorist, and so has his own defenses against the improbabilities of the melodramatic. He delights in comic scenes and epi- sodes—Newman's early talks with M. Nioche, Newman and his confidante Mrs. Tristram talking over the head of her stupid husband, Newman's travels with the seri- ous Mr. Babcock, Newman being studied at the Belle- garde's huge party, Valentin de Bellegarde with Mlle. Nioche, Mlle. Nioche in England with Lord Deepmere, even Newman meditating on Mme. de Cintré's Catholi- cism. The tone here, managed most often by under- or overstated dialogue, goes counter to that of the melo- drama and thereby points it up. In a "romantically" comic scene, Mme. de Cintré, having finished telling a fairy tale to her niece, tells Newman: "I like to talk with [children], . . . we can talk with them so much more seriously than with grown persons. That is great nonsense that I have been telling Blanche, but it is a great deal more serious than most of what we say in society." And Newman laughs and replies: "I wish you would talk to me, then, as if I were Blanche's age." Newman can go along with James' joke, because James

251

makes it the quintessential joke that the American must learn to tell about himself.

Moreover, James himself would—by way of essential make-believe—convince us that he disavows responsibility for Newman's story, jokes and all. Granting that Newman is what he is, granting that Newman did what he did, this is how it was. James, to use a phrase of his, "goes behind" Newman steadily—but "goes behind" him as a biographer would. One is made to feel that in this novel all is over before the novelist (as biographer) begins to tell it; and that he is "merely" reconstituting it, filling it out, so as to make us see how it really was—melodrama, American humor, pathetic-heroic denouement and all. In the later novels of the "advanced" class, the case is different; there we are made to feel that all is happening now—that the novelist's art is to make the "then" into "now." There James not only "goes behind" but "goes into." Here he is the helplessly honest biographer; and when he comments, it is explicitly after the fact and doesn't really make much difference to the progress of the story except to free its teller from responsibility for everything but telling the truth. When Newman looks at the Bellegardes' villa at Poitiers and says "to himself," " 'It looks like a Chinese penitentiary,' " James breaks Newman's sentence in two with "—and I give the comparison for what it is worth—. . . ." The device is habitual in the novel and serves to remind us not only where we stand, but where Henry James stands: on the outside, "going behind," but only to return to the outside, with us.

There is a prime irony in the fact that James in his art should have protected himself thus. For in actuality his view of the French was, at the time he was writing *The American*, at least as melodramatic as Newman's. Writing the reviews and essays which in 1878 he collected as *French Poets and Novelists*, he regularly remarks that, whatever their powers of temperament and style, the French are on the whole terribly flawed moralists. He wrote his friend Howells in May 1876: "Of pure Parisianism I see absolutely nothing . . ."; and to his brother William later the same year, he admitted his ". . . long encroaching weariness and satiety with the French mind and its utterance" and declared, "I have got nothing important out of Paris nor am likely to." James' naïveté here (for surely that is what it is) is notorious. But it was during part of these "French years" that he wrote *The American*. And we can rightly wonder that his art was by then sufficiently developed to let him add his own melodramatic naïveté to Newman's and then, as novelist, clear himself of responsibility by making himself out to be a helplessly honest biographer of an *almost* helplessly honest man. James, then, had a natural gift for a kind of American humor too.

But in 1907, fully at home in England, James was dissatisfied with *The American*. The Preface to the New York Edition version of the novel gives more than eloquent testimony to his dissatisfaction. It was, he felt, too simple a novel. It was, he wrote, an "arch-romance," yet still had a certain power:

> The thing is consistently, consummately—and I would fain really make bold to say charmingly—romantic; and all without intention, presumption, hesitation, contrition. The effect is equally undesigned and unabashed, and I lose myself, at this late hour, I am bound to add, in a certain sad envy of the free play of so much unchallenged instinct. One would like to woo back such hours of fine precipitation.[2]

The problem of *The American*, then, was the problem of "the romance":

[2] *The Novels and Tales of Henry James*, New York Edition, Volume I, *The American* (New York, 1907), p. x.

The only *general* attribute of projected romance that I can see, the only one that fits all its cases, is the fact of the kind of experience with which it deals—experience liberated, so to speak; experience disengaged, disembroiled, disencumbered, exempt from the conditions that we usually know to attach to it and, if we wish so to put the matter, drag upon it, and operating in a medium which relieves it, in a particular interest, of the inconvenience of a *related*, a measurable state, a state subject to all our vulgar communities. The greatest intensity may so be arrived at evidently—when the sacrifice of community, of the "related" sides of situations, has not been too rash. It must to this end not flagrantly betray itself; we must even be kept if possible, for our illusion, from suspecting any sacrifice at all. The balloon of experience is in fact of course tied to the earth, and under that necessity we swing, thanks to a rope of remarkable length, in the more or less commodious car of the imagination; but it is by the rope we know where we are, and from the moment that cable is cut we are at large and unrelated: we only swing apart from the globe—though remaining as exhilarated, naturally, as we like, especially when all goes well. The art of the romancer is, "for the fun of it," insidiously to cut the cable, to cut it without our detecting him. What I have recognised in "The American," much to my surprise and after long years, is that the experience here represented is the disconnected and uncontrolled experience—uncontrolled by our general sense of "the way things happen"—which romance alone more or less successfully palms off on us. It is a case of Newman's own intimate experience all, that being my subject, the thread of which, from beginning to end, is not once exchanged, however momentarily, for any other thread; and the experience of the others concerning us, and concerning him, only so far as it touches him and as he recognises, feels or divines it. There is

a general sense of the way things happen–it abides
with us indefeasibly, as readers of fiction, from the
moment we demand that our fiction shall be intelligi-
ble; and there is our particular sense of the way they
don't happen, which is liable to wake up unless reflex-
ion and criticism, in us, have been skillfully and successfully drugged. There are drugs enough, clearly–
it is all a way of applying them with tact; in which
case the way things don't happen may be artfully made
to pass for the way things do.[3]

This is in fact only one of a number of James' luridly
honest indictments of his earlier self and his earlier art.
It might well furnish all of us who would be like that
"young man from Texas" the basis for an inquiry into
the art and achievement of the first version of *The
American*, and also an introduction to the "advanced"
novels. The cable *is* cut in *The American*, one might
say; and then point out that James convinces us that
Newman himself has cut it–for the American fun of it;
or perhaps that it has not been quite as strong as Newman's American instincts have led him to believe.
James' manner, thus his method, in this *American* is
to convince us (does he indeed drug us?) that the experience in any case is not ours but Newman's and
that, kept back, held off, by the creature's humor and
the creator's helpless objectivity, we are still at the end
on the ground, waiting for Newman to come back to
earth. We have a certain assurance that when he does
he will henceforth act according to our "general sense
of the way things happen." More's the pity, one might
say. Because when he does so, his name and character
will be those of Lambert Strether; and he will be not
an adventurer but an ambassador.

James' words also furnish us a basis for understanding what he intended to achieve with his revisions of

[3] *Ibid.*, pp. xvii-xviii.

The American. He tried, but in vain, to make it into something like the later "advanced" novels. The plot is meant to be tightened, but it only thickens. And Newman is endowed with a kind of sensibility which is simply inappropriate to his conduct and character. Things are indeed more likely to happen this way, we say, but not to a man like this. The heart of the matter lies in James' way of modifying the way we see Newman. I give a few examples. At one point in the first version, Newman says, "I am not intellectual." He says at the same point in the New York Edition, "I don't come up to my own standard of culture." At a slightly later point, Newman says in the first version, "I am a highly civilized man"; whereas at this point in the New York Edition, he says, "I have the instincts—have them deeply—if I haven't the form of a high civilization." The latter is virtually a new Newman; and since his adventures are changed in no essential way, the self-consciousness James gives him is much too acute for the kind of melodrama he lives out. The new Newman is on the edge of being melodramatic in the bad sense, his behavior not redeemable by his humor nor adequately explicable of the continuing reference to his Western background.

One further example, a longer one. (I take the examples from an excellent study of the two versions of the novel, Royal Gettman's "Henry James's Revision of *The American*," *American Literature*, xvi [1945], 279-295, and advise those interested in the matter to begin there.) In the first version, Newman meditates thus on what he has been able to do for Madame de Cintré:

> She was a woman for the light, not for the shade; and her natural line was not picturesque reserve and mysterious melancholy, but frank, joyous, brilliant action, with just so much meditation as was necessary, and not a grain more. To this, apparently, he had succeeded in bringing her back. He felt, himself,

that he was an antidote to oppressive secrets; what he offered her was, in fact, above all things a vast sunny immunity from the need of having any.

All this is a quite reasonable inference from Newman's actions, speeches, and character; and the last sentence manifests his melodramatic certitude in his mission. In the New York Edition, the equivalent passage reads thus:

> She was a creature for the sun and the air, for no sort of hereditary shade or equivocal gloom; and her natural line was neither imposed reserve nor mysterious melancholy, but positive life, the life of the great world—*his* great world, not the *grand monde* as there understood if he wasn't mistaken, which seemed squeezable into a couple of rooms of that inconvenient and ill-warmed house: all with nothing worse to brood about, when necessary, than the mystery perhaps of the happiness that would so queerly have come to her. To some perception of his view and his judgment, and of the patience with which he was prepared to insist on them, he fondly believed himself to be day by day bringing her round. She might n't, she could n't yet, no doubt, wholly fall in with them, but she saw, he made out, that he had built a bridge which would bear the very greatest weight she should throw on it, and it was for him often, all charmingly, as if she were admiring from this side and that the bold span of arch and the high line of the parapet—as indeed on occasion she stood straight there at the spring, just watching him at *his* extremity and with nothing, when the hour should strike, to prevent her crossing with a rush.

Now Newman "fondly" believes; and the irony communicated by the word forces James to go on and to impute to Newman a quality of sympathetic introspec-

tion which he just can't have and be Christopher Newman. Not this early, before the denouement—before his
discovery that his integrity makes him liable to a weakness which, if only it can be brought into play on the
international scene, if only it can make its possesser
part of that scene, will be transformed into a strength.
Written-up like this, the hero of the arch-romance can
no longer have as his goal the liberating discipline of
his power as a self among selves. In effect, the struggle is over before it begins. Here James *does* cut the
cable for the fun of it—part of the fun being in his
showing us exactly how he does it. This is brilliant expertise, but no longer art.

We can gainsay the Preface to the New York Edition
revision of *The American,* because James in making
the revisions gainsays himself. Or so I think any honest
young man from Texas would have to decide, were he
to embark on a study of the "advanced" novels and carry it through to the end. Surely he would have to decide
that the later novels reveal a quality of sheer "making"
not present in *The American;* and he would as surely
have to decide that his experience of the later novels
is richer than that of *The American,* because their
protagonists' experience so firmly shapes and controls
his—indeed, virtually *becomes* his experience. In *The
American,* because James works to put the reader off
from the experience of its protagonist, such richness is
simply not possible, because not intended, because inappropriate. All of which goes to show that James' fictive world is full of a great number of things: a fact
which it perhaps was not so important for the elderly
James to grasp as it would be for that young man from
Texas, and all of us for whom he stands as surrogate.

I should guess that James found the first version of
The American unsatisfactory because when he made
it into a fairly successful play in 1890, he perforce had
to turn it into a melodrama in which drawing-room

comedy had to serve as an unsatisfactory substitute for American humor. And getting deeply into the play, he was working in a genre wherein his auditors, brought into the presence of a "living" Newman, could hardly see him as one whose story was being rendered by a helplessly objective biographer. The play had to have a happy ending befitting unrelieved melodrama; further, in a revision of the last act, James even allowed Valentin de Bellegarde to survive his duel—which in the play is with Lord Deepmere. Perhaps the memory of the play screened James' memory of the first version of *The American*. At least it would seem that some of his harder remarks in the New York Edition fit the play better than the earlier novel. And some of the unseemly sharpening of motivation which he put into the revision originates in the play.

But then, even some of the readers of the first version of *The American* were a little bewildered by its special kind of melodrama. James' friend, William Dean Howells, then editor of *The Atlantic Monthly*, wrote him that he could not see why *The American* could not, on its own terms, have a happy ending. James replied exasperatedly in March 1877 that Mme. de Cintré and Newman would have made an "impossible couple."

Still, the reviewer of the novel in the July 1877 *Atlantic Monthly* (influenced by Howells?) wrote:

> The plot having been turned into the channel of intrigue, therefore, our aesthetic sense is not satisfied by the event here led up to. Mr. James pleads indirectly for a judgment that this issue was made inevitable by the character of Newman. It was his "fundamental good-nature," we are told, which caused him to refrain from publishing the Bellegarde secret to the *beau monde*; and on this good-nature the Bellegardes relied. Perhaps we ought to accept this reasoning, but

it seems to us that good-nature is a meagre excuse for a man so profoundly in love as Newman with Madame de Cintré. . . . The logic of fiction is not that of philosophy, and this story might have had a different ending without defeating consistency.

The novel that the reviewer wanted might well have been called *Old Tom Sawyer Abroad*; or better, it might well have been written by Old Tom Sawyer himself—an adult version of the raid on the Sunday School picnic in *Huckleberry Finn*. The logic of *The American* is surely not the logic of philosophy, even James' own. It is the logic of Newman's character, an aspect of the logic of the culture which at once made him into a melodramatist and gave him the means to save himself alive just when he was about to lose himself in his own melodramatics. The means was his "natural gift," that American humor, about which the reviewer, unlike James, seems not to have heard very much. The joke, then, is on the reviewer; perhaps even on the later James; surely on us if, entering on the international scene, we would still make the world over into our own image. Perhaps Newman's example, if we can take the joke, is meant to teach us that we might begin to save ourselves if we dare learn the lesson of his life— as James did. I cannot but think that the example taught James how he might conceive of those later, larger protagonists who so richly inhabit the other "advanced" novels on the list he drew up for the young man from Texas.

1962

10

WALLACE STEVENS:
The Last Lesson of the Master

"Brother, he's our father!"
THEODORE ROETHKE, *"A Rouse for Wallace Stevens"*

ACCEPTING the National Book Award in 1955 (for his *Collected Poems*), Wallace Stevens said:

> Now, at seventy-five, as I look back on the little that I have done and as I turn the pages of my own poems gathered together in a single volume, I have no choice except to paraphrase the old verse that says that it is not what I am, but what I aspired to be that comforts me. It is not what I have written but what I should like to have written that constitutes my true poems, the uncollected poems which I have not had the strength to realize.

These words proclaim not only Stevens' imperious modesty but the central being and import of his works: that, as in its totality it forever projected an "ultimate poem," the ground of all poetry, the assured existence of the *possibility* of poetry, it was the work "of the mind in the act of finding / What will suffice." The lines I quote are from "Of Modern Poetry," which is followed almost immediately in the *Collected Poems* by "The Well Dressed Man with a Beard," whose last line is "It can never be satisfied, the mind, never." Both poems were first collected in *Parts of a World* (1942), which is in Stevens' work a kind of resting-place and occasion for self-assessment. In the collections which came after, beginning with *Transport to Summer* (1947), Stevens moved into regions whose rarefied ambiance was yet vigorous enough to sustain the spirit of the man who to his dying days appears to have insisted (the words are from his *Adagia*) that "God is a postulate of the ego."

His later work in the main records the quest of one whose reality principle was so capacious that, through the labors of the mind, it could be made to yield the very means by which it might be transcended, then enlarged—its fullest capacity at long last revealed. (The end of the process was that which Stevens came to call "abstraction"; the method, that which he came to call "decreation.") It had to be not the product of instinct but the cause, indeed not a principle but a kind of sublime therapeutic agent (Stevens would come to say "cure") whereby the limitations that it marked out might be broken through. Again and again in his later poetry Stevens sought to fix once and for all the instant of the breaking-through. In "The Novel" (collected in *The Auroras of Autumn*) a man sits before a fire and reads. The novel he is reading takes hold of him and his little world and transforms them from the merely real to the vitally unreal, the sheer life, in which they have their source. "The fire burns as the novel taught it how." Note: not "*as if* the novel taught it how"; for in its art the novel directly renders appearance into reality and so forces upon the reader the knowledge that the unreal is in the end the real:

> The arrangement of the chairs is so and so,
>
> Not as one would have arranged them for oneself,
> But in the style of the novel, its tracing
> Of an unfamiliar in the familiar room,
>
> *A retrato* that is strong because it is like,
> A second that grows first, a black unreal
> In which a real lies hidden and alive.

The reader is an Argentine; he is reading Camus, but might as well be reading Cervantes. Still, as the poem does its work, the little anecdote proves to be not about the Argentine but about the poet and his reader:

> It is odd, too, how that Argentine is oneself,
> Feeling the fear that creeps beneath the wool,
> Lies on the breast and pierces into the heart,
>
> Straight from the Arcadian imagination,
> Its being beating heavily in the veins,
> Its knowledge cold within one as one's own;
>
> And one trembles to be so understood and, at last,
> To understand, as if to know became
> The fatality of seeing things too well.

Understanding oneself in poetry of this order, then, is to be understood. In the working of the poem the dissatisfactions of the poet's mind become the dissatisfactions of the reader's. Time at best has not a stop but a pause. In its very form and function, the poem is an instance of the reality principle working to achieve its necessary ends as it is empowered by the imagination.

So far as I know, Stevens never uses Freud's term "reality principle," although, striving to "face Freud" (as he said in the lecture "Imagination as Value"), he suggested that in our world there must be a "science of illusions" in which "the imagination" would be "the clue to reality"—which I take to signify an acceptance of the idea of the "reality principle." For surely in the poems before *Transport to Summer* and *The Auroras of Autumn* that is what it is—a terribly bounded assurance of what, in the nature of things, our limitations in this world of rocks and stones and trees "really" are. Thus in "The Snow Man" (1923) the poet is satisfied to know that "One must have a mind of winter" in order to see winter's world as it "really" is; one must imagine oneself as one with "the frost and the boughs / Of the pine-trees crusted with snow" and all else that constitutes the hard particularities of the season and its place. One would "not . . . think / of any misery in the sound of the wind"; for that would be an act of "reading into." One would not try to understand if one wanted absolutely to know. But then one would be

> . . . the listener, who listens in the snow,
> And, nothing himself, beholds
> Nothing that is not there and the nothing that is.

The syntax of these negatives is the syntax necessary to the poetic imagination if it is to comprehend its limitations, so to acknowledge them. The listener, become a snow man, is given to realize that, insofar as he is willing not to try to interpret the natural world as metaphor for the human, he *can* know. Hence he would be nothing himself, and so would be able to behold everything (this is the bearing of the double negative in the last line) that is there—in and of itself, descrete, neither composed nor interpreted. But everything, beheld in this non-human fashion, would add up to nothing, as would he. So too in "Anecdote of the Jar" (1923), the poet, figuring himself as composing, so interpreting, so making amenable to human understanding, the wilds of Tennessee by placing a jar upon a hill, must at the end conclude by postulating the necessarily negative syntax of the imagination as it seeks this order of knowledge.

> It took dominion everywhere.
> The jar was gray and bare.
> It did not give of bird or bush,
> Like nothing else in Tennessee.

To take dominion accordingly is to compose the world, not even in imagination (as in "The Snow Man") to see it as it "really" is. Still, to compose thus is to remind oneself that, beyond our capacity to comprehend, there is "reality," and that such "reality," whatever else it may be, is not a product of human will or imagination. The poet negates (not murders) to create (not dissect). But he creates only himself in the act of creating.

"The Snow Man" and "Anecdote of the Jar" of course are *Harmonium* poems. The situation they pose is, in *Harmonium*, essentially the situation of a number of protagonists who would live through it and achieve more than the lyrical quiescence and satisfaction they offer. The Worms at Heaven's Gate, in the poem by that name, speak of Badroulbadour, within their bellies, whom they bring out of the tomb piece by piece, now on her way to being restored to reality. They negate in fact, not in imagination, and are anti-poets, the only sort who *could* so directly "celebrate" reality. The High-Toned Old Christian Woman, in the poem of that name, is told—in an early announcement of one of Stevens' major themes—that "Poetry is the supreme fiction. . . ." Her moral law composes reality into a church; but then, the poets "opposing law" composes the world into an anti-church. And who is to choose?—even if such "fictive things/. . . wink most when widows wince." The Emperor of Ice Cream leaves off his cigar-rolling to whip such "concupiscent curds" as will serve properly to let those attending a wake for one now absolutely cold and dumb know that "be" must "be finale of seem," as the return to reality must be the inevitable end of the sojourn in the life of the imagination. Still, "The only emperor is the emperor of ice-cream," and the wake itself is a continuing sojourn in the imagination, as is life fully lived. So too, the protagonist in "Sunday Morning," who cannot will herself (if indeed she would) to be a High-Toned Old Christian Woman, comes to know that

> We live in an old chaos of the sun,
> Or old dependency of day and night,
> Or island solitude, unsponsored, free,
> Of that wide water, inescapable.

She depends upon a "reality" she cannot know directly, much less understand. But she will not by that token accept Christianity—however powerful a surrogate for reality it might be, precisely because it is a surrogate. She must compose her life out of the reality she is given, supreme fiction or no. Which is to say, she must compose her self.

In *Ideas of Order* (1936) and *Parts of a World* (1942), the volumes which immediately precede *Transport to Summer* (1947) and *The Auroras of Autumn* (1950), Stevens set himself further to meditate on the implications of his sense of human boundedness. The poems collected in those volumes have a certain, quite deliberate discursiveness—that of the poet who would run the risk of dialectics. The principal poems in these volumes indeed are quite explicitly poems about poetry, or the process whereby poems—figured as central for the exercise of the imagination—come into being. The most celebrated poem in the first of these volumes, "The Idea of Order at Key West," turns on this line: "But it was she and not the sea we heard." Even if there appears to be a congruence between the words of the woman singing beside the sea and the sea itself,

> . . . she was the maker of the song she sang.
> The ever-hooded, tragic-gestured sea
> Was merely a place by which she walked to sing.

And these lines immediately follow:

> Whose spirit is this? we said, because we knew
> It was the spirit that we sought and knew
> That we should ask this often as she sang.

Reality, then, in Stevens' iterated use of the word in his prose, is the place by (and in and through) which we walk as we sing. Singing, we may well sing reality, but by way of composition, not creation, not even something so self-comforting as transformation.

Moving beyond the limits of these "dialectical" poems, Stevens in "The Poems of Our Climate" (collected in *Parts of a World*) begins by writing what amounts to an "objectivist" poem, then recalls the mood of "The Snow Man" and, in his dialectical searching, is unsatisfied:

> Clear water in a brilliant bowl,
> Pink and white carnations. The light
> In the room more like a snowy air,
> Reflecting snow. A newly-fallen snow
> At the end of winter when afternoons return.
> Pink and white carnations—one desires
> So much more than that. The day itself
> Is simplified: a bowl of white
> Cold, a cold porcelain, low and round,
> With nothing more than the carnations there.

Here the sequence of noun phrases, broken only by the "one desires . . ." clause, carries the negative syntax of the end of "The Snow Man" and "Anecdote of the Jar" one step farther—since the negation has been performed, as it were, before this part of the poem was composed. The poem, except for that one fateful clause, is made out to be bereft of the poet. There follows a second stanza:

> Say even that this complete simplicity
> Stripped one of all one's torments, concealed
> The evilly compounded, vital I
> And made it fresh in a world of white,
> A world of clear water, brilliant-edged
> Still one would want more, one would need more
> More than a world of white and snowy scents.

This simplicity is that of "nothing" in "The Snow Man," cleansed of that "vital I" who, being such, could, if he would, hear "misery in the sound of the wind," and would surely understand it as an aspect of his "torments." For the earlier Stevens, it was enough simply

267

to *know* boundedness as such. Now he would indeed *understand* it. Thus the third stanza:

> There would still remain the never-resting mind,
> So that one would want to escape, come back
> To what had been so long composed.
> The imperfect is our paradise.
> Note that, in this bitterness, delight,
> Since the imperfect is so hot in us,
> Lies in flawed words and stubborn sounds.

It had been characteristic, I think, of Stevens' *Harmonium* poems that their end was to put the mind at rest—to push the imagination through lyrical and dramatic exercises whereby, realizing its limitations, it would achieve a certain stasis, if only temporary. Now there is not even a temporary stasis. The first lines of another *Parts of a World* poem, "Of Modern Poetry," put it bluntly:

> The poem of the mind in the act of finding
> What will suffice. . . .

Even, that is to say, as Stevens was projecting what I have called his terribly bounded assurance of what our limitations are, he was perfecting a poetic mode—I have called it dialectical—which would, in its power and precision, take him beyond the very limits he had so painstakingly traced out.

2.

For by the time of "The Rock," the most powerful of the poems first collected in his seventy-fifth year, the assurance had become unbounded, was felt to exist only as it might lead to a certitude in unboundedness. Of the "rock" of reality Stevens could write that man must no longer rest satisfied with knowing it mediately, in poems:

We must be cured of it by a cure of the ground
Or a cure of ourselves, that is equal to a cure

Of the ground, a cure beyond forgetfulness.

Wanting to know so much, wanting in one's knowledge
to be so much—this is a kind of disease, the only cure
for which is more of the same. It is wanting to have
God's mind. It is being willing, thereby, to be responsible for God's thoughts—which are "reality." In this
Stevens, the propositions which emerge from "Notes
toward a Supreme Fiction" (1942) and "Esthétique du
Mal" (1945), both collected in *Transport to Summer*,
are developed *in extremis*. Man suffers as God suffers
so that he may, with God, suffer the world to suffer.

If the "cure" is successful, if man can will its success,
"reality"—the sad, gay, infinitely fragmented world of
which man is a part—will surely turn out to be a kind of
mind, the kind which Stevens most often called "imagination." Then the world, the "real" world, which the act
of the mind has rendered into poems and so fragmented, would, if the process were pushed far enough,
finally be made whole once more. But it would be the
mind's world. God would be of His earth, the earth
would be of its God, and all would be right with the
world. Because it would be the mind's world. Of this
ultimately "real" world, Stevens wrote at the end of
"The Rock":

It is the rock where tranquil must adduce
Its tranquil self, the main of things, the mind

The starting point of the human and the end,
That in which space itself is contained, the gate
To the enclosure, day, the things illumined

By day, night and that which night illumines,
Night and its midnight-minting fragrances,
Night's hymn of the rock, as in a vivid sleep.

The mind, then, would be satisfied—but only in a world like the one in this poem, where the thing contained has become the container; only in a sleep vivid enough to be the sleep of revelation; only, in the title of another late poem, when man can know himself as "A Child Asleep in Its Own Life." God is a revelation of the ego, because reality is.

There remained, however, life day-to-day—with the never-to-be-satisfied mind seeing and knowing reality so sharply as to know itself absolutely cut off from what it sees and knows. Day-to-day, indeed, one might have his proper doubts about the vivid sleep and its night hymn to the power of the mind. Thus Stevens put at the end of his *Collected Poems*, six pages after the ultimate affirmation of "The Rock," this poem, called "Not Ideas about the Thing but the Thing Itself." Note: Not even "thing-*in*-itself," but "thing itself."

> At the earliest ending of winter,
> In March, a scrawny cry from outside
> Seemed like a sound in his mind.
>
> He knew that he heard it,
> A bird's cry, at daylight or before,
> In the early March wind.
>
> The sun was rising at six,
> No longer a battered panache above snow . . .
> It would have been outside.
>
> It was not from the vast ventriloquism
> Of sleep's faded papier-mâché . . .
> The sun was coming from outside.
>
> That scrawny cry—it was
> A chorister whose c preceded the choir.
> It was part of the colossal sun,
>
> Surrounded by its choral rings,
> Still far away. It was like
> A new knowledge of reality.

Here the poet figures himself as being waked by a sound, and then gradually figures that sound—coming at the end of winter, out of the hard, bright morning—as being part of a reality which is absolutely "outside" him. The reward is something "like a new knowledge of reality," as bird and sun are discovered to be colossally present. The cost is the acknowledgment that it is all "far away," "outside." Here the effect of the poet's imaging is to see that, if the image is true to the reality which it bodies forth, it is not the poet's image but its own. The "Seemed" in "Seemed like a sound in his mind" is, as the poem moves, the first, most facile, therefore most mistaken, attempt of the poet to satisfy his mind. But once the mind begins its act, it acts to dissatisfy itself, so as far as it can to be true to the reality of that bright early spring morning. Even so, it cannot be entirely true to that reality. Its mediating presence is registered quite minimally, by that "like" in the next-to-last line. Inside the mind the cry is "scrawny." Outside, it *is*—not is *of*—"A chorister whose c preceded the choir." (The repetition of "*c*"-"pre*c*eded" makes for a kind of pun in which subject is incorporated into verb, all the more to identify it in its absoluteness.) The terrible knowledge earned here is, in the words of one of the *Adagia*, that "What reality lacks is a *noeud vital* with life." The poet's *noeud vital*, which is with himself, at least lets him be the first to face this as a fact.

And, thinking back to "The Rock," we may ask: Did "Night's hymn of the rock" also issue "from the vast ventriloquism / Of sleep's faded papier-mâché . . ."? No. But then "The Rock" is an old man's poem. The first section is called "*Seventy Years Later*" and begins by questioning the kind and range of certitude which are celebrated in "Not Ideas . . .":

It is an illusion that we were ever alive,
Lived in the houses of mothers, arranged ourselves
By our own motions in a freedom of air.

271

Regard the freedom of seventy years ago,
It is no longer air. The houses still stand,
Though they are rigid in rigid emptiness.

Even our shadows, their shadows, no longer remain.
The lives these lived in the mind are at an end.
They never were . . . The sounds of the guitar

Were not and are not. Absurd. The words spoken
Were not and are not.

Of course, "Not Ideas . . ." is an old man's poem too.
But it is not a matter of chronology; for there is no
proper sense of history in Stevens' conception of the
poet's work. ("All history is modern history," he wrote
in the *Adagia*, and meant it.) Instead there is, especially in the later work, a sense of a pure, a-temporal dialectical movement, a fateful opting for one of a pair of
radically opposed alternatives. And so in "Not Ideas
. . . ," sounds like those of Stevens' blue guitar "are"
again, as in "The Rock" they "are not."

I have cited "The Rock" and "Not Ideas . . ." because
Stevens placed them in the *Collected Poems* where
they would mark the extreme, dialectically opposed
tendencies in his work—tendencies which, as we shall
see, he began to resolve only at the very end of his life
in a handful of poems in the *Opus Posthumous*. His
later poems (I mean those from the *Transport to Summer* collection through "The Rock" and "Not Ideas
. . .") characteristically begin by showing us how we
may catch ourselves in the act of reaching out toward
some segment of reality—a place, a person, anything
that is an "other" and therefore may seem to be merely
an "object." The goal is that knowledge in whose perfection we may rest secure. As the poems develop, we
are made to realize that what we do in fact know is not
a segment of reality but ourselves in the act of reaching
out. A segment then is the result of segmenting; reaching out is grasping and seizing upon, shaping. At this

point, the poems may move toward one of two ends: toward celebrating the power of the subject, the mind which not only wills but makes its knowledge; or toward celebrating the givenness of the object, the reality which is unchanging and unchangeable, perdurably out there.

Moving toward the first end, the poems stop short and turn back upon themselves. Moving toward the second end, the poems strive to strike against what ultimately must be discovered to be (by virtue of the very act of striving) the blank wall of reality. The utopian alternatives are pure introspection and pure abstraction—knowledge of pure act as against knowledge of pure substance. In the one mode, we would know ourselves as knowing; in the other, we would know the "object" so completely that we would not be aware of ourselves as knowing. The radical disjunction is, as I have said, between act and substance, and marks the extreme development of Stevens' abiding concern with the relationship between "imagination" and "reality." Neither mode is altogether possible for us—since we have not the power to conceive of abstracting (to use Stevens' word) knowing from the known, or the known from knowing. But, at this stage of his work, Stevens was convinced that by the same token at any given time, in any given poem, the two modes could never adequately coexist, except perhaps in theory, or in what he called the "ultimate poem." And for him theory—at least so far as poetry was concerned—involved an abuse of the power of abstract thinking, and the ultimate poem would necessarily be characterized by a kind of never-to-be-attained perfection by which are measured one's actual attainments. At most we are given, or give ourselves, intimations of subjectivity and of objectivity. And the task of poetry, thus its form and function, is somehow to transform intimations into convictions, to see the dilemma all the way

273

through to an end triumphant in its very bitterness. This was, in words of "The Well Dressed Man with a Beard," the "final no." And it was the necessary condition for whatever "final yes" might be possible:

> . . . the yes of the realist spoken because he must
> Say yes, spoken because under every no
> Lay a passion for yes that had never been broken.
> ("Esthétique du Mal")

3.

As philosophizing all this may well seem to be a naïve treatment of the subject-object problem which is at the heart of romantic poetry. For even non-philosophers expect something more than this from philosophical discourse. But it seems naïve only on first glance—as it seems to be philosophizing only on first glance. Still, we must not be so timid as to refuse to take the first glance: to avoid the philosophy and to seek the poetry. For Stevens habitually began with a specifically philosophical problem and yet insisted on a specifically poetic solution for it. Indeed, in a late essay, "A Collect of Philosophy," he concluded that both philosopher and poet seek to "form concepts"—the "integration" of thought. "The philosopher," he said, "intends his integration to be fateful; the poet intends his to be effective." We may extend this to say that "effectiveness" implies that never-to-be-perfect sense of the complex denied to "fatefulness," which in turn implies the perfection of thought to the point where it is inevitable enough to seem simple. Thus it is of the essence of Stevens' later poetry that it explicate the simple in such a way that its complexity be totally revealed. (His philosophical counterpart—let us think of Wittgenstein—would explicate the complex in such a way that its simplicity be totally revealed.) "The poem," Stevens wrote in "Man Carrying Thing," "must resist the intel-

ligence / Almost successfully." (His philosophical counterpart might well demand that the intelligence resist
the poem almost successfully.)

Stevens' concern for the subject-object problem is
then continuous from that of his romantic forebears.
But for him, particularly in the poems from *Transport
to Summer* through *The Rock* group, the solution of
the problem is not to be authorized by any special poetic
(imaginative, intuitive) access to myth or structure of
symbolic correspondences. (This would be too "intelligent," too "philosophical.") If he must, he will say
NO! in thunder. The poetic power has access only
to itself; it controls only itself; its relation to the reality
on which it is operative is that it "resists" (a word he
uses in a critical essay)—and in resisting, shapes, and
in shaping, seems to control. Surely, at times Stevens
hoped for more than this. Explaining some lines in
"The Man with the Blue Guitar," he wrote to his Italian
translator: "Nature is a monster . . . which I desire to
reduce: master, subjugate, acquire complete control
over and use freely for my own purposes as a poet. I
want, as a poet, to be that in nature which constitutes
nature's very self." He would be "natural." His poetry
after "The Man with the Blue Guitar," however, betrays his wishes. For in discovering his "naturalness,"
he cuts himself off from the substantial and contingent
things which make up the rest of nature. Reducing,
subjugating, controlling, he can never know. Or rather,
he can know that there is a reality whose complexity of
existence he cannot know, yet a reality which in his
very ignorance he can acknowledge as existing, if only
as something so "abstract" that he can say of it no
more than that in its self-sufficiency (a counterpart of
his own) it exists. He can bring himself to affirm that
it will be his fate ever to say that "It can never be satisfied, the mind, never." He can say, "I am." Or he can
say, "It is," even "You are." But he can never connect

275

one proposition to the other with a "therefore." Hence, philosophically speaking, the apparent naïveté. But again and again he remarked in effect that it is the philosopher's "therefore" which is naïve, poetically speaking, as is the "therefore" of ordinary language. What happens in his most difficult, often most rewarding poems of his penultimate period is that philosophy resists the poet almost successfully.

For in "The Man with the Blue Guitar" (1937), he had, even as he hoped against hope to resolve it, written of what he was ever more clearly to see as the poet's characteristic dilemma:

> I cannot bring a world quite round,
> Although I patch it as I can.
>
> I sing a hero's head, large eye,
> And bearded bronze, but not a man,
>
> Although I patch him as I can
> And reach through him almost to man.
>
> If to serenade almost to man
> Is to miss, by that, things as they are,
>
> Say that it is the serenade
> Of a man that plays a blue guitar.

Here the poem is remarked as a kind of inevitably necessary compromise between man and the world he knows. Strive to celebrate man, and you miss things as they are—as elsewhere in the poem what Stevens says amounts to: strive to celebrate things as they are, and you miss man. "Man," of course, and "things as they are" are names for what Stevens most generally called mind (or imagination) and reality. And the record of his life's work is of a struggle to learn to do something more than "patch" as he could. The end of the struggle is recorded in "The Rock," "Not Ideas . . . ," and all the poems which surround them in *The Rock* section of the

Collected Poems. What has happened is that the dialectical compromise, although it is still wished for, is no
longer conceivable. The poet will do one thing or the
other. He will celebrate mind or celebrate things themselves, be either the poet of night or the poet of day,
an old man or a young man. He can, that is to say, take
his position on either side of the dialectical movement
which sets the rhythm of "creativity." He belongs to
both sides of his universe, but never to both sides at
once.

This is, I suggest, because in Stevens' deepest thought,
his universe belonged too much to him. And the division was within him, so that he was not divided but
dividing. The greatness of his poetry is a product of
the greatness of his spirit, of a mind striving so terribly hard to perfect its knowledge of the world, to do
something more than patch the reality it confronted
day-to-day, that it never, until it was almost too late,
found time to consider that it might well have first to
perfect itself, and then see how the world looked. Then
it might well discover that the world looked at it, even
as it looked at the world. It would find its place, that is
to say, in the middle of things, always in the middle of
its dialectical journey. We can say this of Stevens, I
suggest, because he finally said it of himself. The intelligence which his poetry resisted almost successfully
was his own. And it was a great, honest intelligence.

> And one trembles to be so understood and, at last,
> To understand, as if to know became
> The fatality of seeing things too well.

4.

At the very end of his life, Stevens seems to have had
some suspicion that the world his mind had revealed
to him, and likewise the kind of mind he had revealed
to himself in the revealing, was not quite enough, be-

cause not true enough to the facts of the matter as in making poems he could discover them. Thus this poem, first published in 1956, the year after his death—"The Region November":

> It is hard to hear the north wind again,
> And watch the treetops, as they sway.
>
> They sway, deeply and loudly, in an effort,
> So much less than feeling, so much less than speech,
>
> Saying and saying, the way things say
> On the level of that which is not yet knowledge:
>
> A revelation not yet intended.
> It is like a critic of God, the world
>
> And human nature, pensively seated
> On the waste throne of his own wilderness.
>
> Deeplier, deeplier, loudlier, loudlier,
> The trees are swaying, swaying, swaying.

In all his profundity, Stevens had always to be ironic at his own expense. This, to paraphrase a notorious claim of his, is a gentle kind of violence which he employed to protect himself from the violence, the voracious violence, of his own mind. He finds that he is, like all of us, a "critic of God, the world / And human nature." The word "critic" supplies the irony which makes this bearable, especially as it helps us to bear the burden of "the waste throne of [our] own wilderness." This is, as they say, to supply a point of view. But what is seen? Something that is heard, or almost heard. The poem seesaws between "sway" and "say"—the movement of meter and sensibility being enforced by the outrageous adverbs, "deeplier" and "loudlier." The treetops are making an effort; and it is an effort which somehow the poet does not merely imagine. This is no matter of the pathetic fallacy, a too-muted version of

278

"What are the wild waves saying?" For the poet cannot conceive of asking such a simple-mindedly overweening question. The effort of the treetops is "So much less than feeling, so much less than speech." Yet it proves a feeling and speech of some sort; and the poet can suppose that they "say / On the level of that which is not yet knowledge." "On the level of . . ." is "philosophic" diction, and so bids us think with this lyric, not sing mournfully with it. The "not yet intended" of the seventh line is in fact a bit of technical language out of Stevens' dabbling in phenomenology, in whose logic all revelations are nothing if not "intended." Now he decides that, spontaneously, without intention, to be is to say: to say what "It is hard to hear." In short, Stevens is claiming that if the treetops do "say," it is not in the language of any "speech." Thus he will not be caught imputing "humanity," much less "deity," to the treetops—both to be implicated in that "meaning" derivable from myth or a structure of symbolic correspondences. He will not let himself be trapped in the anthropocentricism, as often as not masked as theocentrism, of his "romantic" forebears and contemporaries. He will be a radical humanist to the end. But his humanism now forces him to acknowledge both the virtual life of the non-human and its virtual capacity to "say."

And anyhow: the poet has admitted at the outset that "It is hard to hear the north wind again"—after all those years, all those poems, when if nature did speak to the poet, it was in the end only his own voice coming back to him, as though from a synaesthetic mirror. The point is that the "critic of God, the world / And human nature" has at long last begun to understand what he has so long listened to. There are, it would seem, other kinds of saying than the poet's. And perhaps, just perhaps, he is beginning to wonder if there might not in the end prove to be a continuing dialogue between "mind" and

"reality": expressive of the ineluctable continuity between night and day, old man and young—between God,
if He exists, and man.

One ventures to guess, because Stevens ventured to
guess. And one wonders about those "true poems,"
which at the National Book Award dinner, he said he
would "like to have written." I think that "The Region
November" is one of them and that "As You Leave the
Room" (1955) is another. (It is a doubly retrospective
poem, being an enlargement of "First Warmth," written
in 1947 and, because later enlarged upon, never intended for publication.)

> *You speak. You say*: Today's character is not
> A skeleton out of its cabinet. Nor am I.
>
> The poem about the pineapple, the one
> About the mind as never satisfied,
>
> The one about the credible hero, the one
> About summer, are not what skeletons think about.
>
> I wonder, have I lived a skeleton's life,
> As a disbeliever in reality,
>
> A countryman of all the bones in the world?
> Now, here, the snow I had forgotten becomes
>
> Part of a major reality, part of
> An appreciation of a reality
>
> And thus an elevation, as if I left
> With something I could touch, touch every way.
>
> And yet nothing has been changed except what is
> Unreal, as if nothing had been changed at all.

Now the poet can look at his own work and see that,
even as it argued for the division between mind and
reality, it manifested the poet's central involvement in
both. He refers in turn to "Someone Puts a Pineapple

Together" (1947), where he had seen it as the poet's categorical imperative "to defy / The metaphor that murders metaphor"; to "The Well Dressed Man with a Beard," cited above; to "Asides on the Oboe" (1940), "Examination of the Hero in a Time of War" (1942), and other related poems; and to "Credences of Summer" (1947), where he had put down his most concise statement as to the function of poetry:

> Three times the concentred self takes hold, three times
> The thrice concentred self, having possessed
>
> The object, grips it in savage scrutiny,
> Once to make captive, once to subjugate
> Or yield to subjugation, once to proclaim
> The meaning of the capture . . . .

"As You Leave the Room" is in effect a survey of Stevens' poetry during precisely that period when he began to push it into its most "philosophical" mode. It was in this period that he had begun to try to solve the problems of belief and commitment raised so variously and movingly in "The Snow Man" (also referred to here), "Sunday Morning," "A High-Toned Old Christian Woman," "The Emperor of Ice-Cream," and the rest. From "Notes toward a Supreme Fiction" through the poems grouped in the *Collected Poems* under the title *The Rock* the solutions he achieved served only to make the problems more difficult. And, as I have tried to show in my notes on the title poem in *The Rock* group and on "Not Ideas . . ." (also included in that group), he had come to believe that the solution of the problem was that it was insoluble. Acknowledging the fact of the insolubility, the poet—as surrogate for Stevens' Common Reader, "the man of imagination" whom he saluted so often—might learn to rejoice in both his day- and his night-time powers, but alternatively. Yet now, as he leaves the (lecture?) room, it occurs to him that he is

281

not the sort of "skeleton" that his critics have latterly made him out to be. (We ask, has he lectured or been lectured upon?) He puts the question flatly: has he been a "disbeliever in reality"?—or, one must add by way of recalling Stevens' thinking here, a disbeliever in the mind's capacity to relate directly to the "thing itself," therefore a believer only in mind, therefore a believer in the "unreal," therefore a disbeliever in reality? Again: No. The poet is certain: somehow he has in fact accommodated the mind to reality, the unreal to the real. Even the snow (which, as we have seen, when it became a snow man, in the 1921 poem of that name, bodied forth nothingness, "uncreated" reality as against "pure" mind) has become an "appreciation" of reality. "Appreciation" is used with etymological exactness. The mind has *grown* by at once adding itself to, and being added to by, "major reality." Reality has been enlarged; and mind, for all its "unreality," has been changed. As has the poet. Now, in a kind of afterthought, he can claim that he has been at the center of things all along— as poet, not a divided but a whole man: or at least one capable of imagining himself as being at the center of his world and thereby being, in fact, potentially whole. The glance all the way back to "The Snow Man" makes this poem, for all its emphasis on the work of the forties, an exercise in retrospect become an exercise in redefinition.

The greatest victory in the poem is that Stevens, after a good number of stabbing attempts (see, for example, "The Motive for Metaphor" [1943]), can see himself not only as actually "I" but as possibly "you," and so find his place in the world. It is as though he were now beginning to conceive of the poem not as an "act of the mind" but as the "mind of an act" and to admit to himself— as a kind of "invention"—that "acts" are not all necessarily either of man or an imagined God, that "reality" is characterized by something resembling "mind." Perhaps what is involved is a form of panpsychism. If so, there was for Stevens not one but an infinite number of psyches. In any case, for the last Stevens the world of imagination and reality was not only alive and fragmented but in the very life of its fragmentation capable, when conceived of in poems, of being one.

Retrospection and redefinition on the whole characterize the poems which Stevens wrote in his last years. (There is no clearly chronological development here— just hard-won variations on a theme central to the last years. I date the poems only to place them thus.) Twice, surely in a recollection of Tennyson in the same mood, Stevens makes Ulysses his spokesman, calling him in the title of one of the poems "An External Master of Knowledge" (1954). (The other is "The Sail of Ulysses," a Phi Beta Kappa poem of the same year.) In the first-named poem Ulysses soliloquizes:

> "Here I feel the human loneliness
> And that, in space and solitude,
> Which knowledge is: the world and fate,
> The right within me and about me,
> Joined in a triumphant vigor,
> Like a direction on which I depend . . . ."

In "Conversation with Three Women of New England" (1954), Stevens remarks three "modes" of understanding—what we can categorize as idealism, naturalism, and a kind of humanistic personalism; and he refuses to opt for any, imagining himself capable of comprehending them all, saying that it might be "enough to realize / That the sense of being changes as we talk, / That talk shifts the cycle of the scenes of kings." He is modest in "Local Objects" (1955):

> Little existed for him but the few things
> For which a fresh name always occurred, as if
> He wanted to make them, keep them from perishing,

> The few things, the objects of insight, the integrations
> Of feeling, the things that came of their own accord,
> Because he desired without knowing quite what . . . .

The key phrases in the poems from which I have just quoted are: "direction on which I depend"; "sense of being changes"; and "things that came of their own accord."

The feeling registered by the first two of these phrases is, of course, characteristic of Stevens' work almost from the beginning. But the feeling registered in the third is new; accordingly, the sense of direction and of being is surer, for it is no longer only his own direction and being which the poet can conceive of himself as possibly knowing. Whereas before he had known the other only by a kind of heroic inference (cf. the dialectic of "Notes toward a Supreme Fiction"), now he may know it directly as it is revealed to him. Thus in "Artificial Populations" (1954), he can go so far as to admit quite casually that "a state of mind" is no longer enough for him who would find his proper center:

> The center that he sought was a state of mind,
> Nothing more, like weather after it has cleared—
> Well, more than that, like weather when it has cleared
> And the two poles continue to maintain it
>
> And the Orient and Occident embrace
> To form that weather's appropriate people. . . .

We can read "weather" as a specifying, inclusive term for "ambiance"—or even "culture" or "world"; and then note that the "populations" which are formed by the "embrace" are "artificial" only as they are not the product of "pure" mind or "pure" reality—"Orient and Occident"—but the result of the conjoining of both, a conjoining in which the poet may take part and then acknowledge and celebrate, but still one which he by no means may bring about himself. There is a "making," that is to say, beyond human will, but not beyond human understanding. Indeed, human understanding is, in necessary part, a product of such making. Man must will himself toward such understanding—a condition of his situation as man. In his earlier poetry, Stevens had hoped entirely on his own to manage such conjunctions, thus such understanding; yet by the time of *The Rock* group, he had despaired of the managing, and triumphed in the honesty of his despair. Now he is sure of himself as he had never been; for "This artificial population is like / A healing-point in the sickness of the mind. . . ."

The poet now watches and waits, as in "July Mountain" (1955):

> We live in a constellation
> Of patches and of pitches,
> Not in a single world,
> In things said well in music,
> On the piano, and in speech,
> As in a page of poetry—
> Thinkers without final thoughts
> In an always incipient cosmos,
> The way, when we climb a mountain,
> Vermont throws itself together.

Again, retrospection and redefinition. "We live in a constellation . . ." recalls "Sunday Morning": "We live in an old chaos of the sun"; "patches and . . . pitches," and "single world" recall "The Man with the Blue Guitar,": "I cannot bring a world quite round, / Although I patch it as I can." The fragmented sequence of "music," "piano," "speech," and "poetry" recalls their intended fusion in "Peter Quince at the Clavier." "Thinkers without final thoughts" recalls the iterated motif of the never-to-be-satisfied mind. "Always incipient cosmos" recalls the continuing emphasis on change and process in the earlier poems. And then: "The way . . . / Vermont throws itself together" recalls "Anecdote of the Jar," in which, as we should recall, whatever order given the Tennessee wilderness derives from what Stevens came to call the "act of the mind." The earlier observations are not so much contradicted as accommodated, each to the other. The poet in effect re-figures his role as observer. Taken together, all that he may observe are so many facts of life—not only his but their own. Again he finds a "healing-point in the sickness of the mind."

5.

"Poetry is a cure of the mind," wrote Stevens in one of the *Adagia*. His work through *The Rock* group constitutes, as I have maintained elsewhere,[1] a magnificent series of attempts to work toward realizing the implications of this statement. That, as its implications are realized, the statement is proved wrong does not lessen the magnificence of his achievement. For it is given to the poet to do the right things for the wrong reason. We can ask only that the poems be right, right as poems—let the reasons be what they may. If the poems are right enough, in their rightness they will eventually expose the wrongness of the reasons which inform them. If the reasons by chance are ours, then as we see them fully extended in poems, we shall see how wrong we have been. A means of measuring our wrongness is the rightness of the poetry which exposes it. For, as Stevens said in another note, "Poetry seeks out the relation of men to facts." There is an element of psychic distance here—or better, cultural distance—which often confuses not the issue but us. Our relation to some facts is such as to be beyond poetry's seeking out. *The Cantos* are in many places too strong medicine to work as art; but *The Merchant of Venice* is not.

[1] In my *Continuity of American Poetry* (Princeton, 1961, rev. ed., 1965), pp. 376-419.

Likewise for some of his readers, Stevens' invention of "a cure of the mind" and the meditative and philosophical poetic modes it called forth were too strong medicine to work as art. Such readers were threatened at the very core of their being; and so they longed for more "Sunday Mornings," in which Stevens would assure them that they might yet be safely distanced, on the outside looking in. (They mistook mode for substance.) More fortunate readers, hoping that Stevens' reasons were perhaps the right ones, that poetry might indeed be a cure of the mind, were able to follow him ever inward, until, with him, they found themselves trapped on the inside looking out. (They were willing to be taken in by the mode, so to discover substance.) Outside there was something, and it was real. But the truest domain of man was on the inside, with the unreal—which proved to be the non-real, the imagination, the mind: at best, consciousness fully released; at worst, the power of sympathy with oneself. For this self, at best or at worst, there was in the final analysis no time, no history, no living-in-the-world, except in imaginative acts which, when carried all the way, first transformed and then annulled time, history, and the world. The mind, the self, however, could maintain to the end its powers of postulation.

Thereby it might earn its salvation. For thereby it might imagine that whatever lay outside it was out there looking in, and then it might seek to verify this fact. "Swaying" might well be "saying," as the very act of making such poems might be an "appreciation of reality." "Poetry," Stevens wrote in another of the *Adagia*, "is health." And at the end as at the beginning he was seeking that health. The lesson of his life is surely that it could not come exclusively from "a cure of the mind." Yet it could not be a cure of something from which the mind was utterly cut off—reality, or "the thing itself," or even God. Moreover, were he to remain even minimally himself, man in his capacity as poet could not be derived from "things themselves"—or even from God. In the end, as I think these last poems show, for Stevens poetry must be expressive of a continuing dialogue between mind and reality. So far Stevens was able to go in his old age, and only so far. How much farther he would have gone, "what [he] should like to have written" (to recall a phrase from the speech I quoted at the beginning), we of course have no way of knowing. The trouble is—and it it always the trouble! —there are too few poems.

6.

What would it be like for the mind to enter a dialogue with reality, the "thing itself"? It would be

. . . hard to hear the north wind again,
And to watch the treetops, as they sway.

They sway, deeply and loudly, in an effort,
So much less than feeling, so much less than speech,

Saying and saying, the way things say
On the level of that which is not yet knowledge:

A revelation not yet intended.

At issue is the "appreciation" of reality. And, taken in the context of the continuity of Stevens' life's work, the inevitability of this last phase is such as to tempt us to believe that achieving it should somehow have been easier than in fact it was. We may, as are so many of our younger poets, look at the work of one of his Spanish contemporaries and say: But this is how it has always been! The "cure" has been with us, available to us, all the time! Seeking after the cure was itself a kind of disease—an unnecessary complication (to echo a phrase of Stevens) in the journey of the modern spirit as it seeks to find a home in its world! I think of Jorge Guillén's "Más Allá" ("Beyond"), in which there is

fully realized the kind of perfected relationship of man
and his world which in Stevens' last poems we can only
catch a glimpse of. Some stanzas (from Parts I, II, and
VI) read:

> Todo me comunica,
> Vencedor, hecho mundo,
> Su brío para ser
> De veras real, en triunfo.
>
> Soy, más, estoy. Respiro.
> Lo profundo es el aire.
> La realidad me inventa,
> Soy su leyenda; Salve!
>
> * * *
>
> No, no sueño. Vigor
> De creación concluye
> Su paráiso aqui . . .
>
> * * *
>
> Y con empuje henchido
> De afluencias amantes
> Se ahinca en el sagrado
> Presente perdurable
>
> Toda la creación,
> Que al despertarse un hombre
> Lanza la soledad
> A un tumulto de acordes.[2]

[2] In Stephen Gilman's literal rendering:
All communicates to me—the conqueror, transformed into the
world, its elan for being truly real, triumphant.
I am, but even more, I am here, I breathe. What is profound is
the air. Reality invents me: I am its legend. All hail!
    * * *
No, I am not dreaming. Creation's vigor concludes its paradise
here. . . .
    * * *
And, its impetus swollen with loving tributaries, all creation
fixes itself in the sacred everlasting present. For when a man
wakes up, creation launches solitude into a tumult of harmonies.
(*Cántico* [Buenos Aires, 1962], pp. 16-25.)

At most Stevens can do no more than discover the conditions which may make possible an affirmation such as this: of all-suffusing corporeality. The poet in "Más Allá" wakes up not to something "like a new knowledge of realty," but to that "new knowledge" itself; and he is a necessary part of it. On principle, we may say, Stevens' journey toward this discovery should not have been so long or so difficult. But a poet in a world like ours travels not on principle but on fact. Indeed, he would discover the principle-generating, principle-incorporating facts of our lives (and his) in our culture. He can move only so fast and so surely as the facts of the case will let him. The facts of the case have, in the history of our culture, generated principles (of understanding, communication, relationship, community, identity . . .) which have, it seems, so far barred us from access to the world of "Más Allá"—even as in the bareness and purity of what they do offer us, they can be made (by a Stevens) to suggest that such a world must exist, because only in such a world might we be at long last truly at home. Those for whom a sense of the world of "Más Allá" comes from a struggle less difficult than Stevens' are fortunate—although I should guess that in truth the struggle is not less difficult, only different. I am insisting here only that Stevens' struggle, as his life's work outlines it, is, for well and for ill, an American struggle. Surely, his younger peers, of whatever literary persuasion, can more readily conceive of a world like that of "Más Allá" than he could. But this is to say no more than that they have somehow learned his last lesson—often better than they know.

7.

"Whilst the world is a spectacle," Emerson wrote in "Nature," "something in [us] is stable"—and thus in good part set the American poet off on his phase of that romantic adventure which is the history of modern Western Europe thought. And he went on:

> In a higher manner the poet communicates the same pleasure. By a few strokes he delineates, as on air, the sun, the mountain, the camp, the city, the hero, the maiden, not different from what we know them, but only lifted from the ground and afloat before the eye. He unfixes the land and the sea, makes them revolve around the axis of his primary thought, and disposes them anew. Possessed himself by a heroic passion, he uses matter as symbols of it.

> . . .

> . . . the poet confirms things to his thoughts. . . . To him, the refractory world is ductile and flexible; he invests dust and stones with humanity, and makes them the words of the Reason. The Imagination may be defined to be the use which the Reason [i.e. *Vernunft*/ creative intuition] makes of the material world.

Stevens' version of this in the *Adagia* was: "The imagination is man's power over nature." His life's work was a monument to that "heroic passion"—only in him the passion was so heroic as to force him to deny that his "primary thought" partook, even transcendentally, of God's. If anything, he came to say God's primary thought was a product of his, a supreme fiction. A note in the *Adagia* reads:

> The relation of art to life is of the first importance especially in a skeptical age since, in the absence of a belief in God, the mind turns to its own creations and examines them, not alone from the aesthetic point of view, but for what they reveal, for what they validate and invalidate, for the support that they give.

At the end, or almost at the end, as we have seen, the mind's sole creation was the mind, the revelation that its sole creation was itself. Outside there was yet the "thing itself." Man's power over nature was frustrated in its very exercise. We should recall again, but now exactly, Stevens' notorious "the mind . . . is a violence within which protects us from a violence without."

But another note in the *Adagia* reads:

> Feed my lambs (on the bread of living) . . . the glory of god is the glory of the world. . . . To find the spiritual in reality. . . . To be concerned with reality.

The *Adagia* are, so Stevens' editor indicates, undatable. But most of them certainly belong to Stevens' later life. And as certainly they record not only his sense of what he had achieved but his attempt to reach beyond the limits which, in his achievement, he seemed so triumphantly to have set about himself in the poems through *The Rock*. There is in this *Adagia* note I have just quoted a hint of the concerns of the last poems: "to hear the north wind again." The revelations of Stevens' poetry through *The Rock*, I am suggesting, in all their power invalidated the propositions which informed them and so no longer gave support. But the relation of art to life as Stevens had defined it in the next-to-last *Adagia* note I have quoted still held; and the poet was bound to create new poems, seek for new revelations, discover new validations and invalidations. In the seeking itself lay the source of support. The revelation in the last poems is flickering but sure. At long last, the Emersonian paradox is taken to work both ways. But it is stripped of its resolution in the idea that subject and object, imagination and reality, man and nature are all unified in a God-ordained and God-containing system of symbolic correspondences, to which the poet, by virtue of his being poet, has access. Even in imagination the poet is neither God, nor shares in God's world. He cannot be; so he no longer needs to be. Now the Emersonian paradox is kept ever true to the facts of the case as the poet's creations discover them: the

Imagination may be defined as at once the use which the Reason makes of the material world and the use which the material world makes of the Reason. Poetry is Reason's dialogue with reality, and must begin "On the level of that which is not yet knowledge: / A revelation not yet intended." The poet must master a speech which is not his own, must learn first to listen—then, if he can, to ask as well as to answer, to give as well as to take. Knowing what he knows—himself in "the act of the mind"—he must thereby know more. So Stevens began to learn, and so he began to teach—in his own way moving "Más Allá." As he wrote in the *Adagia*, "One's ignorance is one's chief asset." At the outset.

1965/1968

11

THEODORE ROETHKE:
The Power of Sympathy

"What you survived I shall believe: the Heat,
Scars, Tempests, Floods, the Motion of Man's Fate;
I have myself, and bear its weight of woe
That God that God leans down His heart to hear."
ROETHKE, *"Elegy"*

1.

AT THE END of Wallace Stevens' "The Noble Rider and the Sounds of Words" there is a passage which may serve as prolegomenon to the poetics of our recent past:

> The mind has added nothing to human nature. It is a violence from within that protects us from a violence without. It is the imagination pressing back against the pressure of reality. It seems, in the last analysis, to have something to do with our self-preservation; and that, no doubt, is why the expression of it, the sound of its words, helps us live our lives.

Using the passage, one can trace some of the relationships between the work of the great elder modernists (Stevens and his generation) and of the poets who come immediately after. The work of the former defines the poet's vocation according to an extreme choice, whereby he may attend either to the violence without or to the violence within. Only thus may he master the ways of violence with sensibility and learning; only thus transform violence into process, that process of art which form charts for us. Stevens himself is preeminently the poet of the opposing self; Eliot

294

is the poet of the opposing other. And the poets of the generations after Eliot and Stevens, necessarily mindful of their elders' ways, have as necessarily accepted their elders' definition of the poet's vocation: how, through the exercise of his craft, to contain violence, whatever its origin and end, so as to make it a source of power.

At bottom, then, the issue for the poet is the issue for modern man in all his capacities and institutions: power. The commonplace is nonetheless true for being a commonplace. The conditions of modern life have at once created and tapped sources of a force so great that it must inevitably issue as violence. For the poet what threatens is an entropy of the sensibility as it manifests itself in language. And yet he has access to the sensibility only through language. If language— either as he knows it within or as he knows it without— runs mad with the terror of that to which it refers, the poet must yet live with it, live through it. He needs power; so he must put himself vitally in touch with violence. The touch is everything. He knows that violence cannot be attenuated, much less done away with. But it can be transformed into power, so then to bring into consonance the life of the spirit and the life of society— the self alone and the self as other, coordinate with yet other, perhaps higher, selves.

Theodore Roethke's achievement takes on its special meaning from the fact that he single-mindedly searched out violence in its very sources and strove mightily to find such modes of order as would transform it into power—the power of sympathy, the means to reach across the gulf which separates the sources of the violence within from those of the violence without. The paradigm for his poetry is this: violence transformed into power through order. The structure and technique of the poems enact the transformation and would create a kind of spiritual exercise whereby the reader might learn the lessons of the poet's life.

For in Roethke's work the poet's life is always insistently there. Sometimes it is too much so, to be sure, and the exercise leads to no end but wonderment about the poet as private person. In such cases, the process limits rather than transforms, leading to curiosity rather than self-knowledge. Roethke himself seems to have known this. And as he put his poems into volumes, he tried consistently to eliminate from his collections verses in which the requisite transformative factor, for whatever reason, is absent. "Feud," for example, put into *Open House* (1941) but not reprinted until the appearance of the posthumous *Collected Poems*, begins:

> Corruption reaps the young; you dread
> The menace of ancestral eyes;
> Recoiling from the serpent head
> Of fate, you blubber in surprise.
>
> Exhausted fathers thinned the blood,
> You curse the legacy of pain;
> Darling of an infected brood,
> You feel disaster climb the vein.

The manner is not really Roethke's, we may decide, but, say, Allen Tate's. Still, what is lacking in (not wrong with) the poem—when viewed in the light of the poems as Roethke selected and ordered them in *Words for the Wind*—is a means of involving the reader directly in the lucubrations of the speaker. The reader is that "you," and finds himself accused, but as the later Roethke might have decided, not sufficiently tutored into an understanding of the accusation. "Feud" ends:

> You meditate upon the nerves,
> Inflame with hate. This ancient feud
> Is seldom won. The spirit starves
> Until the dead have been subdued.

The violence remains without, to be stoically resisted, perhaps conquered—in any case, not understood. The violence within—which empowers the resisting—is controlled and focused by rhetoric, and someone else's at that. "Feud" is a considerable poem, and persuasive. The later Roethke—I daresay the authentic Roethke—wanted to do more than persuade. The authentic Roethke, as he sought to define himself, is not he who, in language on loan, would persuade the living that they must subdue the dead. For a poem like "Feud" rather commemorates than celebrates, rather neutralizes violence than transforms it, rather shuns power than seeks it. The authentic Roethke came to be the celebrant of the transformation of violence into power.

It is this growing sense of his own vocation, I think, which led Roethke in his lifetime not to put into his volumes his poems about life in mental hospitals—for example, "Lines Upon Leaving" (1937), "Meditation in Hydrotherapy" (1937), and "Advice to One Committed" (1960). The last named, which is not included in his *Collected Poems* as are the others, begins:

> Swift's servant beat him; now they use
> The current flowing from a fuse,
> Or put you on a softer diet;
> Your teeth fall out—but you'll be quiet;
> Forget you ever were someone—
> You'll get ten minutes in the sun.

There is a fine Swiftian quality to such poems. But they are too neat. They are objectively rather than subjectively personal, and (when viewed in the light of what Roethke came to demand of his verse) just will not do. "The Return" (1946), however, Roethke did put into *The Lost Son* (1948) and kept in *The Waking* (1953) and *Words for the Wind* (1958):

> I circled on leather paws
> In the darkening corridor,

297

Crouched closer to the floor,
Then bristled like a dog.

As I turned for a backward look,
The muscles in one thigh
Sagged like a frightened lip.

A cold key let me in
That self-infected lair;
And I lay down with my life,
With the rags and rotting clothes,
With a stump of scraggy fang
Bared for a hunter's boot.

The importance of specific occasion and locale here is diminished exactly as the significance of the experience is increased; such details as we are given are internalized into a sequence of metaphors which urge us to participate in the poem and to use it as a means of defining our own return to the mental hospitals—if such are meant here—which we perforce make out of our lives. The violence of the controlling metaphor—marked by "circled," "crouched," "bristled," "sagged," "self-infected," and "bared"—such violence is countered, then transformed, by that "And I lay down with my life." For it is the power of lying down—but still *with* one's life—which finally dominates and teaches us to defy the hunter's boot. The difference between "Advice to One Committed" and "The Return" is the difference between death-in-life and life-in-death.

For violence leads to death—alternatively to the death of the self at the hands of the other, or the death of the other at the hands of the self. This Roethke saw and felt and understood more deeply and with greater intelligence than any poet of our time. He sought to find a means of refusing the either/or option which his culture offered him. The design of *Words for the Wind* and *The Far Field* (1964), the last volumes published in his lifetime, manifests that search. In choosing earlier poems to reprint, in adding new poems, in grouping them, he mapped out his quest so as to make it his readers'. He rejected not only such "autobiographical" poems as I have cited but a number of wonderfully funny poems attacking persons who threatened not so much himself as what he increasingly stood for. Also, he rejected a number of poems bitingly observant of modern urban life. One guesses that he was overreacting to his own aggressiveness, as though it too were a form of violence which threatened. (Although he had some of this cake and ate it too: in the pieces he published under the pseudonym "Winterset Rothberg.") He would—as he depicted the growth of the poet's mind—observe violence and carefully annotate it; and he would turn it only upon himself. Thus he discovered the nature and working of violence, studied the transformative role of order, and found the power to become a poet.

2.

The first poem in *Words for the Wind* is the title poem from *Open House*. Preserving it, and the four which immediately follow, Roethke preserves himself as public spokesman. "Open House" is, in contrast to the bulk of the poems, somewhat "rhetorical." Its general mode is like that of "Feud"—persuasive. Moreover, it rather declares than develops:

> My secrets cry aloud.
> I have no need for tongue.
> My heart keeps open house,
> My doors are widely swung.
> An epic of the eyes
> My love, with no disguise.

So many figurations—each to be accepted or declined separately, but each leading to the closing lines:

I stop the lying mouth:
Rage warps my clearest cry
To witless agony.

Roethke was to reverse the order described here: to transform agony, by virtue of the transformation no longer witless, into a clearest cry, hence to transcend rage. Doing so, he was to move beyond rhetoric into the actual processes of consciousness.

He had to begin at the beginning—with primitive things. For him, understanding the natural order of primitive things came to be a means to and model for understanding all in the natural order, himself included, which is beyond the primitive. What the natural order contains, and therefore manifests, is growth—what seems to be violence but is not, for it is directed toward an end, as power must be if it is truly to be power. And in the rest of the poems kept from *Open House* the poet is caught in the excitement of his own crashing-through to the edge of just this insight. After a "Mid-Country Blow," he writes: "When I looked at the altered scene, my eye was undeceived, / But my ear still kept the sound of the sea like a shell." "The Heron" is described with the greatest exactitude as he moves; and then "A single ripple starts from where he stood." Roethke would be following, tracing out, that single ripple the rest of his life. But in these poems it is enough—more would be at this stage too much—that he see it at only the outset; that in "No Bird" he define one dead as being beyond the "breeze above her head" and the "grasses [which] whitely stir"; that (reversing a figure from Marvell) he proclaim "Long live the weeds that overwhelm / My narrow vegetable realm!" Wonderment is enough—the wonderment of the lovely "Vernal Sentiment": "I rejoice in the spring, as though no spring ever had been." Intermixed as it is with such poems, the declarative "Open House," like others

300

of its kind in the *Words for the Wind* sequence after which it is named, gains a vitality which is not its own when it is taken separately. "Night Journey," which concludes the sequence, details a cross-country train trip, with its myriad revelations:

> Bridges of iron lace,
> A suddenness of trees,
> A lap of mountain mist. . . .

Because he can see in such things the kind of vitality and growth revealed to him in the more telling poems of the sequence, Roethke is justified at the end in returning to his declarative mode: "I stay up half the night / To see the land I love."

Inevitably (so the design of *Words for the Wind* indicates), Roethke's journey was—as he said in so many words in the title of a late poem—into the interior. First the interior was that of the natural order, and then his own, to the degree that he was part of the natural order. The design of *Words for the Wind*, as it emerges at this stage, is the design of another *Song of Myself*, or another *Prelude*—as in later poems Roethke himself makes quite clear, perhaps having discovered only later that the design, worked out retrospectively, had a certain necessity of its own. At this point, having discovered the vitality, violence, and power of the natural order, he was obliged to understand it. He had, then, to move away from the rather safe and simplistic forms of *Open House* to forms adequate to the understanding he would achieve: a structure of verse which would articulate the essential facts and qualities of its primitive realm and, at the same time, be expressive of the act of articulation itself. Roethke's was to be a lover's battle with his world; victory would result only if it were fought to a draw. The risks, in the context of modernist verse, were great: to dare the heresy of the pa-

301

thetic fallacy and that of imitative form. And there
were failures, to be sure. One takes them as the price
paid for successes. And, because one can be doubly
retrospective, one looks ahead to the poems beyond
those from *The Lost Son*, which make up the second
sequence in *Words for the Wind*.

At this stage, Roethke is surest of himself in his
greenhouse poems. He seems wholly to comprehend the
natural order and those, including himself, who are
close to it. At first glance, the effect of the poems is to
impute human qualities to the natural world; at second
glance, once the poems have had their way, the effect
is to discover those qualities in great and complex detail. There is then established a new order of understanding: that such qualities, precisely as they are human, are derived from the natural order. A kind of
underground dialectic is everywhere at work, an argument generated by the organization and movement of
the poems.

> Sticks-in-a-drowse droop over sugary loam,
> Their intricate stem-fur dries;
> But still the delicate slips keep coaxing up water;
> The small cells bulge; . . .

("Cuttings")

"Sticks-in-a-drowse" and "coaxing" register human qualities; but "intricate" and "delicate" (such commonplace
descriptive words they are) work to qualify and classify
the implied anthropomorphic claim and to establish a
more-than-analogical relationship between perceiver
and things perceived. The act of perception, when it is
expressed, is one with the growth, the vital principle, of
the things perceived. Thus, in "Cuttings, *later*" the poet
can say that he knows exactly what is going on here,
knows it unmediated:

> This urge, wrestle, resurrection of dry sticks,
> Cut stems struggling to put down feet,

302

What saint strained so much,
Rose on such lopped limbs to a new life?

I can hear, underground, that sucking and sobbing,
In my veins, in my bones I feel it,—
The small waters seeping upward,
The tight grains parting at last.
When sprouts break out,
Slippery as fish,
I quail, lean to beginnings, sheath-wet.

The natural world is not the emblem of self-knowledge and self-realization, but the source and occasion of their being. One sees, one hears, one knows, and one is. Or at least, one begins to be.

The poet discovers this in others—the subjects of "Old Florist" and "Frau Bauman, Frau Schmidt, and Frau Schwartze," for example. But most of all, he discovers it in himself—as a "Weed Puller"

. . . down in that fetor of weeds,
Crawling on all fours,
Alive, in a slippery grave;

and in "Moss-Gathering," when

. . . afterwards I always felt mean, jogging back over the logging road,
As if I had broken the natural order of things in that swamp-land;
Disturbed some rhythm, old and of vast importance,
By pulling off flesh from the living planet;
As if I had committed, against the whole scheme of life,
a desecration.

The "natural order of things" and the "scheme of life," then, must be his central subject. The papa who, in all his power, waltzes so surely; the boy, at sixteen, itching with the lust of good smells in the pickle factory; the mother, dwelling in "That fine fuming stink of particular kettles"—these he must understand because they are closest to the "natural order of things" and the "scheme of life." Yet their world, with all its unself-conscious spontaneity, is lost to him. And, as I have pointed out, he must begin at the beginning, studying "The Minimal," the "lives on a leaf," which are "Cleaning and caressing, / Creeping and healing."

He concludes the poems kept from *The Lost Son* with another one ("The Cycle") in his declarative mode. By now, however, that mode has been qualified by and accommodated to the mode which is dominant in *The Lost Son.*

> Dark water, underground,
> Beneath the rock and clay,
> Beneath the roots of trees,
> Moved into common day,
> Rose from a mossy mound
> In midst that sun could seize.
>
> The fine rain coiled in a cloud
> Turned by revolving air
> Far from that colder source
> Where elements cohere
> Dense in the central stone.
> The air grew loose and loud.
>
> Then, with diminished force,
> The full rain fell straight down,
> Tunneled with lapsing sound
> Under even the rock-shut ground,
> Under a river's source,
> Under primeval stone.

Surely, we are to recall the end of *The Waste Land* here. And Roethke is initiating a grand dialogue with one of his modernist masters. He too would Give, Sympathize, Control—come to know the sources of power, in order at once to make proper obeisance to them and to share in them. The rain that comes to save his land, however, comes from underground, and returns there, only again and again to move through, in the title of the poem, "The Cycle." The poet, in short must discover his own cycle, his own underground, his own relationship to the source under the primeval stone.

In *Words for the Wind* Roethke puts into the section called "Praise to the End" not only poems from the volume of that name (1951) but the closing sequence of *The Lost Son.* This sequence does indeed belong where he places it; for, like the sequence kept from *Praise to the End!*, it most fully manifests the violence of Roethke's journey into the interior—beyond childhood with its order (of a sort), beyond the order of the natural world, to the swirling, threatening, inchoate sources of his very being. The Wordsworthian title of the section, and the *Prelude* passage from which the title comes, are helpful, in that they sum up and categorize Roethke's effort here:

> How strange, that all
> The terrors, pains, and early miseries,
> Regrets, vexations, lassitudes interfused
> Within my mind, should e'er have borne a part,
> And that a needful part, in making up
> The calm existence that is mine when I
> Am worthy of myself! Praise to the end!

Writing a kind of apologia for those poems which comprise the "Praise to the End" section, Roethke explained:

> . . . the method is cyclic. I believe that to go forward as a spiritual man it is necessary first to go back. Any history of the psyche (or allegorical journey) is bound to be a succession of experiences, similar yet dissimilar. There is a perpetual slipping-back, then a going-forward; but there is *some* "progress." Are not some

305

experiences so powerful and so profound (I am not speaking of the merely compulsive) that they repeat themselves, thrust themselves upon us, again and again, with variation and change, each time bringing us closer to our own most particular (and thus most universal) reality? We go, as Yeats said, from exhaustion to exhaustion. To begin from the depths and come out—that is difficult; for few know where the depths are or can recognize them; or, if they do, are afraid.[1]

We need guidance like this, if only to prepare ourselves for the exhaustion which is our proper due.

The style of these poems is regressive, but out of the regression there comes a certain progression, a deepening of one's sense of the fact, the factuality, of consciousness itself. The poems seem to anticipate the effort to comprehend them, and to defy it; yet the thrust of defiance is itself a thrust *toward* the reader and on his behalf—so, paradoxically, a crucial factor in his mode of comprehension. The language is most often that of the earliest stages of childhood, thus only barely language; it is charged with the force of the primary process of consciousness and so threatens always to disintegrate. Roethke is closest to the entropy of sensibility here. That infantile amnesia which psychoanalysis has discovered for us is broken through, or almost.[2]

[1] *Mid-Century American Poetry*, ed. John Ciardi (New York, 1950), p. 69.

[2] I must state flatly that the poems are supersaturated with language out of Freud and Jung, or their myriad exegetes. See, however, Carolyn Kizer, "Poetry of the Fifties in America," in *International Literary Annual*, ed. John Wain (London, 1958), p. 84: "I should probably say here that Roethke has not read Joyce or Jung; and that, in 1952, after all his long poems exploring a child's history of consciousness had appeared, he was discovered in a Morris chair by a friend, with a copy of Freud's *Basic Writings* on one arm, his book *Praise to the End!* on the other, and his notebook in his lap, checking references, and chortling to himself, 'I was right! I was right!' " One can only suppose that the friend mistook Winterset Rothberg for Theodore Roethke.

And yet, as Roethke claims, these are "traditional" poems. The tradition is that deepest in the sensibility of individual men; it is a composite of their childhood experiences, experiences so deeply lived through as to seem the experience of the world from which, as children, they could not yet properly differentiate themselves. Coming at this point in the sequence of Roethke's poems, they establish the conditions under which it is possible to see how, in autobiographical fact, a man is part of the natural order in general and of his own natural order in particular. The literary source of the language is appropriately traditional too, as Roethke noted: "German and English folk literature, particularly Mother Goose; Elizabethan and Jacobean drama, especially the songs and rants; the Bible; Blake and Traherne; Dürer."[3] What the poems demand of a reader is a willing suspension of adult consciousness, and yet a firm and controlled sense of oneself in the act of willing that suspension—which is, indeed, in recording the growth of his poet's mind, what they must have demanded of Roethke.

In a sense, they are not poems but rather pre-poems; so that the reader, working through them, must bring his own capacities as proto-poet most actively to bear on them. In effect, the reader *completes* them. One can hardly talk about these poems, or in terms of them. One can only try to talk through them—which perhaps is a way, a way we too much neglect, of learning, all over again, to talk. Thus the first section of the first poem in the six-poem sequence which begins "Praise to the End," "Where Knock Is Open Wide":

> A kitten can
> Bite with his feet;
> Papa and Mamma
> Have more teeth.

---

[3] *Mid-Century American Poetry*, ed. Ciardi, p. 71.

> Sit and play
> Under the rocker
> Until the cows
> All have puppies.

His ears haven't time.
Sing me a sleep-song, please.
A real hurt is soft.

> Once upon a tree
> I came across a time,
> It wasn't even as
> A ghoulie in a dream.

> There was a mooly man
> Who had a rubber hat
> And funnier than that,—
> He kept it in a can.

> What's the time, papa-seed?
> Everything has been twice.
> My father is a fish.

Let us say that this is an entrance-into-the-world poem. For the child, cause and effect are not "rationally" related—thus it is the knock, not the door, which opens wide on this experience; the kitten's scratches with his feet are in effect identical with teeth-bites; and if time is measured by gestation and birth, it is no matter that cows don't have puppies. When the father will not listen, it is his ears, not his larger self, that decline. And in the deepest world of once-upon, the distinction between time and place is of no significance. Papa generates, therefore must be seed, therefore has a sense of time. Like papa, like son; therefore everything has been twice. And further, in this world, papa is primeval, is therefore a fish, swimming through time. What intrudes itself everywhere is the adult world, which threatens the world of the child, precisely as it promises so much to that world. A real hurt is in fact a hurt, as the child's world is threatened; but it is at the same time soft, as it is a hurt from the adult world which promises so much.

We can read such verse only in this way. Even as in its art Roethke's poem gets us to consent to the world it establishes, we report the news of that world back to the one in which we actually live. We do the world of these verses wrong if we translate it into a language appropriate to ours. Rather we must incorporate it, incorporate its style of apperception and knowing, into our own. Thus the way of exhaustion, the slipping-back so as to go forward, progress.

The progress in the "Praise to the End" sequence is not linear, but rather consists of an increased complexity of the modes of consciousness, an increased capacity to comprehend the world at once in its primeval and in its "civilized" states. "Where Knock Is Open Wide" ends.

> I'm somebody else now.
> Don't tell my hands.
> Have I come to always? Not yet.
> One father is enough.
>
> Maybe God has a house.
> But not here.

"Bring the Day!," the third poem, ends:

> O small bird wakening,
> Light as a hand among blossoms,
> Hardly any old angels are around any more.
> The air's quiet under the small leaves.
> The dust, the long dust, stays.
> The spiders sail into summer.
> It's time to begin!
> To begin!

"O Lull Me, Lull Me," the sixth and last poem of the sequence, ends:

> Soothe me, great groans of underneath,
> I'm still waiting for a foot.
> The poke of the wind's close,
> But I can't go leaping alone.
> For you, my pond,
> Rocking with small fish,
> I'm an otter with only one nose:
> I'm all ready to whistle;
> I'm more than when I was born;
> I could say hello to things;
> I could talk to a snail;
> I see what sings!
> What sings!

From establishing a sense of place, to a sense of the origin of things, to a sense of proper relationship with things—not separated in natural, organic fact, but only in degree and quality of understanding. The effect is of a man finding and piecing together his knowledge of himself, which is a product of his knowledge of the natural order. Power, then—as we had always known but yet had to discover on our own—is knowledge.

Prefaced by the sequence which I have just discussed, "The Lost Son" serves all the more to celebrate that power. Fleeing from his father, the son turns from a knowledge so violent in its destructiveness as, at the outset, to be beyond comprehension. The poet himself seems to be fleeing from Eliot; for there are here too a number of significant echoes.[4] The boy, in any case,

---

[4] For example ("The Flight"):

> Fished in an old wound,
> The soft pond of repose; . . .
> Sat in an empty house
> Watching shadows crawl,
> Scratching.
> There was one fly.

and "Where do the roots go? / Look down under the leaves," which,

flees from "the kingdom of bang and blab" down to a river teeming with primeval creatures; he descends into a pit, where he can "feel the slime of a wet nest"; his world is now one terrifying gibber into whose "dark swirl" he falls. And then, at last, he returns to his father—but now with strength to endure. He can assent to his father's "Ordnung! Ordnung!" to the degree that he understands that the words are necessary, because natural. It is winter; and he lives on, fortified by his memories of what he has learned on his flight—of the spirit within and without himself which he has discovered. In the last poem of the sequence, there is a shift to the second person, where before the first has been used—as though the poet were now sufficiently in possession of himself to achieve a certain objectivity:

> A lively understandable spirit
> Once entertained you.
> It will come again.
> Be still.
> Wait.

At the end, there is a recollection of "Ash-Wednesday." The tranquility in which the recollection comes, however, results from a confrontation, and containment, of the violence within, not—as with Eliot—the violence without.

And the rest of the poems in the "Praise to the End" sequence give analogues of and variations upon this theme. The poem whose title is given to the section celebrates, for the first time in the volume, the power of sexuality. "I'm awake all over:," the poet writes, and continues:

---

with other such passages, seem to point to *The Waste Land* and "Gerontion"— so that the poem constitutes a kind of reply to Eliot, or an alternative. And Eliot would appear to have remained steadily in Roethke's mind. For "Meditations of an Old Woman" (appearing first as a whole poem in *Words for the Wind*) is surely a reply to *Four Quartets*, which it abundantly echoes.

I've crawled from the mire, alert as a saint or a dog;
I know the back-stream's joy, and the stone's eternal pulse-
    less longing.
Felicity I cannot hoard. . . .

I believe! I believe!—
In the sparrow, happy on gravel;
In the winter-wasp, pulsing its wings in the sunlight;
I have been somewhere else; I remember the sea-faced
    uncles.
I hear, clearly, the heart of another singing,
Lighter than bells,
Softer than water.

Wherefore, O birds and small fish, surround me.
Lave me, ultimate waters.
The dark showed me a face.
My ghosts are all gay.
The light becomes me.

These lines mark the poet's sense of his freedom ever
after to know, and so to be, himself. Now he is empowered to live in the most possible of all best worlds.
Out of the underground dialectic there has emerged a
knowledge which is knowing.

Knowing himself in his world, he may know others
in theirs and so demonstrate that the two worlds are
one. The rest of the poems collected in *Words for the
Wind* (about one-half the volume) are such demonstra-
tions. They show a degree of formal, "willed" control—a
capacity to tighten and loosen movement as syntax will
allow it—quite beyond that of the earlier poems. Such
poems—even, as regards substance, the most intimate
of them—have a certain "public" quality, the assured
decorum of the poet as his own kind of noble lord.
Consequently, they also have the quality of a certain
careless ease. It is the case of the poet as Young Pros-

pero. Only, having read the poems which come before, we know that we are yielding not to the poet's magic but to his wholly earned and deserved authority, an authority which manifests itself as the poet's style. Such authority, indeed, enables him to address himself to subjects nominally banal and commonplace and to re-discover their abiding power for us.

The poems record the visitations of spirits other than the poet's own, his definition of the losses which he must encounter day-to-day, rollicking memories of earlier days, his nursery-rhymed farewell-and-hail to childhood, and, above all, the infinite possibilities of love. Love, indeed, is the essential substance of them all. It is by now, and at long last, the love which can be given and can be received. Love in these poems is dif-ferent from love in the earlier poems, precisely as its necessary condition is now both giving and receiving. Consciously, willfully to give and to be given to: this initiates the dialectic of relationship to the other which now moves the poems and gives them the formal con-trol which everywhere characterizes them. Their argu-ment is that in love the flesh becomes spirit; that only in time is love possible; that only in love, so known, is eternity to be glimpsed:

> Let seed be grass, and grass turn into hay:
> I'm martyr to a motion not my own;
> What's freedom for? To know eternity.
> I swear she cast a shadow white as stone.
> But who would count eternity in days?
> These old bones live to learn her wanton ways:
> (I measure time by how a body sways).
>   ("I Knew a Woman")

> Dream of a woman, and a dream of death:
> The light air takes my being's breath away;
> I look on white, and it turns into gray—
> When will that creature give me back my breath?

I live near the abyss. I hope to stay
Until my eyes look at a brighter sun
As the thick shade of the long night comes on.
                    ("The Pure Fury")

Just beyond this world, there is a dark world, transcendent, to be discovered. But meantime, there is yet this world, which love makes go round. Roethke, at this stage, was willing to write poem after poem on that truism—in order to bring it back into the life of modern poetry. The pattern and plot that love gives to human life would restore it to its place in the natural order. In "The Waking," he says:

> Great Nature has another thing to do
> To you and me; so take the lively air,
> And, lovely, learn by going where to go.

And in his great sequence, "Four for Sir John Davies," he celebrates (as the Renaissance poet had done before him) the idea of order. For Roethke order is cosmic because sexual, and sexual because cosmic: "The body and the soul know how to play / In that dark world where gods have lost their way." There is then that dark world (elsewhere Roethke calls it an abyss) which threatens, because it awaits. But:

> The world is for the living. Who are they?
> We dared the dark to reach the white and warm.
> She was the wind when wind was in my way;
> Alive at noon, I perished in her form.
> Who rise from flesh to spirit know the fall:
> The word outleaps the world, and light is all.
>   ("The Vigil")

This world and the abyss, light and darkness, love and death—the motifs are common enough, as is our sense of their paradoxical coexistence. Roethke's way with the commonplace is to penetrate into its very commonality: to see it in the natural order, to turn inward and back-

314

ward upon himself and establish his truest involvement in that order, and then to turn outward, to look forward, to fare forward, and, through an understanding of his relation with all that constitutes the other, to affirm that involvement. His reordering of Eliot's formula is this: Sympathize, Control, Give. He would abolish nothing, transmute nothing—but accept everything, and understand as much of it as he can, love even that which he cannot understand. His verse, then, comes to be a vehicle for understanding—and love its principal mode. "Being, not doing, is my first joy," he came to write in a late poem, "The Abyss," even as he felt himself caught up in "The burning heart of the abominable."

In one of the last poems in *Words for the Wind*, written in memory to Yeats, a dying man speaks:

> "A man sees, as he dies,
> Death's possibilities;
> My heart sways with the world.
> I am that final thing,
> A man learning to sing."
> ("His Words")

Roethke's reply, in "The Exulting," is: "A breath is but a breath: I have the earth; / I shall undo all dying by my death," and

> The edges of the summit still appal
> When we brood on the dead or the beloved;
> Nor can imagination do it all
> In this last place of light: he dares to live
> Who stops being a bird, yet beats his wings
> Against the immense immeasurable emptiness of things.
> ("They Sing, They Sing")

3.

This side of the abyss, the dark world, the edges of the summit—so far Roethke, in *Words for the Wind*,

315

charted the journey of his soul. Behind him lay another abyss, into which he had plunged, another dark world, into which he had journeyed, another summit, over which he had leaped. And he had reported fully on his adventures. The reports are poems; and they are so often major poems because they are reports become interpretations, characterized by self-conscious didacticism and a use of traditions and conventions magisterial enough to transfigure, yet not to distort, the experiences on which they center. It is the poems, not the poet, which are transfiguring and transfigured. Roethke seems to have been overwhelmingly aware of the dangers for the modern poet who would risk the personal heresy. Reading the poems, one sees him courting that heresy, as it were employing it against itself. For underpinning the mere person there is the authentic person. I take Roethke's life-work to have been directed toward enlarging and deepening the sense of the authentically personal. On the whole, recent poets who have been of this persuasion have from the outset worked to resist threats to their own sacred selves; theirs has been the violence within fighting the violence without. Roethke rapidly gave up such a sense of his mission—and taught himself (somehow) that first he must learn not to resist himself. Everything followed.

It did not follow as far as it should have. It did not follow as his work promises it would. Our tragedy is that, dying, Roethke did not come to write the poems which would have undone death—I mean the component of death as in his poems he came more and more to acknowledge its immitigable existence. His poems controlled, they sympathized. They only began, at the end, fully to give. They controlled the wide and deep areas of the personal—the widest and deepest, I am persuaded, in the work of any contemporary American poet. And they demonstrated again and again how we have access to those areas only through sympathy— the power of human sympathy as it at first derives and then differentiates itself from the power which maintains the natural order of things. Roethke began to learn, and to make poems which teach, that out of the power of sympathy there comes the power to give, thus to be given to. He began to comprehend the full range of the other, that chain of being which moves from the minimal to God.

The poems in *The Far Field* indicate the distance he had come. Many of the love poems are centered on the consciousness of woman, an "I" different enough from the center of consciousness of the earlier love poems to manifest not only the power of sympathy but of identity with another. In the process, the poet's separate identity is not lost but, for the sake of the poems and the world they create, put aside. The feminine speaker in these poems has little to do with the exacerbated speculations of the masculine speaker in the earlier ones. As the poet gives her to us, we sense that she has always been steadily enough in touch with her interior past (the past of "Where Knock Is Open Wide" and the rest) to have let herself live, and give, fully in the presence of others:

> We are one, and yet we are more,
> I am told by those who know,–
> At times content to be two.
>   ("The Young Girl")

Before this longing,
I lived serene as a fish,
At one with the plants in the pond,
The mare's tail, the floating frogbit,
Among my eight-legged friends,
Open like a pool, a lesser parsnip,
Like a leech, looping myself along,
A bug-eyed edible one,
A mouth like a stickleback,–
A thing quiescent!

317

But now—
The wild stream, the sea itself cannot contain me. . . .
                       ("Her Longing")

And the poet, as the masculine speaker in some of the poems, has learned too, because he has discovered his beloved as she is necessarily part of the order of great nature:

> My lizard, my lively writher,
> May your limbs never wither,
> May the eyes in your face
> Survive the green ice
> Of envy's mean gaze;
> May you live out your life
> Without hate, without grief,
> And your hair ever blaze,
> In the sun, in the sun,
> When I am undone,
> When I am no one.
>   ("Wish for a Young Wife")

He learns that he must some day be no one. And he knows his own temporal oneness all the more specifically, as he knows that of those who people his world— Aunt Tilly whom he celebrates in an "Elegy"; the heroic "Otto" and all those who have inhabited "my father's world— / O world so far away! O my lost world!"; and, simply enough, his "Chums":

> Some are in prison; some are dead;
> And none has read my books,
> And yet my thoughts turn back to them. . . .

What matters is that such memories no longer threaten. Again, he can write of the dark world, but now with the control which comes from loving understanding. Indeed, now he is ready to establish the crucial identification for the American poet:

> Be with me, Whitman, maker of catalogues:
> For the world invades me again,
> And once more the tongues begin babbling.
> And the terrible hunger for objects quails me. . . .

This passage is from a poem I have already cited, "The Abyss." The manner, the structure, and the movement are superficially like such terrified poems as "Where Knock Is Open Wide." But there is now available to the poet a capacity for objectification, itself a product of a capacity for meditation—meditation outward, as it were. "Too much reality can be a dazzle, a surfeit," he writes, and follows this with: "Too close immediacy an exhaustion." He is free, however, to move through the abyss of exhaustion to the peace beyond, which is the peace of acceptance:

> I thirst by day. I watch by night.
> I receive! I have been received!
> I hear the flowers drinking in their light,
> I have taken counsel of the crab and the sea-urchin. . . .

Again the order of nature—now most surely an ordering, so that the conclusion must come:

> I am most immoderately married:
> The Lord God has taken my heaviness away;
> I have merged, like the bird, with the bright air,
> And my thought flies to the place by the bo-tree.

> Being, not doing, is my first joy.

There are two grand efforts toward synthesis in *The Far Field*. Perfected achievements in themselves, the two poems are nonetheless prolegomena toward poems which Roethke did not live to write, toward a synoptic vision of the condition of modern man which at the end was yet beyond him. In the "North American Sequence," the poet is first the explorer of the natural order; then a part of it; then an explorer into the interior of his own experience, so conceived; then the poet who can "embrace the world"; then the poet who realizes that "He is the end of things, the final man";[5] then he who has been given—or, in his struggle, has given himself—unmediated vision into the very center of being. The argument of the "North American Sequence" works to unify and to make all of a piece the world which has invaded the poet, so as to allow him to invade it. The experience would not seem to be ecstatic; for nothing has been cast off. On the contrary, everything has been grasped at once and together, gloriously; and such unification has become the very process of summing-up. The poet (his mentor is still Whitman) discovers that he is part of that sum, that sacred sum. Thus, at the end:

Near this rose, in this grove of sun-parched, wind-warped
  madronas,
Among the half-dead trees, I came upon the true ease of
  myself,
As if another man appeared out of the depths of my being,
And I stood outside myself,
Beyond becoming and perishing,

[5] The whole passage would seem at once to echo and to salute the later Wallace Stevens, whom Roethke claimed (in his "Rouse" for Stevens) as a father-figure for poets of his generation:

> The lost self changes,
> Turning toward the sea,
> A sea-shape turning around,—
> An old men with his feet before the fire,
> In robes of green, in garments of adieu.

> A man faced with his own immensity
> Wakes all the waves, all their loose wandering fire.
> The murmur of the absolute, the why
> Of being born fails on his naked ears.
> His spirit moves like monumental wind
> That gentles on a sunny blue plateau.
> He is the end of things, the final man.
> ("The Far Field")

This is Roethke's version of the "hero," "the final man," celebration of whom dominates much of Stevens' later verse.

A something wholly other,
As if I swayed out on the wildest wave alive,
And yet was still.
And I rejoiced in being what I was:
In the lilac change, the white reptilian calm,
In the bird beyond the bough, the single one
With all the air to greet him as he flies,
The dolphin rising from the darkening waves;
And in this rose, this rose in the sea-wind,
Rooted in stone, keeping the whole of light,
Gathering to itself sound and silence—
Mine and the sea-wind's.

("The Rose")

The compulsion here, as so often in Roethke's later work, is toward the sacred. The underground dialectic, at once empowered and constrained by the poet's dedication to the ordering of nature, has evolved an idea of God. The "Sequence, Sometimes Metaphysical" treats of that idea. In "In a Dark Time" (as in the last poem in the "North American Sequence") the poet encounters himself as one object among many. They constitute "A steady storm of correspondences," and in their storming put to the deepest doubt his sense of the order of nature —as though the order of nature, if only one knows it unmediated, as it really is, might negate itself, and issue into the ultimate entropy. His doubt now is like that which came to him when he confronted for the first time the possibility of his own authentic existence and that of the persons, places, and things which constituted his world:

Dark, dark my light, and darker my desire.
My soul, like some heat-maddened summer fly,
Keeps buzzing at the sill. Which I is I?
A fallen man, I climb out of my fear.
The mind enters itself, and God the mind,
And one is One, free in the tearing wind.

The logic here is keen. Encountering himself as object, man fights through his terror and so rises from his fallen state. He knows once and for all that the price he has to pay for discovering God as object is the same as that he has had to pay for encountering as object any of the forms of the other: the old divisive agony of meditation. Yet now he has the strength, the power, to will himself into understanding and to make whole what has been divided—himself. So doing, he brings God into his "mind." But now he knows that it is he who has found God, he who has redeemed Him, and made manifest His freedom in that "tearing wind."

Such, I take it, is the central motif in the "Sequence, Sometimes Metaphysical." The "Godhead above my God" whom the poet addresses in "The Marrow" is the source of the power which the poet has always sought; finding it, he will have found the means to redeem the God below:

> I was flung back from suffering and love
> When light divided on a storm-tossed tree;
> Yea, I have slain my will, and still I live;
> I would be near; I shut my eyes to see;
> I bleed my bones, their marrow to bestow
> Upon the God who knows what I would know.

The other poems in the sequence are less "metaphysical" than these two, perhaps; but they nonetheless celebrate those moments of meditation, with its burden of divisiveness, which are the necessary consequences of the poet's search for, and likewise the necessary antecedents of, his discovery of the sacred. For always he demands—"More! O More! visible." He goes on in "Once More, the Round."

> Now I adore my life
> With the Bird, the abiding Leaf,
> With the Fish, the questing Snail,

And the Eye altering all;
And I dance with William Blake
For love, for Love's sake;

And everything comes to One,
As we dance on, dance on, dance on.

4.

I have said that the poems in *The Far Field* indicate how far Roethke had come. They may also indicate how far he might have gone. In the note of explanation he wrote for John Ciardi's anthology, *Mid-Century American Poets*, Roethke concluded: "The next phase? Something much longer: dramatic and *playable*. Pray for me." He did not live long enough to reach that phase. In his last poems, he did discover one of the necessary means to the dramatic: a full sense of the other. But the discovery was longer in the making, and surely more painful, than he seems to have imagined it would be. For whatever reason, he could not undertake the compulsive twentieth-century quest for identity via the route of alienation—which, we are told, is in our time the only proper route for the man of high imagination. His was the way of sympathy, and he kept to it as long as he lived. In his work there are many moments of alienation; but they are associated with violence, and he works to transform the violence into power, thus alienation into identification.

Had he lived longer, he might have written a poem of power and identification, a *Jerusalem* for our age. Truly, his beginning was in his end. Even his discovery of God, the ultimate other, could promise him no respite. For God had to be fought toward, and the fighting-toward threatened always to be a fighting against: if not against God, against man. But Roethke was always bound not to be against. The ordering of the "Sequence, Sometimes Metaphysical" registers just this movement, and proves it out. Thus I suggest that perhaps Roethke would have turned to Blake as his great model. (He was always nobly blatant in his study of models.) Calling to mind Blake's *Tiriel*, he pleads with Mnetha (whom Foster Damon calls Blake's Athena), mother of Har (whom Damon calls poetry degenerated), in "The Long Waters" section of the "North American Sequence." And he associates himself with Blake in "Once More, the Round," the last poem in the "Sequence, Sometimes Metaphysical." Perhaps, then, his vision would have become as large as Blake's; and, like Blake, he would have been able to put into his poems the awareness of the concrete and particular conditions of modern life, the biting hatred of abusers of power, even the wonderful comedy which, as he selected his poems for *Words for the Wind*, for the most part he set aside. A Blakean poem—narrative, prophetic, lyric, diatribic— we may guess, was his life's project, as was his life. For him the world was first I, then (from the minimal to God) thou—but not yet, as with Blake, he, she, or they. Learning the lessons of his work, we can say only that in our time, the world (too much with us) is inhabited by third persons, fearing to be first, therefore unable to reach toward the second.

To have revealed the sacredness of the second person, of all persons (and places and things) as they in truth are second—this is Roethke's achievement. And more than that: to have made known that our world of third persons is one in which the power of sympathy, if it exists outside the order of nature, becomes one of violence, now murderous, now suicidal, now both; to have transformed suicide into a means of rebirth and rediscovery; to have "undone" death, and to have dared to "do" love. Freed in the process, Roethke might have indeed become his own kind of Blake.

In a posthumously published piece (*Encounter*, December 1963)—it was intended to be one of the "Winterset Rothberg" tirades and is not included in his *Collected Poems*—Roethke, in fact, wrote in the mode of Blake's *Descriptive Catalogues*. He addressed his "more tedious contemporaries":

> Roaring asses, hysterics, sweet-myself beatniks, earless wonders happy with effects a child of two could improve on: verbal delinquents; sniggering, mildly obscene souser-wowsers, this one writing as if only he had a penis, that one bleeding, but always in waltztime; another intoning, over and over, in metres the expert have made hideous; the doleful, almost-good, over-trained technicians—what a mincing explicitness, what a profusion of adjectives, what a creaking of adverbs!

He went on in this vein, and at length, telling the violent truth. Yet at the end, in Blake's manner, he shifted to verse, characterized by his immense power of sympathy.

Was it reading you I first felt, full in my face, the hot blast
    and clatter of insane machinery?
Yet heard,
Beneath the obscene murderous noise of matter gone mad,
Whose grinding dissonance threatens to overwhelm us all,
The small cry of the human?

I, the loneliest semi-wretch alive, a stricken minor soul,
Weep to you now;
But I've an eye to your leaping forth and fresh ways of wonder;
And I see myself beating back and forth like stale water in
    a battered pail;
Are not you my final friends, the fair cousins I loathe and
    love?
That man hammering I adore, though his noise reach the
    very walls of my inner self;

325

Behold, I'm a heart set free, for I have taken my hatred and
  eaten it,
The last acrid sac of my rat-like fury;
I have succumbed, like all fanatics, to my imagined victims;
I embrace what I perceive!
Brothers and sisters, dance ye,
Dance ye all!

To have heard always the small cry of the human and
to have amplified it and extended its range—that, as
things came to stand with Roethke, had to be enough.

1965

12

WHITMAN AND OUR HOPE
FOR POETRY

"Whitman was wrong about the People,
But right about himself. The land is within.
At the end of the open road we come to ourselves."
LOUIS SIMPSON, *"Lines Written Near San Francisco"*

1.

I TAKE as an initiating text part of the second section of
Robert Duncan's "A Poem Beginning with a Line by
Pindar." Here Duncan looks back toward an aging
Whitman; tries to recover a sense of Whitman's special,
if waning, authority as poet in the Gilded Age; imagines
how it was to be that Whitman—his stroke-affected
speech at once a literal and symbolic vehicle—now fumbling for the words with which to comprehend his society, its politics, and its failure to find leaders it does
not quite deserve. Duncan sees the failure; and, like
Whitman, he will not interpret it as a betrayal of the
poet. For Duncan sees that Whitman as poet succeeded
not as he portrayed failure, but rather as he gave us
the means to measure success, thus to know that our
forebears' failures, and our leaders', may well be our
own. A society does not betray its poets—the argument
implicitly goes; rather, it betrays itself. Its poets may
indeed betray themselves—when they refuse to, or
simply cannot, bear witness to what they see. If, bearing witness, they falter as did the aging Whitman,
theirs are not failures but rather "glorious mistake[s]."
The line from Pindar with which Duncan's poem begins is "The light foot hears you and the brightness

begins." And it is the light-footed poet of our age who
listens to Whitman and sees illumined his world—and
ours—in its present condition.

This is the passage from Duncan's poem:

> . . . It is toward the old poets
> we go, to their faltering,
> their unaltering wrongness that has style,
> their valuable truth,
> the old faces,
> words shed like tears from
> a plentitude of powers time stores.

> A stroke. These little strokes. A chill.
> The old man, feeble, does not recoil.
> Recall. A phase so minute.
> Only a part of the word in- jerrd.

> *The Thundermakers descend,*

> damerging a nuv. A nerb.
> The present dented of the U
> nighted stayd. States. The heavy clod?
> Cloud. Invades his brain. What
> if lilacs last in *this* dooryard bloomd?

Hoover, Roosevelt, Truman, Eisenhower—
where among these did the power reside
that moves the heart? What flower of the nation
bride-sweet broke to the whole rapture?
Hoover, Coolidge, Harding, Wilson
hear the factories of human misery turning out commodities.
For whom are the holy matins of the heart ringing?
Noble men in the quiet of morning hear
Indians singing the continent's violent requiem.
Harding, Wilson, Taft, Roosevelt,
idiots fumbling at the bride's door,
hear the cries of men in meaningless debt and war.

Where among these did the spirit reside
that restores the land to productive order?
McKinley, Cleveland, Harrison, Arthur,
Garfield, Hayes, Grant, Johnson,
dwell in the roots of the heart's rancor.
How sad "amid lanes and through old woods"
    echoes Whitman's love for Lincoln!

There is no continuity then. Only a few
    posts of the good remain. I too
that am a nation sustain the damage
    where smokes of continual ravage
obscure the flame.
            It is across great scars of wrong
    I reach toward the song of kindred men
    and strike again the naked string
old Whitman sang from. Glorious mistake!
    that cried:

    "The theme is creative and has vista."
    "He is the president of regulation."

I see always the under side turning,
fumes that injure the tender landscape.
    From which up break
lilac blossoms of courage in daily act
    striving to meet a natural measure.[1]

Duncan's discovery of Whitman is like that of many
of his contemporaries. I have chosen to begin with a
lengthy passage from his work rather than with a
florilegium of bits and pieces from poems of his contemporaries, because bits and pieces, however many
of them there could be, simply will not convey the

---

[1] *The Opening of the Field* (New York, 1960), pp. 63-64. The
mock-litany of names of course recalls Emerson's ironic litany of
"earth-proud" men in "Hamatreya."

particular import of this, the newest version of our poets' continuing discovery of Whitman.[2]

For the history of American poetry could be written as the continuing discovery and rediscovery of Whitman, an on-going affirmation of his crucial relevance to the mission of the American poet: which is, as it is everywhere, simply to tell us the truth in such a way that it will be a new truth, and in its newness will renew us and our capacity to have faith in ourselves, only then together to try to build the sort of world which will have that faith as its necessary condition. Our great modernist poets—Eliot, Stevens, Pound, Crane, and Williams—of course all registered in their poems their dis-

[2] Were the florilegium an anthology, it might well include these widely and sometimes wildly various poems: Edwin Honig, "Walt Whitman," *The Gazebo* (New York, 1959), p. 44; Denise Levertov, "A Common Ground," *The Jacob's Ladder* (New York, 1961), pp. 1-3; Allen Ginsberg, "A Supermarket in California," *Howl* (San Francisco, 1956), pp. 23-24; James Wright, "The Morality of Poetry," *Saint Judas* (Middletown, 1959), pp. 18-19; Charles Olson, "I Mencius, Pupil of the Master . . . ," *The Distances* (New York, 1960), pp. 61-63; Louis Simpson, "Walt Whitman at Bear Mountain," "Pacific Ideas," and "Lines Written Near San Francisco," *At the End of the Open Road* (Middletown, 1963), pp. 64-70; Galway Kinnell, "Vapor Trail Reflected in the Frog Pond," in R. Bly and D. Ray, eds., *A Poetry Reading against the Vietnam War* (Madison, Minn., 1966), pp. 61-62 and also, in a slightly different version, in Kinnell's *Body Rags* (Boston, 1967), pp. 7-8; Jack Spicer, "The Book of Galahad," Part 1, *The Holy Grail* (San Francisco, 1964); Ted Berrigan, "Real Life—1. The Fool," the tenth of *The Sonnets* (New York, 1964); Robert Lowell, "Words for Hart Crane," *Life Studies* (New York, 1959), p. 55; David Ignatow, "Walt Whitman in Civil War Hospitals," *Say Pardon* (Middletown, 1961), p. 31, and "Envoi," *Rescue the Dead* (Middletown, 1968), p. 21; Roland Johnson, "Letters to Walt Whitman," *Poetry*, cviii (1967), 152-161; and two broadsides—Tuli Kupferberg, "I say / To masturbate is human / To fuck divine . . ." (New York, 1966) and Lawrence Ferlinghetti, "One Thousand Fearful Words for Fidel Castro" (San Francisco, 1961). Louis Zukofsky, at long last coming into his own as an Elder Statesman of the newest poetry, in his essay, "Poetry: For My Son When He Can Read," appended to his *"A": 1-12* (Ashland, 1959), pp. 269-288, concludes by quoting the whole of Whitman's "Respondez!" as a "definition of the poetry we anticipate."

covery of Whitman, a discovery made sometimes, as it were, in spite of themselves. Their Whitman, however, is not quite the Whitman of Duncan and his contemporaries—our contemporaries—as their hope for poetry is not quite that of Duncan and his, and our, contemporaries. Their Whitman was the lonely Adamic figure—in Emerson's phrase, the self against the world; the poet struggling to define his vocation in a world which seemed to have no place for him; the shape-shifter who at the end tricked himself into believing that it was more important to be a divine than a literatus. Their concern, one with their commitment to define their vocation in their time, was to separate the literatus from the divine and to learn from him all they could. They were little interested in—indeed, were suspicious of—the poet as directly critical of and deeply involved in society, politics, the structure and function of American life and its sheer busyness. They were reacting, of course, against the quasi-deification which was Whitman's boon at the end of his life and immediately after—and also against the politically reductionist understanding of his work in interpretations like those of Parrington and Arvin. They wanted clarity, even if it meant sacrificing charity. And their poems show that they achieved it, and so often precisely at such a cost.

The situation is otherwise now—as Duncan's lines show. Duncan sees those "lilac blossoms of courage in daily act / striving to meet a natural measure." And he will say, with Whitman, that he too is "a nation" which sustains "the damage / where smokes of continual ravage / obscure the flame." And, like Whitman, he is concerned with our leaders, our *political* leaders. In 1860, Whitman had written "To a President":

All you are doing and saying is to America dangled mirages,
You have not learn'd of Nature—of the politics of
    Nature you have not learn'd the great amplitude,
    rectitude, impartiality.

331

You have not seen that only such as they are for
    these States,
And that what is less than they must sooner or later lift off
    from these States.[3]

Duncan, in his address to Presidents, is contemporary by virtue of being Whitmanian. For his peers in our time are—whatever their local affiliations—determined to put political and social criticism back into their poetry. Clarity, yes. And often bitterness of apocalyptic depths; often barbaric howls over the rooftops of our world; often a deliberate and vulgar courting of confusion; often a seeking of shortcuts to poetic insight, which manifest themselves as short-circuits in communication. But still at the end: charity. Such charity demands an unflinching attempt at scope and inclusiveness, and so urges our poets to see the poet involved in the whole of his world, to claim—often tendentiously—that a condition of the whole poet is a commitment to understand the whole world. Duncan of course knows the work of Pound and Williams well; he has gone to school to Charles Olson, and he is immensely learned—a poet-scholar. Still, on behalf of the poets of our age, he evokes Whitman as he would seek the spirit "that restores the land to productive order." This is, in our time, our poets' hope for poetry. And they would make it ours.

2.

My task thus is to be exegete and advocate of that Whitman who sought the spirit "that restores the land to productive order." There are other Whitmans, of course, and valid ones. But this is the one whom we appear to need now. I must accordingly turn to an old

[3] Here and in what follows I quote the poems, except when noted, from *Leaves of Grass*, Comprehensive Reader's Edition, ed. H. W. Blodgett and Sculley Bradley (New York, 1965).

problem in Whitman criticism: that of the poet as critic of society. And I shall hope to show that the Whitman Duncan has recently discovered is one of the Whitmans American scholar-critics have also recently discovered. At the very least, the one discovery— by the poet—illumines the other—by the scholar-critics —and vice-versa. I should like to think that each entails the other. That is one of my hopes for poetry.[4]

The difficult fact is that we know almost too much about Whitman as critic of American society, pre- and post-Civil War. Inevitably, those who interpret Whitman must write about his "social thought"—inevitably, because it is an integral aspect of his life's work that he should have been a "social critic." In this role he is regularly present in histories of American thought— social, political, and otherwise. This is only proper. For with great and glorious ease and freedom, the newspaperman become poet tells us in the Preface to the 1855 *Leaves of Grass* that as poet he is nothing if not critic of society. He will make his society know all its possibilities and how it may realize them.

Now, the way to that realization is, in the poems of the 1855 *Leaves of Grass*, not so much social as individual, as we all by now surely know. And the tendency of that recent strong line of interpreters of Whitman which prefers the 1855 version of his book to all others is, in fact, to deny him, as poet, much of a role as social critic—or at best to deny him a covert role. Yet even this line of interpreters sees the journalistic work

[4] Perhaps the hope is merely academic. At least I worry that it might be when I read the conclusion of Charles Tomlinson's "conversation" with Robert Creeley (*The Review*, No. 10 [1964], p. 35:

Creeley: . . . And there is one much earlier poet who is far, far more available than Eliot . . .
Tomlinson: And that is?
Creeley: That is the figure the New Critics and the universities to this day have conspired to ignore: that is Walt Whitman.

I trust that by now Mr. Creeley is talking to the right people, who are sending him to the right books.

which surrounds the 1855 *Leaves of Grass* as geneti-
cally related to it. That is to say, as journalist, Whitman
came to know his world in closely examined and expressed detail; and consequently as poet he came to see
that what his world needed was a new, or renewed,
image of man, whereby it might at long last realize its
potentialities. The poet offers himself to his society,
offers himself as archetypal for all selves, and thereby
rests assured that it will henceforth be whole. The
genetic line is from Whitman's journalistic social criticism to his earliest important poems. Out of the world
described in the journalism the poet was precipitated.
Or rather, out of that world that poet precipitated himself, and in what came to be called "Song of Myself"
with loving and daring precision described the act of
precipitation, which was in fact an act of self-creation.

But the genesis did not stop there. For now the *poet*,
by virtue of being a poet, surely had to continue to be a
kind of social critic. True enough, he was no longer
particularly a critic of issues and events—except when
he wrote something other than poetry, which of course
he continued to do. As poet, he had to find a way of
speaking about his world and the facts of its life—a way
which would let him be a critic by virtue of being a poet.
The facts of which he came to speak were not quite
those of which he could treat in his journalism, or even
in his programmatic prefaces. No longer free soil, abo-
lition, political compromises, forms of manifest destiny,
and the like. Indeed, as his recent interpreters have
uniformly noted, especially after the Civil War crisis,
Whitman, even in his prose writing, was much less interested in specifically sociopolitical issues than he had
been before. They have, as a consequence, tended to
judge him as a social critic only in contexts outside his
poetry, even when they have tried to interpret his post-
Civil War poetry as somehow tending to pull (or push)
him toward a definite political stance—ranging from

that of utopian socialist to anti-ideological conservative. At this point, I must demur. For I think that Whitman, after the Civil War and into the Gilded Age, yet tried, as poet, to be social critic, and succeeded; and that the sort of social criticism he got into his poems was, when, occasionally, it worked as poetry, all the more powerful because it was not so much *pro-* or *anti*-political as *pre*-political.

I want to inquire a little into Whitman's attempt to find a means of dealing in his poetry with the *products* of the sort of world about which he had written at length in his journalistic prose. What—again to echo Robert Duncan—were the conditions which would have to obtain if the land were to be restored to productive order? For one of Whitman's great insights as poet—an insight which makes him so truly the poet of whom Duncan writes—is that the world of post-Jacksonian democracy, of the common man, of the Gilded Age, was for good and for bad, one in which, through its increasingly rationalized social and political and economic structure, producers were increasingly bowed down under the weight of their products. Whitman not only generalized, as had Emerson, that "Things are in the saddle,/ And ride mankind." He *observed* the "things" as they were at once bound to mankind and also bound it. And in his post-Civil War poetry—or in some of it—he not only declared his insight but gave his readers a means of weighing its significance for them precisely as they would find themselves bowed down under the weight of their products, or their society's. Whitman was only fitfully successful in this vein; and toward the end, so the poems show, the burden of his insight was too great for him. He faltered. Yet it is not his failure which I would like to emphasize, but his success, however small: his "glorious failure"— to quote Duncan again. It is a success story which we have not yet read clearly, and one which, so the work

335

of our poets now indicates, has increasingly great significance for us.

These are the basic facts of the case: the 1855, 1856, and 1860 versions of *Leaves of Grass* are stages in the development of an essentially autobiographical poem. In this poem, or in these versions of it, the poet discovers first himself, then society, then again himself. The 1860 *Leaves of Grass* is Whitman's attempt to write a totally humanistic poem; in it even the cycle of love and death is contained in the magnificently autobiographical humanism which it projects. The Civil War put this humanism into doubt, manifesting to Whitman not only anti-humanism (which he had successfully contained in the 1860 *Leaves of Grass*) but dehumanization. The Civil War poems show the poet's sense of the razor-edge balance between humanism and dehumanization; and he survives, when he does, only by appealing to supra-human forces, as so memorably in "When Lilacs Last in the Dooryard Bloomed." The war, then, was for Whitman a new kind of extreme situation—unlike the terrors and torments confronted in the 1855, 1856, and 1860 *Leaves of Grass*, one outside of himself, a product of forces he could in no way imagine himself or any man as containing and controlling. The technique of the pre-Civil War poems had been that of total empathy and total sympathy: Give, Sympathize, Control. And the events of the war, like the social and personal catastrophes it produced, simply were beyond Whitman's, or any man's, powers of poetic empathy and sympathy. One could give and sympathize—as is shown by Whitman's prose memoranda on his hospital journeys and his letters to the soldiers he so lovingly tended. But one could not control. The poet was called upon to enlarge his technique, to amplify his capacities, to examine anew his role as poet. He was faced, crucially, with the discovery that a society, a community, is greater than the sum of its individual parts; that the sum somehow generates ac-

tions and events and things which may destroy the
parts. The poet, in short, was now called upon to deal
with the sum, whereas before he had dealt only with
the parts (and with himself as the greatest part, as he
had said).

"Long, too long, O land," Whitman wrote in 1865—
later changing "O land" to "America."—

Long, too long, O land,
Traveling roads all even and peaceful you learn'd
        from joys and prosperity only,
But now, ah now, to learn from crises of anguish,
        advancing, grappling with direst fate and
        recoiling not.
And now to conceive and show to the world what your
        children en-masse really are,
(For who except myself has yet conceiv'd what your children
        en-masse really are?)

It was an enlargement of his conception of the poet
which Whitman quite carefully announced in the first
of the "Inscriptions" which open the 1871 version of
Leaves of Grass:

One's-self I sing, a simple separate person,
Yet utter the word Democratic, the word En-Masse.
Of Physiology from top to toe I sing,
Not physiognomy alone nor brain alone is worthy for the
        Muse, I say the Form complete is worthier far.
The Female equally with the Male I sing.

Of Life immense in passion, pulse, and power,
Cheerful, for freest action form'd under the laws divine,
The Modern Man I sing.

The poem puts precisely Whitman's attempt to con-
ceive anew of his capacities as poet—here, as if by *fiat*.
Note the burden of meaning which is carried by the
"Yet" of the second line:

One's-self I sing, a simple separate person,
Yet utter the word Democratic, the word En-Masse.

337

Not the coordinating "and" nor the subordinating "but." Rather the concessive "yet": which is to say, to claim, that even as the poet celebrates himself as an archetypal ego for us all, he celebrates us (including himself) as we (with him) compose a group. The one celebration is claimed to be precisely the same as the other. So it follows a few lines later that we are to have "freest action form'd under the laws divine." Individual freedom is one with the law which governs the group, the mass, to which the individual belongs. This is but an extrapolation of the heroically confident doctrine of the 1855, 1856, and 1860 versions of *Leaves of Grass*, of course. But at this point in Whitman's career—as in the career of his society—it becomes an issue which must be boldly, bluntly, and at the outset, proclaimed. If he protests too much, we must at least be grateful that he has the courage to protest.

The argument of this little poem is repeated in others of the "Inscriptions" series: in "In Cabin'd Ships at Sea," "Eidolons," and in "For Him I Sing," for example. And the confidence it expresses is manifest in a significant number of poems published in 1871 and beyond—in the Gilded Age. I shall want later to look at one of those poems and see in somewhat formal terms just how Whitman strives to enlarge his capacity as poet, so to treat of the word Democratic, the word En-Masse, by virtue of treating of the simple separate person; how he conceives of freedom under law; how he would celebrate the group's product in such a way as to teach its producers how to relate it to themselves; how, in short, as poet he is critic of society.

But first we must note some of the consequences of this expanded conception of poetry for Whitman's conception of the poet. The major text here is *Democratic Vistas* (1871), which derives in good part from slightly earlier prose writing. A few quotations will serve our purpose:

View'd, to-day, from a point of view sufficiently over-arching, the problem of humanity all over the civilized world is social and religious, and is to be finally met and treated by literature. The priest departs, the divine literatus comes.

It may be argued that our republic is, in performance, really enacting to-day the grandest arts, poems, &c. by beating up the wilderness into fertile farms, and in her railroads, ships, machinery, &c. And it may be ask'd, Are these not better, indeed, for America, than any utterances even of greatest rapsode, artist, or literatus?

I say that our New World democracy, however great a success in uplifting the masses out of their sloughs, in materialistic development, products, [note that word: *products*] and in a certain highly developed superficial popular intellectuality, is, so far, an almost complete failure in its social aspects, and in really grand religious, moral, literary, and esthetic results.

[After detailing the objects and events and excitements of Brooklyn and New York]: But sternly discarding, shutting our eyes to the glow and grandeur of the general superficial effect, coming down to what is of the only real importance, Personalities, and examining minutely, we question, we ask, Are there, indeed, *men* here worthy the name?

For to democracy, the leveler, the unyielding principle of the average, is surely join'd another principle, equally unyielding, closely tracking the first, indispensable to it, opposite . . . and whose existence, confronting and even modifying the other, often clashing, paradoxical, yet neither of highest avail without the other, plainly supplies to these grand cosmic politics of ours, and to the launch'd forth mortal dangers of republicanism, to-day or any day, the counterpart and offset whereby Nature restrains the deadly original relentlessness of

WHITMAN AND OUR HOPE FOR POETRY

all her first-class laws. This second principle is individuality, the pride and centripetal isolation of a human being in himself—identity—personalism.

The word of the modern . . . is the word Culture.

We find ourselves abruptly in close quarters with the enemy. This word Culture, or what it has come to represent, involves, by contrast, our whole theme, and has been, indeed, the spur, urging us to engagement. Certain questions arise. As now taught, accepted and carried out, are not the processes of culture rapidly creating a class of supercilious infidels, who believe in nothing? Shall a man lose himself in countless masses of adjustments, and be so shaped with reference to this, that, and the other, that the simply good and healthy and brave parts of him are reduced and clipp'd away, like the bordering of box in a garden. You can cultivate corn and roses and orchards—but who shall cultivate the mountain peaks, the ocean, and the tumbling gorgeousness of the clouds? Lastly—is the readily-given reply that culture only seeks to help, systematize, and put in attitude, the elements of fertility and power, a conclusive reply?

I should demand a programme of culture, drawn out, not for a single class alone, or for the parlors of lecture-rooms, but with an eye to practical life, the west, the working-men, the facts of farms and jackplanes and engineers, and of the broad range of the women also of the middle and working strata, and with reference to the perfect equality of women, and a grand and powerful motherhood. I should demand of this programme or theory a scope generous enough to include the widest human area.

In short, and to sum up, America, betaking herself to formative action (and it is about time for more solid achievement, and less windy promise,) must, for her

340

purposes, cease to recognize a theory of character grown of feudal aristocracies, or form'd by merely literary standards, or from any ultramarine, full-dress formulas of culture, polish, caste, &c., and must sternly promulgate her own new standard, yet old enough, and accepting the old, the perennial elements, and combining them into groups, unities, appropriate to the modern, the democratic, the west, and to the practical occasions and needs of our own cities, and of the agricultural regions.[5]

Thus Whitman in the process of enlarging his sense of himself as critic of society. Central to the enlarging is the introduction of the word "culture" as subsuming and interrelating art, religion, politics, family, trade—all American institutions—as "products": products which, as they are produced, at once make possible the good life in society and yet, because they transcend the individual, threaten that life. If we can trust the standard Whitman concordance, the word—and the concept—"culture" comes first into Whitman's vocabulary in *Democratic Vistas*. Where he got the word we do not know. We do know that it was much on his mind in the years around 1870. He planned, apparently, to write an essay called "The Theory of Culture." In the Feinberg Collection of Whitman manuscripts there are his notes for that essay. With Mr. Feinberg's permission, I quote what I take to be the most important of them:

> The theory of culture fits the specialities of scholars & the literary class; Personalism is for universal use of living men in the practical world, with its qualities, fibre, storms, mixture of good & evil. The latter of the two has heights & flashes to which the former can never

[5] *Collected Writings: Prose Works*, ed. F. Stovall (New York, 1964), II, 365-403.

WHITMAN AND OUR HOPE FOR POETRY

attain. The latter is for the Soul, the other for the Intellect. . . .

In short, Whitman was concerned to put "culture" to
the test of "personalism," so to distinguish what has in
our time been called authentic from inauthentic culture, that which enables and that which disables the
American as he seeks to live the life of the simple
separate person, yet democratic, en masse. To discriminate between authentic and inauthentic culture, to
write poems which would be the instrument of discrimination—this was the task of the divine literatus.
Such discrimination would be a necessary condition
of the discovery, or recovery, of that of which Robert
Duncan writes: "the spirit . . ./ that restores the land
to productive order."

Whitman strove to write poems of this order before
the period of *Democratic Vistas*, of course. I think of
parts of "A Song of Joys," "Starting from Paumanok,"
and "As I Walk These Broad Majestic Days"—all of
which come into the 1860 version of *Leaves of Grass*,
all of which mark Whitman's awareness of the tension
between the claims of his radical humanism (that is,
his "personalism") and the claims of his burgeoning
world (that is, its "culture"). And there is "Years of the
Modern," put first into the 1865 *Leaves of Grass*, and
also "Respondez!" put into the 1856 and 1860 editions
but subsequently (I think mistakenly) dropped. Still,
the tension is somewhat slack in these poems, as the
claims and counterclaims seem naturally and easily to
resolve themselves.

The tension is as tight as Whitman could allow it to
be in a poem first published in the 1871 *Leaves of
Grass*, the poem which became "Song of the Exposi-
tion." Under its original title, which is its first line as
I quote it, Whitman recited it at the opening of the
Fortieth Annual Exhibition of the American Institute,

in New York, September 7, 1871. Retitled and some-what changed, it went into the 1876 *Leaves of Grass* in part prefaced thus, the language recalling that of *Democratic Vistas*. The preface enunciates the hope of Institute:

> Struggling steadily to the front, not only in the spirit of Opinion, Government, and the like, but, in due time, in the Artistic also, we see actual operative LABOR and LABORERS, with Machinery, Inventions, Farms, Prod-ucts, &c., pressing to place our time, over the whole civilized world. Holding these by the hand, we see, or hope to see, THE MUSE (radiating, representing, under its various expressions, as in every age and land, the healthiest, most heroic Humanity, common to all, fus-ing all) entering the demesnes of the New World, as twin and sister of our Democracy—at any rate we will so invite Her, here and now—to permanently infuse in daily toils, and be infused by them.
>
> Ostensibly to inaugurate an Exposition of this kind—still more to outline the establishment of a great *perma-nent* Cluster-Palace of Industry from an imaginative and Democratic point of view—was the design of the following poem. . . .

"Holding these by the hand. . . ." The phrase, as does so much of Whitman's self-indulgent prose, makes us uncomfortable. It is important, nonetheless; for it is yet another attempt of the poet to indicate how, as social critic, he might envisage the things, the products, of his world as at once of the simple, separate person and of the mass. This is his "programme of culture," and it entails no less than the humanization of the actually or potentially dehumanized, the products and institutions of an industrial society moving even in the 1870's precipitously toward overdevelopment.

The poem, in its 1871 version, begins:

After all not to create only, or found only,
But to bring perhaps from afar what is already founded,
To give it our own identity, average, limitless, free,
To fill the gross the torpid bulk with vital religious fire,
Not to repel or destroy so much as to accept, fuse, rehabili-
    tate,
To obey as well as command, to follow more than to lead,
There also are the lessons of our New World.
While how little the New after all, how much the Old, Old
    World![6]

Then, following immediately upon this call to give identity and freedom to all that which bulks large in the world, there is a small lyric intrusion, a recollection of the primal power celebrated from the beginning in *Leaves of Grass*:

> Long and long has the grass been growing,
> Long and long has the rain been falling,
> Long has the globe been rolling round.

The body of the poem consists of Whitman's attempt to indicate just how that primal power may be discovered in what he had called in *Democratic Vistas* "culture"—culture in its largest, quite modern, extended sense. He asks at length that the Muse come to America from the Old World and find her place here. He sees her

Making directly for this rendezvous, vigorously clearing
    a path for herself, striding through the confusion,
By thud of machinery and shrill steam-whistle undismay'd.
Bluff'd not a bit by drain-pipe, gasometers, artificial ferti-
    lizers,
Smiling and pleas'd with palpable intent to stay,
She's here, install'd amid the kitchen ware!

[6] I quote the poem from the pamphlet, *After All, Not to Create Only* (Boston, 1871).

Once in the New World, the Muse finds herself at home in a land where

> We plan even now to raise, . . .
> Thy great cathedral sacred industry, no tomb,
> A keep for life for practical invention.

But how does Whitman conceive that the products of "practical invention" may be those of authentic as opposed to inauthentic culture? The answer is one the reader of earlier versions of *Leaves of Grass* would expect: by seeing precisely, by expressing precisely, the degree to which these are specifically human products; products of the simple, separate person as he is caught up in the communal life of the mass; if not the poet's own creations, nonetheless genuine creations as they are communal creations:

Here shall you trace in flowing operation,
In every state of practical, busy movement, the rills of
    civilization,
Materials here under your eye shall change their shape as
    if by magic,
The cotton shall be pick'd almost in every field,
Shall be dried, clean'd, ginn'd, baled, spun into thread and
    cloth before you,
You shall see hands at work at all the old processes and all
    the new ones,
You shall see the various grains and how flour is made and
    then baked by the bakers,
You shall see the crude ores of California and Nevada pass-
    ing on and on till they become bullion,
You shall watch how the printer sets type, and learn what
    a composing stick is,
You shall mark in amazement the Hoe press whirling its
    cylinders, shedding the printed leaves steady and fast,
The photograph, model, watch, pin, nail, shall be created
    before you.

The technique and the form here are familiar to us: the loving catalogue; the careful singling out of the specifically human act involved in industrial production; a dependence upon particularized nouns and verbs of human agency; an essential vitalism. I suggest that in these lines—certainly not among Whitman's greatest, but cumulating toward a certain kind of power—we know again what James Wright has recently called Whitman's "delicacy."[7] It *is* a delicacy, the total delicacy, of the human, of a poet who would (as Whitman says a few lines later) "exalt the present and the real." And he would do so by conceiving of the artisan as artist. The literatus can and must do this. So that, passing in review the very things which, produced en masse, might threaten the simple separate existence of the producers, he can in his art inquire as to the degree that they are and are not integral in the authentic existence of the producers. And at the end he can address the Muse—not God, but the Muse—simply and straightforwardly:

Our farms, inventions, crops, we owe in thee! cities and
    States in thee!
Our freedom all in thee! our very lives in thee!

The specific mode of this poem is one with a few others out of Whitman's later career—"Song of the Redwood Tree" (1874) and "To a Locomotive in Winter" (1876). And it has affiliations with the mode of "Passage to India" (1871). Moreover, it is a mode which we know well in Whitman's earlier poetry—particularly in the last segment of "Song of Myself." The difference between the mode in the post- as against the pre-Civil War poems is this: that in the earlier poems (not only "Song of Myself," but poems like "Salut au Monde" and "Crossing Brooklyn Ferry"), the poet reads himself *into*

[7] "The Delicacy of Walt Whitman," in R.W.B. Lewis, ed., *The Presence of Walt Whitman* (New York, 1962), pp. 164-188.

his world, whereas in the later poems he reads an enlarged sense of other men, of humanity, *out* of his world. The aim in the earlier poems was to discover himself; that of the later poems, to discover others. The later task was the more difficult, and was performed with significantly less success, because there the poet had wherever possible to point toward the possibility of the reassociation of that which had been, or was in danger of being, disassociated: producer from product, actor from act, agent from deed. He had to find a source of what he called (in "A Backward Glance O'er Travell'd Roads,") that "ultimate vivification" which would endow "facts," "science," and "common lives," "with the glows and glories and final illustriousness which belong to every real thing, and to real things only." He had, in short, to locate them in social and communal reality, to find in them at once a source and an end of culture.

"The chief trait of any given poet," he wrote in the same essay, "is always the spirit he brings to the observation of humanity and nature—the mood out of which he contemplates his subjects. What kind of temper and what amount of faith report these things?" Whitman's humanist temper and faith—for that is what the aspect of his spirit I have been discussing comes to—only falteringly sustained him after the Civil War. It would not sustain him throughout the history of "Song of the Exposition." For the 1881 version of that poem, he added at the beginning a stanza unhappily out of phase with what adamantly follows it:

> (Ah little recks the laborer,
> How near his work is holding him to God.
> The loving Laborer through space and time.)

The stanza is in parentheses (as a comforting afterthought) and is meant, I suppose, to divinize the all-too-human Muse whom the poet would bring from abroad to dwell among the kitchenware. Only as God could the Muse find safe-conduct in the New World. The literatus would become more divine than literate—as in so much of Whitman's later verse, with its passages to everywhere except home, the only place where the poet could honestly confront the problem of the simple separate person and its productions en masse. But, with other scholar-critics, I have regretted this change of phase before. I regretted it, I regret it, because it diminishes Whitman's power, and his significance, for us.

3.

Here, however, I would dwell undiminishingly on that power and that significance. I suggest—as a way of thinking about the poet as critic of post-Civil War society—that in his own way, according to his own style, he was discovering what Marx called alienation, the alienation of the laborer from the product of his labor, in that mass-industrial society in which all men willy-nilly become laborers. The "realization of labor," so go Marx's famous words of the 1840's, "appears as *loss of reality* for the workers; objectification as *loss of the object* and *object-bondage*; appropriation as *estrangement, alienation.*"

And with my quotation from Marx I return to our own time, and to the text from Robert Duncan, with which I initiated this inquiry. Let me modify two of Duncan's lines:

> Where among *us does* the spirit reside
> That restores the land to productive order?

"Productive order" is precisely the opposite of Marx's "appropriation as *estrangement, alienation.*" And "alienation" is a word which is perhaps too much with us these days. In any case, it is a word—and a concept—central to that which is most fruitful and promising in radical political thinking in our time. And, in point of

348

fact, poets like Duncan and his peers all over our land share with all of us the discovery of "alienation" and all it implies for the fate of our culture. As I have said, they are putting politics back into our poetry. But it is a politics shot through with their sense of the matter of authentic as against inauthentic culture. They show that in an alienated world, proper politics is impossible, because it is cut off from the human values and capacities from which derives the very power it must organize. For them, as recent events have shown, free speech and free verse are of a piece. Accordingly, the Whitman to whom they look—although not often with Duncan's superb (and scholarly) awareness of what he is doing—is that Whitman whom I have been discussing.

Let it be freely admitted that this Whitman is, as poet, far from the greatest Whitman. "Song of the Exposition" is, as I have said, not one of the poems which stick with us; nor are the other poems in its vein, including "Passage to India." In all of them a certain religiosity and self-indulgence dull and diffuse, as if Whitman could not bear to carry out the task he set for himself. He faltered. Together, nonetheless, these poems matter deeply to us—if only in falling short of their goal, they help us all the more clearly establish our own. They show, perhaps, that Whitman was successful as prophet inversely as he was successful as poet. Together, perhaps, they amount to that "glorious mistake" over which Duncan exclaims. In all honesty, acknowledging the mistake may well be the price we must pay for apprehending the glory. And it might be possible—if we are lucky—that our poets, apprehending the glory, will not make the mistake. As ever, that must be our hope for poetry.

Whitman knew this well. We should recall that one of the key inscriptive poems to *Leaves of Grass* reads thus:

Poets to come! orators, singers, musicians to come!
Not to-day is to justify me and answer what I am for,
But you, a new brood, native, athletic, continental, greater
    than before known,
Arouse! for you must justify me.

I myself but write one or two indicative words for the future,
I but advance a moment only to wheel and hurry back in
    the darkness

I am a man who, sauntering along without fully stopping,
    turns a casual look upon you and then averts his face,
Leaving it to you to prove and define it,
Expecting the main things from you.

I add: We yet expect the main things from our poets—
our poets to come—as did Whitman. Our hope for poetry
now lies precisely in its search for the spirit which will
restore the land to productive order.

1968

INDEX

Aalto, Alvar, 89
Abrams, Meyer, *The Mirror and the Lamp*, 212
Adams, Samuel, 138n
Adkins, Nelson F., 147n, 150n
Allen, Gay Wilson, 201n, 217
Alonso, Amado, 60
Altick, Richard, 86n
Anderson, Sherwood, "I Want to Know Why," 98
Asselineau, Roger, 217
American Literature, 256
Arvin, Newton, 331
Atlantic Monthly, 240, 259
Auerbach, Erich, *Mimesis*, 23, 24, 24n, 48
Avalon, Frankie, 86

Babbitt, Irving, 192
Bachelard, Gaston, 60
Baldwin, James, 94
Bancroft, George, 164, 165
Barnaut, Elsa, 30n
Baudelaire, Charles, 212
Beardsley, M. C., and W. K. Wimsatt, Jr. "The Intentional Fallacy," 47
Bellow, Saul, *The Adventures of Augie March*, 57-59; *Henderson the Rain King*, 59
Bennett, Emerson, 111n
Beowulf, 6
Berrigan, Ted, 330n
Bible, 210, 307
Bird, Robert Montgomery, 111n
Blackmur, R. P., 54
Blake, William, 207, 307, 323-325; *Descriptive Catalogues*, 325; *Jerusalem*, 323; *Tiriel*, 324
Bowers, Fredson, 201n, 225
Brooks, Van Wyck, 54
Brownson, Orestes, 79-80
Bryant, William Cullen, 51
Bush, Douglas, 21n
Brooks, Cleanth, 21, 21n

Bultmann, Rudolf, 5n; *Essays, Philosophical and Theological*, 34
Burke, Kenneth, *The Philosophy of Literary Form*, 34
Burroughs, William, *Naked Lunch*, 68

Castro, Américo, 18; *The Structure of Spanish History*, 34, 60
Catton, Bruce, 7
Cervantes, Miguel de, *Don Quixote*, 59
Chayefsky, Paddy, 89
Chekov, Anton, 89
Ciardi, John, 306; ed., *Mid-Century American Poets*, 323
Coleridge, Samuel Taylor, 40
Collingwood, R. G., 39
Cooper, James Fenimore, 24, 51, 109-136, 165, 168; *The Deerslayer*, 125; *Home as Found*, 128; *The Last of the Mohicans*, 125, 128; *Leatherstocking Tales* (1850), Preface, 130-131; *The Pathfinder*, 123, 125, 126; *The Pioneers*, 123-125, 126-127; *The Prairie*, 125, 126, 128, 134
Cope, Jackson, 25
Cozzens, James Gould, *By Love Possessed*, 83
Crane, Stephen, 330
Creeley, Robert, 333n
Crews, Frederic C., 106n
Croce, Benedetto, 5n
Cunningham, J. V., 24; *Woe or Wonder: The Emotional Effect of Shakespearean Tragedy*, 25
Curtius, Ernst Robert, 60

Daedalus: Journal of the American Academy of Arts and Sciences, 84, 90, 94
Daily Times, Brooklyn, 200
Dallam, James W., 111n

Thorp, Willard, 198
Thwing, Annie Haven, 138n
Tocqueville, Alexis de, 50
The Token, 138, 138n, 147
Tomlinson, Charles, 333n
Traherne, Thomas, 307
Trilling, Lionel, 48; *Freud and the Crisis of Our Culture*, 30; "The Sense of the Past," 20, 29
Troeltsch, Ernst, 24
Trollope, Anthony, 198
Tuve, Rosemond, 24
Twain, Mark, 248, 260; *Huckleberry Finn*, 260

Van Tassel, David D., 163n

Waggoner, Hyatt H., 105n
Warren, Austin, 193; and René Wellek, *Theory of Literature*, 9, 10, 15n, 24n
Warren, Robert Penn, 7, 9, 10, 24n, 62; *Brother to Dragons*, 45, 145; *Promises*, 42-44; "Pure and Impure Poetry," 44
Wasserman, Earl, 24
Watt, Ian, 24
Weber, Max, 33
Wellek, René, 24n; and Warren, Austin, *Theory of Literature*, 9, 10, 15n, 24n
Wells, William V., 138n
Wheelwright, Philip, 20
White, David, and Bernard Rosenberg, ed. *Mass Culture: The Popular Arts in America*, 84
Whitehead, Alfred North, 16n
Whitman, Walt, 54, 69-70, 71, 160, 200-239, 320, 327-350; *American Primer*, 214, 216, 233; "Are You the New Person Drawn toward Me?" 225; "As Adam Early in the Morning," 236; "As I Ebb'd with the Ocean of Life," 219, 236; "A Backward Glance O'er Travel'd Roads," 204, 209, 347; "Base of All Metaphors," 237;

"Burial," 227; "By Blue Ontario's Shore," 219; "Calamus," 217, 223-228, 230, 233, 237; "Chants Democratic," 203, 219, 229; "Crossing Brooklyn Ferry," 214, 227, 230, 346; *Democratic Vistas*, 154, 205, 208, 338-344; "Earth, My Likeness," 225; "Eidolons," 338; "Enfans d'Adam," 223-228, 230, 233; "Europe," 223; Faith Poem," 221; "For Him I Sing," 338; "Here the Frailest Leaves of Me," 226; "I am He that Aches with Love," 236; "I Hear America Singing," 219; "I Sit and Look Out," 236; "In Cabin'd Ships at Sea," 338; Inclusive Edition, 238; "I Sing the Body Electric," 235; "I Was Looking a Long While," 219; "Kosmos," 227; "A Leaf of Faces," 223; "Leaves of Grass," 229; *Leaves of Grass* (1855), 80, 202, 209, 210, 214, 239, 333-338; *Leaves of Grass* (1856), 200, 209, 210, 214, 336-338, 342; *Leaves of Grass* (1860), 203, 205, 209, 210, 211, 213, 214, 336-338, 342; *Leaves of Grass* (1865), 342; *Leaves of Grass* (1867), 235, 236, 238; *Leaves of Grass* (1871), 237, 238, 337, 342, 343; *Leaves of Grass* (1872), 204; "Me Imperturbe," 219; "Messenger Leaves," 227, 230; "Miracles," 221; "Myself and Mine," 221; "Night on the Prairies," 234; "On the Beach at Night Alone," 222; "Out of the Cradle Endlessly Rocking," 218, 223, 234; "Passage to India," 204, 346, 349; "Poem of Joys," 223, 229; "Poets to Come," 203; "Respondez," 342; "Salut au Monde," 223, 229, 346; "Sleep-Chasings," 227; "The Sleepers," 214; "So Long!," 222, 228; "A Song for

356

Occupations," 219; "Song of Myself," 11, 218, 224, 334, 346; *Song of Myself,* 301; "Song of Prudence," 220; "Song of the Answerer," 220; "Song of the Broad-Axe," 219; "Song of the Exposition," 342-348, 389; "Song of the Redwood Tree," 346; "Starting from Paumanok," 218; "The Theory of Culture," 341-342; "There Was a Child Went Forth," 221; "This Compost," 220; "To a Locomotive in Winter," 346; "To a President," 331-332; "When Lilacs Last in the Dooryard Bloomed," 336; "Years of the Modern," 342
Whittier, James Greenleaf, 81
Whorf, Benjamin Lee, 12
Williams, Raymond, *Culture and Society, The Long Revolution,* 91

Williams, Ted, 89
Williams, William Carlos, 330, 332
Williamson, George, 25
Wimsatt, W. K. Jr., and M. C. Beardsley, "The Intentional Fallacy," 47
Winsor, Justin, 138n
Winters, Yvor, 54
Wittgenstein, Ludwig, 274
Wolfe, Thomas, 43n
Wordsworth, William, 24; *The Prelude,* 301, 305
Wright, James, 330n, 346

Yeats, William Butler, 207, 315
Yerby, Frank, 7
Young, Samuel, 111n
Young, Stark, 240

Zukofsky, Louis, 330n